Not Yet...
And That's
OK

How Productive Struggle
Fosters Student Learning

PEG GRAFWALLNER

Solution Tree | Press
a division of
Solution Tree

555 North Morton Street
Bloomington, IN 47404
800.733.6786 (toll free) / 812.336.7700
FAX: 812.336.7790

email: info@SolutionTree.com
SolutionTree.com

Visit **go.SolutionTree.com/instruction** to download the free reproducibles in this book.

Printed in the United States of America

Library of Congress Cataloging-in-Publication Data

Names: Grafwallner, Peggy J., 1960- author.
Title: Not yet...and that's ok : how productive struggle fosters student
   learning / Peg Grafwallner.
Description: Bloomington, IN : Solution Tree Press, 2021. | Includes
   bibliographical references and index.
Identifiers: LCCN 2021014237 (print) | LCCN 2021014238 (ebook) | ISBN
   9781952812255 (paperback) | ISBN 9781952812262 (ebook)
Subjects: LCSH: Student-centered learning. | Cognitive styles in children |
   Learning, Psychology of.
Classification: LCC LB1027.23 .G728 2021 (print) | LCC LB1027.23 (ebook)
   | DDC 371.39--dc23
LC record available at https://lccn.loc.gov/2021014237
LC ebook record available at https://lccn.loc.gov/2021014238

Solution Tree
Jeffrey C. Jones, CEO
Edmund M. Ackerman, President

Solution Tree Press
President and Publisher: Douglas M. Rife
Associate Publisher: Sarah Payne-Mills
Art Director: Rian Anderson
Managing Production Editor: Kendra Slayton
Copy Chief: Jessi Finn
Senior Production Editor: Todd Brakke
Content Development Specialist: Amy Rubenstein
Copy Editor: Evie Madsen
Proofreader: Elisabeth Abrams
Editorial Assistants: Sarah Ludwig and Elijah Oates

Acknowledgments

This book would not be possible without the support of the professional educators at Ronald W. Reagan College Preparatory High School and the many professional educators I've met online and throughout my teaching career. I appreciate you taking the time to offer your experience, your expertise, and your excitement. I could not have written this book without you. A heartfelt thanks to:

- Chey Cheney and Pav Wander, middle school teachers and creators of *The Staffroom Podcast*

- Melissa Chouinard, seventh-grade science teacher, Beckendorff Junior High School, Katy, Texas

- Kathleen Dimmer, middle school music teacher, Brown Deer Middle School, Brown Deer, Wisconsin

- Jennifer Inaba, seventh-grade science teacher, Ann Arbor, Michigan

- Teri Knight, language acquisition teacher, Ronald W. Reagan College Preparatory High School, Milwaukee, Wisconsin

- Aubrey Lynn, special education teacher; author of *#lessonsandlattes* on Instagram

- April Nagel, special education teacher, Ronald W. Reagan College Preparatory High School, Milwaukee, Wisconsin

- Willie Patterson Jr., former student and engineer, Milwaukee Water Works, Wisconsin

- Andy Schoenborn, English teacher, Mt. Pleasant High School, Mt. Pleasant, Michigan

- Chad Sperzel-Wuchterl, 2020 Wisconsin Teacher of the Year, and art teacher, Ronald W. Reagan College Preparatory High School, Milwaukee, Wisconsin

- Victoria Thompson, STEM coach, Tacoma, Washington
- Robert Ward, English language arts teacher, Los Angeles, California

In addition, thank you to my editor, Todd Brakke, who spent countless hours listening and brainstorming with me to make this book the very best it could be.

Finally, a warm hug to Claudia Wheatley, author liaison. Claudia has been my writing guiding light and biggest supporter. Thank you, Claudia. I am so very appreciative of you.

Last, but not least, a big hug and smooch to my husband, Mike. Thanks for always giving me the time to make it work!

Solution Tree Press would like to thank the following reviewers:

Tonya Alexander
English Teacher (NBCT)
Owego Free Academy
Owego, New York

Kelly Hilliard
Mathematics Teacher
McQueen High School
Reno, Nevada

Eric Lindblad
English Teacher
Andover High School
Andover, Minnesota

Shanna Martin
Social Studies and Technology Teacher,
    Instructional Coach
Lomira Middle School
Lomira, Wisconsin

David Pillar
Assistant Director
Hoosier Hills Career Center
Bloomington, Indiana

Visit **go.SolutionTree.com/instruction** to download the free reproducibles in this book.

Table of Contents

Reproducible pages are in italics.

About the Author ix

Introduction 1
A Problem of Practice 3
About This Book 7
Conclusion 8

PART 1
Foundations of the Not-Yet Approach

1: The Challenge of Failure 11
The Long-Term Effects of Failure 13
Failure as an End and as a Beginning 17
Conclusion 19
Ruminate and Respond *20*

2: Grading and the Not-Yet Approach 21
Points and Zeroes 23
Standards-Based Grading 26
The Gradeless Classroom 29
Conclusion 34
Ruminate and Respond *36*

3: Concepts to Support the Not-Yet Approach 37
The Growth Mindset 39
Grit 42

The Abolitionist Teacher. 45
Conclusion. 48
Ruminate and Respond. 49

4: Vigorous Learning Intentions and Scaffolded Success Criteria

4: Vigorous Learning Intentions and Scaffolded Success Criteria. 51
Initiating the Not-Yet Approach in Your Classroom. 53
Crafting Vigorous Learning Intentions and Scaffolded Success Criteria. 54
Applying Vigorous Learning Intentions and Scaffolded Success Criteria. 65
Using Data to Personalize Learning Intentions and Success Criteria. 69
Conclusion. 72
Ruminate and Respond. 75
Not-Yet Learning Intention Template. 76
Not-Yet Success Criteria Template. 77

PART 2
The Not-Yet Classrooms

5: The Practical Classroom

5: The Practical Classroom. 81
The Not-Yet Approach in the Practical Classroom. 82
Deficit Language in Disciplinary Instruction. 83
Not-Yet Language for Learning Success. 86
Conclusion. 88
Ruminate and Respond. 90

6: The Transformational Classroom

6: The Transformational Classroom. 91
The Not-Yet Approach in the Transformational Classroom. 92
Ensuring Feedback for Academic Transformation and Personal Success. 95
Using Best Practices for Feedback. 100
Transforming Grading Practices. 102
Conclusion. 105
Ruminate and Respond. 107
Academic Transformation and Personal Success Feedback Form. 108

7: The Productive Classroom

7: The Productive Classroom. 111
The Not-Yet Approach in the Productive Classroom. 112
Differentiation and Creativity in the Learning Process. 115

The Joy of Learning 117
Conclusion 120
Ruminate and Respond *123*

8: The Supportive Classroom 125

The Not-Yet Approach in the Supportive Classroom 126
Supportive Check-Ups 129
Tools to Support Choice 133
Conclusion 140
Ruminate and Respond *142*
Two-Week Instructional Calendar *143*

9: The Flexible Classroom 145

The Not-Yet Approach in the Flexible Classroom 146
Teacher Self-Reflection 148
Student Reflection 154
Student Feedback on Teaching 158
Conclusion 162
Ruminate and Respond *164*
Professional-Reflection Form *165*
Professional-Observation Form *166*

10: The Constructive Classroom 167

The Not-Yet Approach in the Constructive Classroom 167
Time 170
Space 174
Process-Driven Improvement 178
Conclusion 183
Ruminate and Respond *185*
Constructive-Focus Chart *186*

11: The Connective Classroom 187

The Not-Yet Approach in the Connective Classroom 188
Collegial Observation 190
Pedagogical Guiding Questions and Comments 192
Opportunities for Collaboration 195
Conclusion 197
Ruminate and Respond *200*

12: The Inclusive Classroom 201

The Not-Yet Approach in the Inclusive Classroom 202
Student-Teacher Relationships 203
Inclusive Curricula 206
Conclusion 208
Ruminate and Respond *212*

Epilogue 213

References and Resources 215

Index 233

About the Author

Peg Grafwallner, MEd, is an instructional coach and reading specialist at Ronald W. Reagan College Preparatory High School, an urban International Baccalaureate school located on the south side of Milwaukee, Wisconsin. Peg has more than twenty-five years of experience in education. She began her career as an English teacher at a private high school and eventually became an alternative education teacher in a suburban district. She has taught graduate-level courses on reading and writing in the content areas, with an emphasis on differentiation and interventions. She now supports teachers in seamlessly embedding literacy without disrupting their classroom objectives. Peg models how to create comprehensive literacy lessons that enhance skill-building; she coaches and assists teachers in creating these lessons.

Peg is a member of the Wisconsin State Reading Association (WSRA), Wisconsin Council of Teachers of English (WCTE), National Council of Teachers of English (NCTE), and Association for Supervision and Curriculum Development (ASCD). As the parent of a gifted and talented son and a daughter receiving special education, Peg offers a unique educational lens that focuses on supporting students of all abilities in realizing their potential in the classroom and beyond. She is a blogger, author, and national presenter whose topics include coaching, engagement, and inclusion. Her articles have appeared in *The Missouri Reader*, *Exceptional Parent*, *WSRA Journal*, and *Illinois Reading Council Journal*. She has written for several websites and blogs, including *Edutopia*, *ASCD Inservice*, Education Week's *Classroom Q&A With Larry Ferlazzo*, KQED's *In the Classroom*, and *Literacy & NCTE*. She has also appeared on numerous podcasts such as *Cult of Pedagogy*, *BAM! Radio*, and *Ed: Conversations About the Teaching Life*. Peg is also the author of *Lessons Learned From the Special*

Education Classroom: Creating Opportunities for All Students to Listen, Learn, and Lead and *Ready to Learn: The FRAME Model for Optimizing Student Success.*

Peg earned a bachelor's degree in English and a mentoring certification from Cardinal Stritch University, a master's degree in curriculum and instruction and an alternative education certification from Marian University, and a reading specialist certification from the University of Wisconsin–Milwaukee.

To learn more about Peg's work, visit www.peggrafwallner.com and follow her on Twitter @PegGrafwallner.

To book Peg Grafwallner for professional development, contact pd@SolutionTree.com.

Introduction

Spend any amount of time in the classroom—providing instruction, issuing assessments, and reviewing data about student learning—and you'll see a spectrum of learning outcomes. On one end, there are students who seem to effortlessly absorb learning material and, on the other, are students who encounter obstacles and soon give up, accepting failure as inevitable. In the span between are students who encounter challenges as they learn but engage in productive struggle to overcome those challenges. Regardless of where your students reside on this spectrum, as a teacher, it's your responsibility to ensure they all meet with content that challenges them to overcome struggle, maximize their learning, and eventually master learning standards. But what does productive struggle look like, and how can it be achieved?

As an instructional coach and reading specialist at a large, urban high school, I work with teachers in all content areas to seamlessly embed literacy into their daily lessons without disrupting the focus on activities that support students in learning curriculum content. Literacy skills are a critical component of every content area, and students who lack foundational skills for their grade level or course will inevitably struggle to learn (Onuscheck, Spiller, Argentar, et al., 2020; Onuscheck, Spiller, & Glass, 2020). For this reason, I often collaborate with teachers to create differentiated and scaffolded lessons for all student abilities so every student engages in what many educators refer to as *productive struggle* (Blackburn, 2018) or *desirable difficulty* (Bjork & Bjork, 2014). Educator, speaker, and consultant Barbara R. Blackburn (2018) defines *productive struggle* as the sweet spot in students' learning relative to teacher-provided scaffolds and supports:

> Rather than immediately helping students at the first sign of trouble, we should allow them to work through struggles independently before we offer assistance. That may sound counterintuitive, since many of us assume that helping students learn means protecting them from negative feelings of frustration. But for students to

become independent learners, they must learn to persist in the face of challenge.

As you will explore in this book, there are numerous variables that inform and affect how students respond to obstacles in their learning and how quick they are to give up. The challenge for teachers is to create a culture where any failure to learn is simply a common and natural indicator that the learning hasn't happened *yet*. But it will. This is the essence of the not-yet approach. It's about how teachers allow for and even encourage setbacks in the classroom, recontextualizing them for students as a crucial and mandatory part of learning. Teachers who foster a not-yet approach and culture in their classroom do the following.

- Empower students to realize that setbacks and obstacles are a beginning point to learning and not an end point.

- Normalize encountering and overcoming obstacles so they become part of the learning process as students produce new products (completed classwork, essays, projects, and so on).

- Contextualize setbacks and obstacles as trial-and-error opportunities that assist students in process-based learning and, ultimately, progress.

- Model how to graciously accept setbacks and obstacles as part of every student's social-emotional endeavor to better themselves and those around them.

Classrooms that offer systems and routines around these actions inspire process (the learning), product (the result of that learning), and progress (the reflection of that learning). In doing so, teachers create classrooms that embed effective action as something ordinary rather than reactive. Teachers in such classrooms allow students the opportunity to overcome academic fear and replace it with a mindset that any struggle to learn simply means that learning hasn't been accomplished *yet*. You will see the terms *process*, *product*, and *progress* laced throughout this book because, by looking at each through multiple, unbiased classroom lenses, the not-yet approach ensures students realize *not yet* means learning obstacles or setbacks are just part of the ongoing journey toward achievement.

In the rest of this introduction, you will read about the problems of practice common to conventional classroom approaches that inhibit a not-yet approach to learning. I then establish this book's structure to help you understand the many factors that influence how students respond to obstacles and failure and how dedication to a series of classroom lenses ensures that productive struggle and a not-yet approach are norms for your students.

A Problem of Practice

In a traditional grading model, when a student fails or fails to complete an assignment, test, essay, or other graded work, the teacher enters the grade in his or her gradebook without the student being able to revise or redo the work. *The grade was the grade*, and the student simply had to live with it. Writing for *Edutopia*, high school English language arts (ELA) teacher and adjunct professor of education Monte Syrie (2016) argues that as much as teachers assess "under the pretense of validity, reliability, and infallibility," most teachers "end up grading the way they were graded." In my experience, teachers who are not part of a collaborative team seldom discuss their grading practices other than to explain them to their students when distributing the syllabus or classroom expectations at the start of the year. Such practices are typically inconsistent from teacher to teacher. According to Seth Gershenson (2020a), an associate professor of public policy at American University who conducted a series of interviews with secondary teachers:

> Teachers may base their grades on a mix of both results and pupil effort, and the meaning of each letter grade is neither clear nor consistent for these teachers. Some hold onto the traditional view that "C is average," while others indicate that a B is the new average. (p. 18)

Such unconstructive and inconsistent academic experiences can cause students to feel disheartened with the learning process and eventually put them on a path to dropping out before graduation. In *"Why We Drop Out,"* authors Deborah L. Feldman, Antony T. Smith, and Barbara L. Waxman (2017) write:

> The overwhelming majority of interviewed youths experienced academic challenges that undermined their faith in themselves as learners, leading to a debilitating sense of helplessness and hopelessness, academic failure, and, ultimately, a rejection of school. (p. 2)

This finding is not surprising to experienced teachers, who can easily think of a student whose reaction to failing or falling behind amounted to, "Why should I keep trying? No matter how hard I work, I won't be able to dig myself out of this hole."

But here's the part that no one wants to talk about—even the most successful among us have experienced educational disappointments. We remember the test score that was less than what we were hoping for and the group project where we did *all* the work for the presentation but suddenly couldn't remember the topic when it was time to present. Instead of accepting that such educational interruptions happen and growing from them, many teachers errantly convey to students the idea that they should never experience a lack of success by saying to both students and their parents the students will always achieve.

But can educators really make that promise?

In a world that continually reinforces the notion that *failure is not an option*, teachers and students alike feel the constant pressure of high expectations. But just having high expectations doesn't mean anything if the learning process doesn't support achieving them. Veteran education consultant and teacher Marie Amaro (2016) details the critical importance of the connection between high expectations and achievement, listing the following seven traits as essential for setting those expectations.

1. Believe in all your students.

2. Do not give up on students.

3. Do not make excuses for students or give them an easy way out.

4. Provide high levels of support and nurturing.

5. Show students you believe they can achieve.

6. Demonstrate high-level professionalism.

7. Use strategies that reduce students' anxiety.

The Education Hub (n.d.) further connects the importance of *acceleration* to setting high expectations, noting the need for teachers to adopt practices that advance student performance beyond whatever their current proficiency level is. While it's easy to accept the idea of teachers believing in students' ability to achieve, the means of that achievement must be based on students' individual abilities and not on a blanket belief that *all* students will be successful *all* of the time. Unfortunately, traditional grading based on points accumulation and obscure participation grades is not a pedagogically sound pathway to achievement (Townsley & Wear, 2020).

Authors Douglas Reeves, Lee Ann Jung, and Ken O'Connor (2017) explain:

> Whether the issue is classroom scores on daily work or final report card grades with consequences for scholarship opportunities and university admissions, grading remains the wild west of school improvement, in which policy coherence is more apparent in claims than in practice and anyone armed with a red pen can make decisions with devastating instructional consequences.

This wild-west approach—red pens slung from their holsters ready to score at any time—can have devastating consequences for students and their academic-emotional health. Therefore, if educators cannot accept failure as the status quo—which they can't!—then they must empower students to be masters of their own learning. However, students receiving poor or failing marks on their work—and, by extension, their class grade—is only one piece of a bigger problem.

Unfortunately, a common method teachers use to avoid addressing student failure is to simply avoid giving failing grades at all costs. While the retakes and redos might help alleviate those failing grades, do they really support improvement in students' process, products, and progress? One has to wonder if all of the retaking, redoing, and so on are merely steps taken to forego an administrative showdown. After all, if the student is failing, the inquiry begins with the teacher, not with the student.

Throughout my career, I often see this disturbing trend in grading. When students fail a graded assignment or an assessment, teachers simply allow a redo or retake. Although this gives students the opportunity to raise their grade, it raises an important question: In doing the redoing and retaking, how can teachers ensure students aren't simply going through the motions to get a better grade by memorizing previous content without necessarily mastering the learning standards? To avoid this, teachers often write a new assessment for students to retake, or they might assign a new essay topic for students to write. These approaches require hours of work on teachers' part, work that could be spent creating new process-focused learning opportunities or determining new scaffolds to support students through a setback or obstacle. Many teachers require students to be caught up with their homework before they are allowed a retake or a redo. This step can help ensure students take a more active part in overcoming a learning challenge, but does that get to the root of the question: How can teachers create opportunities where those redos or retakes are part of the learning process and not simply implemented as a way for students to play catchup with their learning?

Another route schools and teachers often take to avoid poor grades from showing up in a gradebook or report card is for teachers to meet with students before, during, or after school in individual conferences to help students make up or redo work. Many large districts have after-school tutoring labs where content-area teachers facilitate learning well into the dinner hour, Saturday classes when students can make up late work, or credit-recovery classes after school and in the summer in which students attend an abridged version of a course—often just a couple of weeks—to make up a quarter's or semester's worth of learning. Such efforts can be effective, but they often place the onus on teachers to get students to pass the class, abdicating students' role in their own learning. Thus, the question remains: Are students truly mastering the learning, or are they merely regurgitating information that has barely been digested?

Or worse, are they succumbing to the feelings of helplessness and hopelessness that Feldman and colleagues (2017) describe?

Consider also that, while teachers might consider using after-school time for redos or retakes for students to complete at home, this can still be problematic for students who may not have the time or capacity for such measures. It's not unusual for secondary-level students to be unable to do redos or complete those retakes because they are working a job (often for the sake of the household) or babysitting siblings while family members work two or three jobs. Nor do all elementary students have the supports at home to understand how to establish productive homework practices. After- or before-school supports or weekend interventions face similar hurdles if students are unable to attend, and teachers and schools should never require students to attend them as part of needed instruction. Therefore, it becomes even more important to support students in using a process-driven learning approach during classroom time that enables them to embrace and overcome academic setbacks.

None of this is to argue that ensuring students have multiple opportunities to show their learning or access teacher-provided supports is unnecessary or counterproductive. It's not unusual or problematic for students to need and benefit from extra help from their teacher. I vividly remember needing extra support in science when I was in high school. In college, I attended study group sessions to help me better understand course content. Students getting a little extra help with a skill or knowledge item they're struggling with isn't the problem I present with the preceding scenarios. Rather, these scenarios reflect situations where redos and retakes become norms, and failure is submissively accepted or avoided altogether. These are scenarios in which more students end up requiring interventive measures than teachers can possibly hope to provide. Further, school- and teacher-provided supports can't be stopgap measures in which the goal shifts from the learning process to simply getting a grade.

Instead, what if teachers built into school culture a *not-yet* attitude as an expected part of learning, an attitude where productive struggle during daily lessons is part of academic growth, and students can learn from and reflect on their learning process independently? The not-yet approach is all about designing and creating a classroom culture that encourages the learning process while accepting setbacks and obstacles as part of that process. The belief is that *not yet* means there is more to learn, more to assess, and more to reflect on. Often, the connotation of failure to students and parents is an end point. It isn't. As veteran educator and author Robert Ward (2017) writes, educators should not focus on that *end* perception but "on the multiple little triumphs, enlightenments, and headways likely gained in the process." This is the essence of the not-yet experience.

About This Book

I wrote this book for upper-elementary and secondary educators to take inspiration from the practical and research-backed ideas, suggestions, and reproducibles it offers and apply them in their own classrooms in ways that meet their students' unique needs. Even if you're an early elementary teacher (K–3), the flexibility is here to easily adapt and transition this book's practices to your students.

To support you in learning about and applying the not-yet approach, I've divided it into two parts. Part 1 focuses on the foundations for this approach. Chapter 1 discusses failure and how deeply rooted it can be in students' psyche—prohibiting even elementary-level students from valuing themselves as learners and risk takers. Chapter 2 examines the sometimes contentious relationship between engaging students in productive struggle and grading practices. I briefly describe the journey from traditional grading to standards-based grading to the gradeless classroom—a journey many teachers are experiencing, regardless of content area or grade level (Gonser, 2020). Chapter 3 then highlights three important aspects of the not-yet approach: (1) growth mindset (Dweck, 2016), (2) grit (Duckworth, 2016), and (3) abolitionist teaching (Love, 2019a). Chapter 4 illustrates how to write vigorous learning intentions and scaffolded success criteria that use setbacks and obstacles as part of learning.

With a foundation established for the not-yet approach, part 2 introduces and details eight lenses (core traits) of classrooms that reinforce a not-yet culture: (1) the practical classroom, (2) the transformational classroom, (3) the productive classroom, (4) the supportive classroom, (5) the flexible classroom, (6) the constructive classroom, (7) the connective classroom, and (8) the inclusive classroom. Chapter 5 shows how to modify your classroom language from a deficiency model to one focused on practical, not-yet language for learning success. Chapter 6 is about transforming your approach to instruction and grading based on feedback from students and their parents or guardians. Chapter 7 explains the importance of joy and creativity to a productive classroom. Chapter 8 clarifies the difference between providing students with necessary *supports* but not *help* when encouraging them to adopt a not-yet approach in a supportive classroom. Chapter 9 highlights the need for classrooms to be flexible, with appropriate attention given to reflection on teachers' practice in a safe and encouraging environment. Chapter 10 details how teachers can maximize classroom time and space to be constructive and ensure every lesson offers students the best possible learning experience. Chapter 11 explains the importance of having a connected classroom built on collaboration with other teachers to ensure all students benefit from teachers' collective knowledge and experience. Last, chapter 12 emphasizes the importance of inclusivity to classroom culture.

Chapters 4–12 also end with A Look Inside elements containing the reflections of many educators who have successfully defined, described, and demonstrated the not-yet approach. These scenarios serve as instructional models demonstrating how you can embed the not-yet approach into your teaching. Use their suggestions to further your own not-yet classroom or adopt and adapt their practices in ways that work best for you and your students.

To assist teachers in creating a classroom that encourages productive struggle, every chapter in this book offers detailed step-by-step instructions, concrete examples, strategies, and reproducible tools. As a classroom teacher, I have always appreciated these elements and have found that even if I don't necessarily use the book's offerings exactly, I am inspired to create my own based on what I have read. I hope you feel enthused to do the same. To that end, all chapters conclude with one or more reproducible pages, including a "Ruminate and Respond" reproducible designed for teachers to reflect on and journal about their actions and practices. I encourage you to take the time to pause and consider the process, progress, and products in your classroom. Not only should you use the questions for personal growth, I encourage you to apply them in broader settings—like in collaboration with other teachers on your team or in your department. Being reflective with other teachers is a critical part of your teaching practice; you grow when you learn from your peers and when you implement that growth for the sake of your students' success (DuFour, DuFour, Eaker, Many, & Mattos, 2016).

Conclusion

The not-yet approach creates an authentic classroom experience where students value setbacks and obstacles as ways to grow, learn, and develop. Instead of allowing failure to define the student, the not-yet approach creates opportunities to normalize development and empowers students to realize learning takes time and that mastery isn't the end of growth. The not-yet approach provides authentic classroom lenses that give teachers and students flexibility.

Note that, for the purposes of this book, I occasionally use the word *failure*, but most often, I concentrate on classrooms that utilize failure as an empowering opportunity to grow. The classroom themes that underpin each chapter topic in part 2 are meant to honor the not-yet approach and inspire student learning. Ultimately, *Not Yet . . . And That's OK: How Productive Struggle Fosters Student Learning* celebrates the academic experience and all it has to offer both teachers and students. I encourage you to join together with your colleagues to move to a not-yet approach that better supports learning for *all* students!

PART 1
Foundations of the Not-Yet Approach

The Challenge of Failure

It's easy to think back to a time when you failed at something. By that, I don't mean those little everyday inconsequential failures, like forgetting to pick up more napkins from the grocery store. Think of something you did or avoided doing as an adult that had a real cost to you or others and the resulting feeling of fear, deep in the gut, that can paralyze even the most confident individual. What is it about failure that causes people to fall apart? Is it that you feel you've let someone down? Is it that your own self-worth has been put into question? Is it that you have created an image of yourself that, upon failing at something, you sadly realize isn't true? Many people feel so paralyzed by fear of failure they're afraid to do anything that feels like a risk (Martin, 2012; Zakrzewski, 2013).

Now, apply that trepidation to your elementary school, middle school, or high school years. Did a teacher ever hand back a mathematics test with an *F* engraved in red ink at the top of your paper? Or did an ELA teacher adorn an essay you wrote with the words *See me*, summoning a feeling of anxiety? Did you have a science lab project or experiment that didn't get the expected results? Many remember such experiences so vividly that, for some, it can still cause a visceral reaction.

Classic definitions of *fail* typically invoke actions that fell short of success when achievement was expected or strongly desired (Fail, n.d.b). They also often use labels like *deficient* or *lacking* (Fail, n.d.a), implying a failure not just in action but of self and character. Such definitions aren't technically inaccurate, but consider: Does anyone really fail? Certainly, if there were risks you chose not to take, you really haven't failed. After all, you didn't actually try. But if you did try, is it truly a failure not to have succeeded? Surely you gained or learned something in the attempt. In so doing, you have achieved something, just not the task you expected, attempted, desired, or approved.

This thinking applies in all avenues of life but especially in the classroom. As an instructional coach and reading specialist, I collaborate with teachers to design lessons that embed literacy into all content areas without disrupting classroom objectives. While meeting with a teacher, I might suggest a differentiation technique or scaffolded approach to the lesson. If the teacher wants to try another method, I certainly don't think I failed in my attempt to support the teacher. In these circumstances, I've tried an approach that's worked in the past; however, this time, it didn't work out. But a teacher's rejection of the idea (not me!) gives me more information I can use to brainstorm another idea and offer another suggestion to better support that teacher (which I do).

Ward (2017) contends, "Seldom are the instances when a person does not achieve some degree of accomplishment, improvement, or understanding while engaged in a serious endeavor, no matter how short of one's goals they may have fallen." By applying Ward's (2017) perspective, I've achieved some understanding of what the teacher might want, even though initially, I might have fallen short of my goals.

This perspective and experience are equally adaptable between teachers and students. For example, if you assigned students to write an *analytical* paragraph in response to who was at fault for the deaths of Romeo and Juliet (Shakespeare, 1597/2004), and a student wrote a *thesis* sentence, did that student fail? While he or she might have fallen short of the expectation or desired outcome, he or she did, in fact, attempt to write something. Further, there certainly was some degree of understanding since he or she *was* able to write the thesis sentence.

The idea of failure becomes even more problematic if you apply labels like *deficient*. Yes, the student in this example lacked understanding of what the teacher wanted in that assignment, but with just a little discussion with the teacher, he or she could certainly use and adjust the original thesis statement to then construct an analytical paragraph.

It's not unusual for students to fall short of understanding a topic or be deficient or lacking in knowledge until teachers have had the opportunity to fill in the gaps. In fact, it's expected. Through conversation, reading, experiments, video, and personal narratives, along with thinking tools like graphic organizers or choice opportunities, teachers build foundations and scaffolds from which students will eventually comprehend new material, eliminating their preliminary lack of knowledge. Attaching the word *failure* just because students haven't achieved the learning *yet* is unjust and unwarranted (and quite a label to attach to any human being).

Utilizing Ward's (2017) view, accomplishment becomes an iterative process. Students may lack understanding of new information prior to teaching, but they begin to accomplish their teacher's goals for them simply by absorbing new information as part of direct instruction. When students then engage in additional activities, such as reading and taking notes about learning the content or engaging in classroom activities to build knowledge about it, they further that accomplishment. Most students consistently accomplish something in class; it is rare for any of them to be lacking some kind of achievement. Perhaps that accomplishment is not always what the teacher wants or how he or she wants it, with learning setbacks causing students to fall short of success or achievement, but something is happening. Further, a lack of success represents a temporary state, not a constant. Engaging in productive struggle, confronting and eventually overcoming such challenges, ensures students don't stay in one place; they move forward. That moving forward—no matter how small the steps—can be empowering to students because it represents progress. When students are able to see that progress as a tangible thing, they are more willing to continue in that struggle.

This book concentrates on teachers establishing and sustaining classroom environments that utilize educational setbacks as empowerment opportunities from which students grow. As Ward (2017) writes, those setbacks focus teachers and students "on the multiple little triumphs, enlightenments, and headways likely gained in the process" of learning. In the rest of this chapter, you will explore the long-term effects of failure and learn how failure is, in fact, both an ending *and* a beginning.

The Long-Term Effects of Failure

When students think they have failed, the consequences of that perceived failure can last far beyond the moment. Some students come to expect failure as part of their academic career. It is a part of their worldview. Traditional assessment and grading practices, as you'll read more about in chapter 2 (page 21), often exacerbate this toxic expectation because they don't allow for revisiting sources of struggle or allowing for alternate solutions, which impacts all parts of a student's day, from the classroom to the hallway to the lunchroom and bathroom (Hilppo & Stevens, 2020).

Consider the following: according to Valerie Strauss (2017), education writer for the *Washington Post*, "Algebra is the single most failed course in high school, the most failed course in community college, and, along with English language for nonnative speakers, the single biggest academic reason that community colleges have a high dropout rate." The connection to dropout rates is clear evidence these students have encountered walls they don't believe they can climb. They expect to fail. David Rubel (2018), an education policy consultant for the state of New York, offers this ominous report about the Regents Exams necessary for high school graduation in New York:

These students need more help than just their first year Algebra class (which is typically a large classroom of 27 students with a diverse range of learners); if the extra help is not made available, these students are basically doomed to struggle with failure with little chance of graduating. (p. 3)

Clearly, educators must do more to eliminate that failure expectation. Rubel further states, "On day one, in ninth grade, every high school knows exactly how many students aren't going to pass. You have a prediction system in place" (as cited in Barshay, 2019). Imagine being a student and knowing that you are taking a course where even *the teacher* expects a majority of students to fail. With such a mindset, it would be unusual if you *didn't* fail.

As that failure cycle spins, many students just don't see a reason to stay in school. Because they have not explicitly been shown the process of productive struggle and how it works, they have not had opportunities to practice how to fail and rise back up again or reflect on failure and use that reflection to improve next time. Put simply, they don't know that failure can be a temporary state, and so they associate it with dread and despair.

A failure mindset doesn't magically appear in middle or high school. Unfortunately, you can trace failure patterns back to elementary school. In an iconic article in *Educational Leadership*, coauthors Robert E. Slavin, Nancy L. Karweit, and Barbara A. Wasik (1992/1993) note, "Success in the early grades does not guarantee success throughout the school years and beyond, but failure in the early grades does virtually guarantee failure in later schooling."

You can often recognize the well-worn verbal and body language of the middle or high school student whose academic career has encompassed patterns of failure leading back to their elementary years. You might have to routinely remind the student to take his or her seat and get out his or her materials—a pen to write with and a notebook in which to take notes. You might have to cajole the student into taking notes. You might encourage the student to ask a question or ask the student if he or she has any insight on the topic only to see a complete lack of engagement in the learning. When you ask to meet with the student after school to learn how you can help him or her, the student either doesn't show up or might just blurt out: "I never understood this stuff," "I'm dumb," or "None of this makes sense to me." Spend enough time in the classroom, and you'll surely see this behavior and hear these dejected phrases.

A common consequence of failure early in students' academic lives is that failure in elementary school often leads to in-grade retention, in which students repeat an entire year instead of just an individual course (Intercultural Development Research

Association, 2018). When it comes to the deep scars that result from in-grade retention, teachers can be unaware of how that experience influences attitudes toward
struggle and learning. Some teachers might think holding a student back to repeat
a grade is a positive thing; after all, the student will have the opportunity to learn
the material again, and then it will really stick. However, *Education Week* bloggers
Deborah Stipek and Michael Lombardo (2014) caution, "Retention does not help
most children who have fallen behind, primarily because they are exposed to the
same material in the same way that didn't work for them the first time around."
When students are placed in the same class with the same teacher moving through
the same curriculum, it's the equivalent of thinking that teaching *louder and slower*
is likely to lead to new understanding.

Researchers Francisco Peixoto, Vera Monteiro, Lourdes Mata, Cristina Sanches,
Joana Pipa, and Leandro S. Almeida (2016) followed a fifth- and seventh-grade
cohort to study the effects of retainment and conclude, "Retention leaves a significant mark that remains even when students recover academic achievement and
retention is in the distant past." Retained students often carry a negative self-image
throughout school and into adulthood, always assuming they are not smart enough
to take the educational risks that confident students look forward to trying (Peixoto
et al., 2016). Derrick Meador (2018), the superintendent of Jennings Public Schools
in Oklahoma, writes, "Grade retention can also have a profound impact on a student's socialization. This becomes especially true for older students who have been
with the same group of students for several years." As one's friends move on to the
next grade, the retained student may develop poor self-esteem and behavioral issues
(Meador, 2018). Research across generations of students continually affirms the negative academic and social outcomes associated with academic failure and retention
(Crosnoe, 2002; Johnson, 2018; Miller, 1998; Needham, Crosnoe, & Muller, 2004;
Rosenbaum, DeLuca, Miller, & Roy, 1999).

Many years ago, I taught English 11 in what educators referred to then as an
alternative classroom setting. I remember working with a student, Willie, helping
him write an analysis of Elie Wiesel's (2006) *Night*, the iconic story of a teenager's
firsthand account of the horrors of the Holocaust. I asked Willie what he thought of
the book. He responded that he really didn't care about the story and that he was a
"bad" reader. We had read the book in class, and I had supplemented the book with
videos, poems, and other resources to help it become more accessible to students. I
gently pressed Willie, asking him what he meant. "I don't read good, and I hate to
read," he answered. I then asked him if he liked to write. He shook his head *no*. "I
don't write good, neither." It was obvious Willie felt he was unable to write an analysis because he believed he would fall short of success or achievement in something I,

as his teacher, expected and desired. Willie was, in his opinion, deficient and lacking in reading and writing. For him, it was easier not to try to write the analysis than to write it and risk being a failure.

I remember asking Willie who had ever told him he wasn't a good reader or wasn't a good writer? He didn't respond and just shook his head. I have since realized that we tell students so much without even using words. I began to prompt Willie about certain parts of the book and asked his opinion on what Wiesel (2006) might have been thinking when he wrote about his father, mother, or sisters. What was Willie's opinion about Elie wanting to become a rabbi, Madame Schächter's haunting behavior in the cattle car, or Elie not answering his father when he called out his name in his dying breath? As Willie started to share his ideas—hesitatingly at first—I began typing his responses for him. Eventually, Willie and I wrote that analysis together. As the year went on, Willie's confidence as a reader and writer grew. As his teacher, I knew something he didn't: he was not, nor had he ever been, a reading or writing failure. He was simply behind in his grade-level reading and writing skills and needed intervention to supplement and accelerate his learning to catch him up to grade level (Buffum, Mattos, & Malone, 2018).

Willie and I have kept in touch, and I asked him if he remembered this experience. He did. He said when he was in class, teachers would ask him if he wanted to read: "If I said no, I wasn't reading (aloud especially), the teacher would just move on. Psychologically, I guess that was it, [the teacher was] giving up on me, which only shielded me to not want to read at all" (W. Patterson Jr., personal communication, March 16, 2021). Willie believed he was a poor reader and poor writer because teachers, as far as he was concerned, didn't push him to read or write, but that didn't mean Willie wasn't looking for a reason to read:

> For me, there were three things about reading that I could not get past. Why am I reading this, why is it purposeful for me, and am I really engaged in what I'm reading? Reading aloud was our issue for me, but reading to myself was never really an issue because I would skip right to the point. (W. Patterson Jr., personal communication, March 16, 2021)

Willie would go on to graduate from the University of Wisconsin–Madison in mechanical engineering and is a chief operating engineer at Milwaukee, Wisconsin's water plant. About this formative experience, Willie says:

> [Peg] took reading and writing to a whole other level for me by showing effort. I just gave the same in return. As of today, learning from Peg was a life-changing experience for me. It made me want to go further in life career-wise, and school-wise. (W. Patterson Jr., personal communication, March 16, 2021)

The takeaway of this experience is the importance and value of disrupting patterns of failure. Willie always had the capacity to read and write. He just needed the scaffolds in place to struggle productively and develop those skills. According to sports psychologist, parenting expert, professor, author, and speaker Jim Taylor (2011), there are three ways students learn to avoid failure.

1. By not engaging in an activity

2. By having an excuse

3. By becoming successful, so the threat of failure is removed

In Willie's case, it was easier for him not to engage in writing the *Night* analysis since he perceived the experience to be a certain failure. Because Willie believed for some time in his lack of reading and writing skills, he had developed a pattern for how to respond. For him, it wasn't relevant that the pattern held him back. He didn't know any other way. He didn't know he *could* learn.

Countless students like Willie would rather walk away from a situation than look like a failure, especially in front of their teacher or peers. I've seen students run and hide metaphorically by slumping down in their chair and pulling their collar up as high as possible to avoid eye contact, and I've seen students literally run to the bathroom to hide (always a discreet spot!), avoiding anything that remotely reminds them they will be unsuccessful. Fear of failure can cause children to experience debilitating anxiety before they take a test, compete in a sport, or perform in a recital (Taylor, 2011). As a result, they will put themselves through "unbelievable psychological machinations in order to avoid failure and maintain the sense that they are worthy" (Zakrzewski, 2013). These psychological machinations can eventually cause a student and his or her adult self to avoid anything perceived as a questionable risk. After all, there is no failure if one chooses never to take the risk. When teachers encounter students with a failure mindset, it is incumbent on them to help students reframe failure not as an end but as a beginning.

Failure as an End and as a Beginning

Unfortunately, the lovable loser is an accepted trope in pop culture (Taylor, 2011). Such characters are typically defined as poor, anonymous, powerless, unpopular, or physically unattractive and are the butt of most jokes. Think of the unattractive wingman or sidekick who has a low-paying job but provides comic relief for the more attractive and successful lead character. Taylor (2011) writes that such characters, who are emblematic of failure cliches, are "teased, bullied and rejected." Social media helps magnify this image of failure, such that people can see the failures of their neighbors or complete strangers alike and share them with all their friends. The damage for students comes when they see or feel identified as one of those failures or losers in some way. They see themselves in these caricatures and feel as if they're already at the end of their life's journey, wondering if they will live aimless, despondent, or lonely lives.

Think back to my conversation with Willie; he had already pegged himself as permanently lacking in reading and writing skills. It was as if he felt born without some natural ability to read and write well. He needed someone who could not only tell him that failure is not an endpoint but a beginning, but also someone who could provide the scaffolds he needed to find success.

At an abstract level, students who fear or expect failure must inherently know that everyone fails—this commonality alone makes us human. But it is difficult for them to imagine the valedictorian or their teacher ever failing. Ironically, even the most successful adults often feel just as much fear of being seen as failures. Entrepreneur Sebastian Kipman (2021) explains that Sir James Dyson went through nearly 5,126 prototypes during the course of fifteen years before creating the "eponymous best-selling bagless vacuum cleaner that led to a net worth of $4.5 billion." Not bad for being a vacuum guy.

Toxic perceptions about failure being an endpoint make it paramount for teachers to be open to their own so-called failures in the course of instruction. When you experience a misstep in the classroom, model for students why that mistake is just a beginning. Instead of ignoring or covering up mistakes, immerse yourself in them and model for students how mistakes become a part of the learning process. By knowing there will be setbacks and obstacles, students can anticipate that the work they do will be hard and the task will be vigorous, but the essential productive struggle will lead to a satisfying accomplishment.

Social psychologist Susan Newman (2015) writes, "By *not* allowing children to falter or experience disappointment, you render them helpless—the precise opposite of what most parents hope to achieve." Former middle school language arts teacher and college-level teacher of teachers Jennifer Gonzalez (2015) agrees, "That means if we make life too easy for our kids, if we rescue them from every fall, they will never learn the important lessons that will carry them through life." Teachers must allow these experiences and then be there to support students in determining how to overcome those experiences. Tell students in advance they will encounter failure and, when failure inevitably happens, embed those setbacks and obstacles into the course of teaching, ensuring students have access to the tools, resources, and time they need to try again. Teachers must make it clear that those setbacks and obstacles do not define who students are or their aptitude. Show them a way out. Make your classroom community a place that overcomes mistakes and rises above failure.

Given all the negativity packed into the word *failure*, you will see it infrequently over the rest of the book. This is not a matter of misrepresenting or softening this text; rather, it is a means to build up the not-yet mentality, which dictates that failures are their own endings, but the learning is just beginning. From this point forward, you will learn how you can support your efforts and those of your colleagues and students in utilizing academic setbacks to offer opportunities that embed ongoing learning into classrooms so students understand that obstacles are a valuable part of the learning process. Remember, experiencing setbacks and supporting growth and achievement—whatever that achievement might look like—are what make learning so purposeful, worthwhile, and beneficial.

Conclusion

Failure and its long-term effects can cause the most confident individual to shrink from taking risks to further his or her personal life and professional opportunities. But, the word *failure*, especially in education, has a negative connotation. Too often, educational communities proclaim that failure will never happen and, as a result, students will never experience failure. Educators know this is false. Instead of declaring students will never encounter failures, the not-yet approach creates a new mindset—one where students experience and embrace setbacks and obstacles and learn that the process of engaging in productive struggle is the foundation of learning.

Ruminate and Respond

Consider what you've learned in this chapter, and individually or with your team, answer the following questions.

1. What is your personal definition of *failure*?

2. Have you ever suffered setbacks? How did they make you feel?

3. How can you consider those setbacks a beginning?

4. What are some ways you can support students struggling in your classroom to embrace setbacks and engage with them productively?

5. How have you helped your students use setbacks in a positive way?

Grading and the Not-Yet Approach

When I was student teaching in September of 1992, my cooperating teacher showed me how she graded homework and assessments for her secondary-level ELA students. As she showed me her gradebook, it looked like a coloring book halfway finished—she marked certain homework assignments, such as weekly vocabulary worksheets, with one color, other homework assignments received another, and various assessments also had a color set. The colors meant a different weight percentage based on the assignment or assessment. For example, she highlighted vocabulary homework in light blue because it was worth 10 percent of students' overall final grade; because she used these assignments for formative purposes, she deemed the grades students received as less important than what students' work communicated about their learning progress. Items she highlighted in red, such as essays, represented 50 percent of students' overall score; she deemed these assignments far more important because they reflected whether students had acquired unit or grade-level learning goals.

She told me this was how I should grade too.

As the end of the first quarter approached, she explained to me how to add and average all the numbers. I'll be honest; I couldn't figure out her system. It just seemed so cumbersome and subjective. There was no specific set of academic standards to apply to the homework or assessments except what she (as the teacher) thought of as *poor*, *good*, or *excellent*. In addition, if a student was hovering between a B+ and an A- and was "a strong participator," she recommended giving the student an A-. However, there were no guidelines on how to be a strong participator—that was subjective too. I thought to myself: "When I have my own classroom, I'll just weigh everything equally." I decided that vocabulary homework should be worth the same as an English essay because, after all, some students are better at the weekly homework than essay writing. Why not reward them for their strengths? Also, the mathematics of averaging all the grades just seemed so much easier—*easier for me.*

Ken O'Connor (2018), an author and independent consultant specializing in grading and reporting, explains that "traditional grading, grades as adults mostly knew them, is grading based on assessment methods and giving or taking away points for almost everything students did and then calculating the mean for those points" (p. 2). This is exactly what my cooperating teacher and I both did when calculating grades, and so did nearly every other teacher I knew. Much like dictators, we giveth, and we taketh away.

Because I had little or no training in how to grade other than during my student teaching, I used the method that made the most sense to me. For example, I liked my cooperating teacher's idea of bumping up a student's grade if the student participated in class. If a student raised his or her hand consistently to answer questions or was an effective small-group leader, I would reward the student by moving the grade to the next grade band. Of course, I determined what was consistent and effective. As Ken O'Connor (n.d.) finds, this was hardly atypical: "Most teachers have little training in how to grade, so grading has developed into a private and idiosyncratic practice."

Since I didn't want my grading to be a mysterious thing, I made sure I could explain it to students, parents or guardians, and administrators. I thought that by explaining my grades and showing what I believed to be transparency in grading— after all, I *could* explain them so, of course, I was transparent—my grading practice was sound and just.

Of course, I now realize the inequity and injustice of how I graded. I look back on those early years of teaching and realize I seldom took into account the student's home life. I didn't wonder *why* the student didn't get the work done. I just knew it wasn't done. *Edutopia* editor Emelina Minero (2018) writes, "Many educators argue that home-life factors create barriers to student learning, that low grades encourage struggling students to give up, and that teachers who can't get their kids to comply use grades to punish rather than to assess knowledge."

Was I a teacher who subconsciously used grades to control my students? In truth, I don't know. I know that the use of points was easier for *me.* Minero (2018) continues, "A significant number of teachers simply considered [points] draconian arithmetic—a grading strategy that, once triggered, torpedoed any record of progress and learning across the remainder of the grading period." That was certainly true in my class. If a student failed a major assignment, assessment, or project worth a lot of points, it would be nearly impossible for him or her to crawl out from under that burden. My "draconian arithmetic" didn't allow for students to try again; it didn't allow for a new mindset; it didn't allow for a new beginning. Unfortunately, my practices were, in most respects, typical of most traditional grading practices throughout North America.

In this chapter, I reflect on how and why grading practices have evolved and how they impact the not-yet approach of using productive struggle to achieve high-level learning. I start with an exploration of a traditional system based on points and zeroes, highlight the benefits of standards-based grading, and explore the merits of having a gradeless classroom.

Points and Zeroes

I began full-time teaching in December 1993 at a small private all-girls high school in Milwaukee, Wisconsin. I was the lone freshman ELA teacher, and I taught six sections of freshman English, starting with a section on William Gibson's (1959) *The Miracle Worker*.

As a new teacher, I believed I was implementing what I learned in my teacher-preparation programs. I had a set of chosen themes to teach and used various engaging resources to teach those themes. I gave students what I believed to be worthwhile homework, and I graded the homework and returned it to students the following week. After students read every act in the play, I gave a summative test on that particular act. At the end of the play, I assigned an essay. I graded the essay and returned it with plenty of red-pen feedback. Being the revolutionary teacher I was, I allowed students to redo the essay to earn more points.

I graded everything—homework assignments, assessments, and projects. Everything was given a point value. As an example, if the test had ten questions, it might be worth one point per question or two points per question or three points. I determined how much it was worth. An essay was always worth one hundred points. I have no reason or research to explain why I valued homework, assessments, or projects as I did. I just made the mathematics of it as simple as I could. I simply added up the numbers and averaged them out based on the total number of graded items. It was easy and obvious. I could effortlessly explain my system to students, and I thought it provided them necessary transparency. I also created a rubric for writing based on the components I thought were essential to writing a stellar English paper. And if students failed to turn in work, they got a zero.

Many teachers believe that the use of zeroes teaches students lifelong lessons, like time management or motivation. Other teachers feel zeroes are punitive and demotivating, opting instead to give 50-percent grades or a similar floor for grading.

While writing on the merits of zeroes, ELA teacher and education blogger Ray Salazar (2019) summarizes the thinking behind 50-percent scores: "Fifty percent on a one hundred–point scale, after all, still equals failing. Lots of 50s should still equal an F for students, so a zero isn't necessary." Minero (2018) writes that many teachers believe a no-zero policy "allows students to do minimal work and still pass, pushes students forward who haven't mastered the content, and doesn't teach students the real-life consequences of not meeting their responsibilities."

In the ten years I taught at the private school, I only had two late papers. I was very proud of that and considered it a benchmark of good teaching. But while the points-and-zeroes system might have worked for me (or seemed to), I'm not sure how well it worked for my students. Think of it this way: Is it even true a zero can be an accurate measure of learning? In *Charting a Course to Standards-Based Grading*, author Tim R. Westerberg (2016) writes:

> It is unlikely that a student knows nothing—zero—about the content or skills under study. . . . A zero for missing work undermines the validity of any cumulative grade of which it is part in that it measures something other than mastery of course content and skills. (p. 12)

Reflecting on my own grading practices, I wasn't giving students a chance to try again to actually learn the material. In a way, I was giving them the easy way out. Once they "earned" that zero, they didn't have to *do* anything. Teacher and author Gary Armida (2018) agrees:

> We must make every effort possible to have the student complete the work. We have to create an environment that tells the student that the work is more important than filling a column in the book. We have to create a climate that shows that we value the work so much that we will do anything and everything to get them to do it.

The work students don't do, whatever the reason, should not be forgotten as soon as teachers turn the page to the next lesson or unit. Students can't simply move on from a zero because it's never erased from memory. It shows up every time a student or teacher refers to that particular lesson, every time that incomplete work represents the foundation for attaining a new skill, and every time the student or teacher calculates the grade for that course or subject. It's always *there*, even if the student has or attains mastery of the intended learning.

In my grading, I thought I was helping students work toward their strengths; however, I wasn't supporting them in working toward improving the aspects of the work students found challenging. Put another way: I wasn't helping them build up the academic muscle that most needed exercise. Instead, I was encouraging them to play a points game where the pursuit of abstract numbers is supposed to signify the quality of a student's learning. Not only do points and zeroes not accurately represent high-level learning, they create toxic and disproportionate grading practices (Chiaravalli, 2017). Crucially, they also don't facilitate students engaging in the kinds of productive struggle necessary for a not-yet mindset. Instead, teachers are left with students whose learning has been compromised and conceded.

Curriculum and instruction coordinator Matt Johnson (2018) asserts, "We sometimes forget that learning something new is *hard* work and takes effort. It is such a labor-intensive process that the human brain is physiologically designed to *avoid* the difficulty associated with learning a new task." For example, consider a student (Susan) who doesn't have much writing practice or perceives herself as a poor writer. In the class I conducted, she might either turn in a subpar analysis or, worse yet, nothing at all. A student like Susan could get by just doing well on homework assignments that were already part of her strengths, but she doesn't get the chance to dive into the *hard* work of writing an essay; instead, she can *avoid* it by focusing on something she is already good at doing. Consider for a moment your own approach to assignments and grading, what your practices communicate about student learning, and whether they challenge students to successfully meet curriculum goals. Are you supporting students by helping them build those academic muscles and a not-yet mindset? Are you providing challenging work that is thought-provoking, effortful, and, ultimately, empowering? Or, are you assigning zeroes and allowing academic atrophy?

Johnson (2018) continues, "We also know that when learning is *appropriately* difficult, the brain must work intentionally to overcome barriers." This is synonymous with the concept of productive struggle that is at the core of the not-yet approach. As a teacher, your goal isn't to ensure your students pass. It's to ensure they learn the required skills that enable them to not only pass your grade level or course but find success with their future learning, comfortable in the knowledge that any learning challenge they meet, they can overcome. That productive struggle means the answer may not come right away or at all; productive struggle helps students "build the habits necessary to embark on projects in which the outcome is not immediately apparent" (Kallick & Zmuda, 2017). Productive struggle is what makes the not-yet approach so accessible for all students; everyone, teachers and students, works together, using process to attain progress.

When I used zeroes-based grading in my own practice, I believed I was motivating students by teaching the value of deadlines, the importance of organization, and the significance of timeliness, along with a little ELA on the side. Douglas Reeves (2004) describes this thinking as "an almost fanatical belief that punishment through grades will motivate students" (p. 325). While I didn't consider myself fanatical, I knew that a zero motivated the student not to turn in a late paper—right? Given that only two students turned in a late paper over nine years, one might even argue such thinking is correct. However, consider that I taught private-school classes with students who had deeply involved, committed, and wealthy parents with plenty of privilege. Would my approach have worked at a priority school where dropout rates are high, parents are too overstretched to support their children the way they wish to, and most students struggle to achieve? How many zeroes would I have handed out? What would that have done to the students who received them? Remember my student, Willie, from chapter 1 (page 11)? When he was called on to read and chose not to, he explained the feeling he had that the teacher was simply giving up on him. The very nature of a not-yet approach demands that teachers support students through productive struggle so that they never feel their teachers have given up on them.

Getting rid of zeroes in any points-based grading system is part of this approach. As author, associate partner with the International Center for Leadership in Education, and former principal Eric Sheninger (2019) explains:

> As a principal, I worked with my staff to tackle this issue as well as the overall practice of grading. I'm not going to lie; it was one of the hardest change initiatives I ever engaged in during my tenure as principal. Now I am not saying our solution was perfect or the best by any means. However, it did represent a step in a better direction in that we focused more on learning as opposed to grades and marks.

Focusing more on learning—on that productive struggle—inspires and motivates students toward their own learning goals and, ultimately, their own personal success.

Standards-Based Grading

As you read about traditional points-and-zeroes grading systems and my approach to grading early in my career, you probably asked yourself, "Where do students fit into this scenario?" It's the right question to ask, because I used (and many teachers still use) what education coauthors Grant Wiggins and Jay McTighe (2005) refer to as content-focused design and not results-focused design. *Content-focused design* focuses on the "*teaching* and not the *learning*" (Wiggins & McTighe, 2005, p. 15). With this mindset, teachers focus first on the inputs (textbooks, favorite lessons, long-used activities) instead of the outputs (the desired results) those inputs are meant to support. As a novice teacher, I used content-focused design. I began with the text, designed some lessons, and found worthwhile activities that I thought aligned well with the text. Conversely, in a classroom featuring *results-focused design*, the learning is centered around purposeful questions, such as, "Why are we asking students to read . . . ?" "What learnings will they seek . . . ?" and "What should students be expected to understand . . . ?" (Wiggins & McTighe, 2005, p. 15). Some teachers never think to ask *why* they assign students specific tasks or what *standards* their assessments are meant to measure. In a results-focused classroom, the not-yet approach supports students in asking these questions since students have the opportunity to wonder and analyze for the sake of learning, not the convenience of grades or marks.

All teachers need to be prepared to routinely ask themselves *Why?* and *What?* As Wiggins and McTighe (2005) put it, "Why are we asking students to read this particular novel—in other words, what *learnings* will we seek from their having read it?" (p. 15). For example, as a new teacher, I simply picked up where the former teacher had left off. Drama was the next thing on her list, and *The Miracle Worker* (Gibson, 1959) was the only full play in the anthology. When discussing the play, I encouraged students to use textual evidence to corroborate their inferences or assumptions, but I didn't cite a learning standard. (Note that, although these examples depict secondary and ELA-specific content, this thinking is equally applicable to any content area or grade level.)

Standards-based grading is based on assessing students on learning goals and performance standards, with one grade or entry per goal. The focus is on the "outputs—what students will know and do—rather than on inputs—the opportunities that will be provided to students and/or what teachers are expected to do" (O'Connor, 2018, p. 4). Instead of random numbers, percentages, and good teaching (as each teacher individually defines it), a specific set of learning goals and performance standards ensures teachers grade students on uniform competencies. Standards-based grading's focus on outputs makes it well aligned with the not-yet approach, which encourages a growth mindset (see chapter 3, page 37) while applying rigorous standards that communicate specifically what teachers want students to know and be able to do. Like most approaches to standards-based grading (Townsley & Wear, 2020), the not-yet approach offers multiple opportunities for students to demonstrate their understanding and apply that understanding to learning targets that are real, relevant, and relatable.

Although the standards-based education reform movement began in the 1980s, in 1992, there still was not a consistent set of national standards for teaching and learning. At the time, states were testing "students using state-developed, state-selected, or

state-approved tests and assessing student performance against state-established performance standards" (Coley & Goertz, 1990, p. 3). As a result, each state designed,
created, administered, and assessed its own set of standards. A state-developed test
in Georgia could test a very different set of performance standards than a state-
developed test in New York; each test was based on what those states thought their
students should know and be able to do.

In many cases, schools didn't even teach to their own state's standards. As a new
freshman ELA teacher at a private school, my focus was not on the standards or how
the state of Wisconsin would ultimately assess students. In truth, our school really
didn't pay much attention to the Wisconsin educational standards, and the ACT was
the only standardized test that mattered. I taught the curriculum my predecessor
had used and tried to make it engaging and purposeful while testing and grading the
heck out of my students based on what I thought was most important.

The Common Core State Standards (CCSS) Initiative (n.d.) launched in the
United States in 2009 as an effort that included state leaders and education commis-
sioners from forty-eight U.S. states and the District of Columbia and members of the
National Governors Association (NGA) Center for Best Practices and the Council
of Chief State School Officers (CCSSO). The idea was to have a uniform, national
approach to learning based on a common set of standards that would support all
students to be successful. Fast forward to 2018 and, as veteran English teacher and
Forbes senior contributor Peter Greene (2020) states:

> These days, it's considered more appropriate to talk about "col-
> lege and career ready." Meanwhile, while many states still have the
> Common Core Standards in place, many other states have made
> a show of throwing them out, then re-installing them under some
> new name.

It's not unusual to find elements of the CCSS redesigned across the United States
(Sawchuk, 2017a). For example, the state of Minnesota has adopted only the ELA
standards; the state of South Carolina has created the South Carolina College and
Career-Ready Standards and Indicators; Nevada calls their standards NVACS
(Nevada Academic Content Standards) because they include the Next Generation
Science Standards (NGSS) and their state's social studies standards; Texas uses Texas
Essential Knowledge and Skills; and Indiana uses the Indiana Academic Standards.
However, the common threads through all of these are remnants of the CCSS.

In a standards-based grading environment, points accumulation is not the goal of
teachers or students. Instead of the content driving the learning, the content is meant
as a vehicle to teach those standards (Heflebower, Hoegh, Warrick, & Flygare, 2019).

This is a step forward, but a standards-based approach is only part of a not-yet mindset. Some educators don't know much about the standards movement because it simply hasn't been a part of their teaching lives, in school or in practice. As a result, these teachers still set a goal to teach with a content-focused mindset, thinking this will enable their students to be well-rounded in specific content areas, be they ELA, science, mathematics, or others. With this mindset, some teachers aren't necessarily concerned about what their students *do* with what they learn.

This mindset also affects how teachers approach assessment. For example, as a young educator, I was far more interested in teaching and assessing content based on what I deemed important from my chosen themes, but such subjective mindsets aren't aligned with an assessment's proper role. The purpose of having standards is for teachers to have consistent learning targets that ensure rigor and transparency. As EdTech editor and former department chair and instructional coach Lauren Davis (2020) puts it, "The focus has been to create fewer, more challenging standards that make students think deeper and work towards more meaningful understandings and applications." Consultants Tammy Heflebower and colleagues (2019) sum up the implications of standards-based assessment: "Instead of assessing specific content in, say, a unit test, the unit test will assess certain standards by asking students to use the content they've learned to show their growth on the standards" (p. 3). Whether the standards come from national, state, or provincial origins, applying standards-based education reform is not about passing, failing, numbers, percentages, or points; it is about empowering students to master a standard and demonstrate what they know and can do.

Whether or not the CCSS or other specific sets of standards remain in use long into the future, the CCSS and similar efforts shifted discussion about learning to a results focus that values objective measurement of learning. The impact is to level the learning field for students, giving educators a place to start when determining what essential curriculum knowledge and skills are necessary for students to have. The not-yet approach encourages the use of such vigorous standards as a way to begin the learning for students and help teachers determine what students should know and be able to do while supporting them through setbacks and obstacles that are necessary to overcome when learning.

The Gradeless Classroom

As the standards-based education reform movement expands, several school districts across North America have chosen to enhance the benefits of a focus on standards by also moving toward a gradeless system. Despite what the label implies, going gradeless doesn't mean these schools have stopped assessing student learning, but it does mean a change in thinking about how teachers evaluate that learning. Starr Sackstein, author of *Hacking Assessment* (Sackstein, 2015), describes to me the key benefit of a gradeless classroom is how it enables teachers to put students first: "Students are empowered to be a part of the assessment process, and teachers readily provide feedback to ensure optimal student growth. Students spend time reflecting on their progress rather than negotiating points" (personal communication, March 17, 2021). It's an initiative meant to give teachers, students, parents, and administrators new ways to think about student performance and how to assess that performance utilizing feedback, clear learning targets, and scaffolded success criteria, and applying a growth mindset. As authors and science teachers Elise Burns and David Frangiosa (2021) further summarize, "The main goal of a gradeless classroom is to provide a learning environment that allows students to grow as learners without the constant fear of a single assessment having a devastating effect on their grade" (p. 1).

Student goals are an integral part of the gradeless classroom because this approach tasks them with monitoring their own understanding of learning goals. As you have likely guessed, this thinking aligns with the very heart of the not-yet approach. Gradeless classrooms develop efficacy around goal setting, and teachers encourage students to reflect and self-assess regularly to track their progress toward goals.

As a teacher, when you help students focus on goals, you are concentrating on more than just numbers, percentages, or averages. Grades must cover a lot of ground when incorporating what students are supposed to know and be able to do. It's nearly impossible to "combine aspects of students' achievement, attitude, responsibility, effort, and behavior into a single grade that's recorded on a report card" (Guskey, 2011, p. 19). And yet, that's what schools often expect teachers to do. Grades offer a mere snapshot of what a student can do at that moment; goals give a student the chance to focus on the process of progress. In the not-yet classroom, goals provide student ownership of his or her learning and support the student in monitoring that learning. As students self-assess their success in meeting scaffolded success criteria (which you'll learn about in chapter 4, page 51), they can discern if they have met their goals; if not, students have the opportunity to try again.

Susan M. Brookhart (2019), professor emerita of the School of Education at Duquesne University in Pittsburgh, Pennsylvania, explains the importance of clear learning goals to the success of a gradeless classroom. Whether teachers write goals in the form of learning intentions (see chapter 4) or students write their own goals, it is vital that students master goals that demonstrate their understanding of a particular standard. While it may seem essential that teachers be the ones to determine goals, giving students the opportunity to participate in writing their own goals makes the goals more practical, purposeful, and personal. What does the student want to know? What specifically does the student want to accomplish? What does the student want to do with what he or she has learned? Student-created goals offer students the chance to dive into a passion and dig deeper for their own learning's sake.

Of course, the teacher is responsible for delivering a curriculum based on vigorous standards. However, within that curriculum, it is imperative to make room for student interests and student suggestions. As an example, in teaching a social studies unit on individual development and identity, give students the time and space to create their own goals. If a student wants to research, analyze, and share a topic within that unit that he or she finds interesting, what goals does the student need to accomplish to show growth? Likewise, in a mathematics classroom focusing on the importance of predictions and inference, give students the opportunity to learn more about their neighborhood through various mathematical lenses: what do they predict is the current demographic of their neighborhood? How do they know? How could they determine if their prediction was correct? What does that demographic infer about the age or income of that neighborhood? Students could create interesting questions regarding the world in which they live and create mathematical opportunities based on what they want to learn. This type of responsibility propels students toward success.

For this approach to work, however, teachers must understand their role in facilitating effective student goals. Chase Nordengren (2020), a research scientist for the Northwest Evaluation Association, defines effective goals as a "set of practices for helping individual students understand their academic performance, identify concrete goals for future performance, and collaborate with their teacher on the behaviors and practices that will get them there." These tangible indicators (sets of practices, concrete goals, and teacher collaboration) are all authentic tools that students can use to begin an effective goal-setting process. As the Midwest Comprehensive Center (2018) explains, goal setting in this way "may be associated with multiple, positive benefits, for a range of ages and abilities, across academic subject areas and in varying geographic locations in the United States and abroad." These numerous benefits include enhancing students' learn-to-learn skills, increasing students' sense of agency and motivation, and developing students' capacity to manage their learning (Midwest Comprehensive Center, 2018). Therefore, student goal setting must be a shared activity, one where students collaborate with their teachers to design a goal or goals that help them achieve curriculum learning standards. Nordengren (2019) writes:

> Goal setting in isolation, then, is far less likely to be successful than when it is part of a culture where goal setting is common, goals are linked to learning, and students continue goal setting as they change teachers and grades.

Nordengren (2019) further explains, "Through goal setting, students develop the skills to reflect on their learning and turn their understanding of their current knowledge and skills into a drive to learn more." In other words, time spent on meaningful and purposeful reflection empowers students to metacognitively think about their own thinking and what they need to do to be successful. Instead of putting that onus solely on the teacher, students have the ability to create individualized goals that are uniquely interesting and exclusively personal while still meeting curriculum standards. Creating a classroom centered around goal setting encourages students to create goals for learning's sake while also motivating them to overcome setbacks and obstacles.

Another feature of a gradeless classroom is portfolios. When I began teaching, my ELA students kept their work in a portfolio—a manila folder where their tests, homework, and essays were saved. Even now, there's nothing more to portfolios than that. The difference is that, where portfolios used to be cumbersome and unorganized, in the digital age, they can serve as a high-tech showcase of student work in various artistic ways. As an example, teacher and certified technology integration specialist Mary Beth Hertz (2020) explains that "rough copies of student work may be included to show growth. If students are able to create a portfolio that spans multiple years, they can see growth over a longer time."

The ability for students to see their own growth is uniquely powerful and uncommonly purposeful. Principal Matt Renwick (2017) explains:

> When student work is housed in an online space for others to see, the importance for the learning naturally increases. Parents, peers, and even the world can be a potential audience. And when there is an authentic audience, there is the opportunity for feedback.

Thus, the opportunity to garner other voices to critique and evaluate gives students more chances for meaningful discussion and reflection. Education technology expert and researcher David Niguidula (2010) coined the term *digital student portfolios* and defines them as "a multimedia *collection* of student work that provides evidence of a student's skills and knowledge" (p. 154; as cited in Renwick, 2017). Renwick (2017) takes the definition of *digital portfolios* one step further, explaining digital portfolios are "dynamic, digital collections of information from many sources."

In a gradeless classroom, portfolios give students the chance to share their work and demonstrate growth over a period of time. They further encourage respectful conversations from various perspectives, and they inspire critical self-reflection and self-assessment meant to support students' learning. Given these factors, portfolios, as part of a gradeless classroom, are certainly a concept envisioned within the not-yet approach. The not-yet approach, like portfolios, also champions growth over time, the opportunity for students to experience setbacks without academic consequences meant to lessen a student's abilities, and the chance for students to routinely reflect on their learning process. Portfolios show personal growth, no matter how small that progress may seem. Students can see where they were and realize that within their own productive struggle, they utilized process to improve their products and achieve progress.

Consider for a moment the powerful synergy that occurs when teachers use student goals and digital portfolios as part of a not-yet approach. In his Michigan high school classroom, veteran ELA teacher Andy Schoenborn develops his curriculum and assesses student learning using a combination of National Council of Teachers of English (NCTE) standards (NCTE, 1996), CCSS (NGA & CCSSO, 2010), and International Society for Technology in Education (ISTE) standards (ISTE, n.d.). He then uses student goals and digital portfolios together to show literacy growth. For example, one of his students needed to improve her writing quality and commented that one of her goals was to "enhance my writing using stronger claims and evidence and diving deep into the meaning of the words" (personal communication, May 24, 2020). To ensure students' goals and portfolios align, Schoenborn designed his curriculum to present obstacles that ensure students engage in productive struggle to meet curriculum standards. Giving students time to revise and space to struggle through learning roadblocks and revise their work to meet standards empowers them to accept setbacks as a natural part of the learning process. There is no one-and-done mentality because the workshops he designs give students the opportunity to practice and process based on concrete feedback.

Brookhart (2007/2008) explains that when grading digital portfolios, "the most useful feedback focuses on the qualities of student work or the processes or strategies used to do the work." For example, in middle school German and coding teacher Kathy Rogers's (2019) classroom, students and teachers work as a collaborative team to ensure students have explicit feedback to support them in meeting learning goals: "Our focus is on the detailed feedback we share throughout the semester. We work together to evaluate the data in their portfolios to determine which learning targets are being met, and which ones may need additional work." Note that assigning grades isn't a factor here, just providing instructive feedback.

Similarly, Schoenborn explains that he uses learning workshops (writing workshops, in his case) to give students space and time to "set their own goals, work at their own pace, and receive one-to-one writing support with me during conferences" (personal communication, May 24, 2020). Creating opportunities to phase out "traditional graded transcripts in favor of digital, interactive portfolios that show academic and enrichment skills, areas of growth, and samples of students' work" (Gonser, 2020) is far more reflective of what students know and are able to do than a collection of letter grades culminating in a single overall grade.

In a final example, the 2020 Wisconsin Teacher of the Year Chad Sperzel-Wuchterl, a high school visual arts teacher, uses digital portfolios in his classroom as a way for his students to work and reflect as artists. Professional artists use digital portfolios to showcase their art and share it with others. In this class, the digital portfolio is an adaptation of traditional art processes of refining and reflecting. Sperzel-Wuchterl uses digital portfolios for a very real reason—he wants his students to think and behave as visual artists: "It has been common practice for years for artists of all kinds to use a portfolio to look back on successes and challenges" (personal communication, May 27, 2020). When his art students create their digital portfolios, his use of technology also ensures the artists have constant access to their work and can provide access to others for impromptu critiques. As a result, the artist is not tethered to the classroom to receive feedback; the artist's work and research can be accessed anywhere for immediate feedback and evaluation.

It's understandable that going gradeless might not sound realistic, given many teachers are beholden to school system or district mandates that require teachers to adopt specific grading practices. However, there are many concepts within this philosophy of a gradeless classroom that align with a not-yet approach that teachers can apply in their classrooms as part of daily instruction. Remember, the not-yet approach champions growth over time. Students may experience setbacks, but teachers and students accept them as normal and authentic opportunities to reflect, learn, and grow. That goal is achievable for any classroom.

Conclusion

According to progressive educator, author, and lecturer Alfie Kohn (2017), "There is never a need to reduce a student's performance to a letter or a number," and yet that has been the basis of education since the early 20th century. Kohn (2017) goes on to say, "[Students] are less likely to play with ideas because they are more concerned with doing only what is necessary to get the correct answer and secure the higher grade." This idea of *playing with ideas* is what makes learning a unique concept and not a condition for accumulating points.

Traditional grading systems have become antiquated, as statewide and national performance standards give teachers the opportunity to align their content and instruction to standards that ensure learning. Teachers should no longer teach to the content; but, instead, align their content to learning standards. Whether teachers utilize a standards-based grading system based on learning goals and performance standards or use a gradeless digital portfolio, where student learning goals and feedback are essential to students' development, the ultimate purpose of grading is student growth. Educators want students to explore new perceptions and wonder about the unknown because, in those explorations, there will be time and space to try again—to experience setbacks and obstacles as examples of process and progress.

Ruminate and Respond

Consider what you've learned in this chapter, and individually or with your team, answer the following questions.

1. What is your current grading practice (traditional, standards-based, gradeless, or other)? Is it effective? How do you know?

2. If you moved from a traditional to a standards-based grading system, think back to that particular change of practice. Is it an effective grading system in your classroom? How do you know?

3. If you still work within a traditional grading system, what could you do to ensure your instruction focuses on allowing students to experience setbacks while learning to incorporate agreed-on standards?

4. Would you consider using learning portfolios as a key part of showing student learning in your classroom? Why or why not? If yes, what format would you use (physical, digital, or both)?

5. In reflecting on your approach to grading, what concepts of the not-yet approach do you see in your classroom?

3

Concepts to Support the Not-Yet Approach

For many teachers, grading remains a necessary evil within the teaching profession. As a twenty-year teaching veteran who has been an instructional coach and reading specialist since 2013, I have seen anxious students crying in the classroom as they explain, cajole, and eventually beg their teacher for a chance to try again, and I have seen teachers do whatever they could to help those students pass a class—from offering make-up classwork and allowing them to retake tests and redo projects to setting aside personal time to support and reteach course content and standards. When I was a classroom teacher responsible for student grades, I often thought, "If I could just teach, just learn with my students, wouldn't that be great? If I didn't have to assess and worry about the implications that grading brings with it, I would be a much better teacher."

Classroom teachers often feel stuck between a rock and a hard place, thinking, "If I pass the student, what will the student have learned . . . that he or she can just wait until the last minute, offer a sad story, and pass on sympathy?" Sometimes teachers think, "If I do teach the student a lesson, and the student fails the quarter or the semester, I will have to endure the wrath of the parent and ultimately justify this failure to the administration."

Neither line of thinking focuses on the most critical aspect of the equation: students will not learn necessary standards from merely passing a class out of convenience. Similarly, while an F might accurately reflect a lack of learning, it doesn't provide a pathway to learning students *need*. Students learn best by *doing* something—something authentic and rewarding. Jennifer Gonzalez (2018a), host of the *Cult of Pedagogy* website and podcast (www.cultofpedagogy.com), explains:

> If we want our students to actually learn the facts and concepts
> and ideas we're trying to teach them, they have to experience those
> things in some way that rises above abstract words on paper. They
> have to process them. Manipulate them. To really learn in a way that
> will stick, they have to DO something.

To do something is to learn and to share that knowledge in engaging and passionate ways. My experience with the not-yet approach tells me students want to learn, and they want to share their knowledge with the world around them. Begging for an unearned passing grade or accepting failure is the student admitting he or she has no power, and when students feel powerless over their education, they quit trying. Amy L. Eva (2017), associate education director for the Greater Good Science Center, explains, "One surefire way to make students feel powerless is to focus on everything they are weak and failing at. When problems loom large, they can undermine your students' sense of self and capacity to engage in class." That loss of self or loss of capacity can cause students to reconsider their motivation and become frustrated.

To move students beyond that resignation—that something is happening *to* them—teachers must include them in the learning process and all the successes and challenges that process entails. Most of all, teachers must support students in accepting those challenges, that even though the classroom work will be difficult, students will have their teacher's support and that of the classroom community, including explicit and timely feedback. In short, teachers and students alike must adopt a mindset that unsuccessful attempts to learn don't reflect a lack of ability to learn but the need for another approach. The learning hasn't happened *yet*, but it will. With this support and through the application of a few essential concepts of the not-yet approach, students will know success and thrive.

For the not-yet approach to thrive, teachers and students alike must adopt and develop mindsets that accept obstacles as normal, always learning from overcoming them and moving forward. There are three specific research-backed mindsets that I find particularly helpful for unlocking students' capacity: (1) a growth mindset (Dweck, 2015, 2016), (2) grit (Duckworth, 2016), and (3) an abolitionist approach to teaching (Love, 2019a, 2019b). While the work supporting each mindset offers contrasting viewpoints, each mindset gives classroom teachers flexibility in laying the groundwork for their not-yet classroom. So, in this chapter, we explore these essential mindsets and show how each is fundamental to developing a not-yet classroom culture. By fostering a classroom culture around these elements, you instill in yourself and your students a not-yet approach to learning that ensures students leave your class with the essential knowledge and skills they need for the next grade or course.

The Growth Mindset

Carol S. Dweck (2006, 2016) introduced the growth mindset with her iconic bestseller, *Mindset: The New Psychology of Success*. In it, she explains that a "growth mindset is based on the belief that your basic qualities are things you can cultivate through your efforts, your strategies, and help from others" (Dweck, 2016, p. 7). She goes on to explain that growth mindsets view setbacks and feedback not as a reflection of one's innate abilities but as information to use to help oneself learn (Dweck, 2016). Conversely, someone with a fixed mindset believes their core qualities are carved in stone.

Dweck (2015) explains that fixed mindsets in students are common:

> They believe their talents and abilities are just these fixed traits. They have a certain amount, and that's it. This makes them afraid of learning. They're so worried about looking smart and not looking dumb that they back off from challenging learning.

Particularly for students with a track record of "failure" leading back to elementary school (see chapter 1, page 11), this worry manifests itself into an almost fearful attempt to try anything difficult. Mathematics teachers Tessa Kaplan and Rozlynn Dance (2018) explain, "Many students come to us afraid of making mistakes or getting the answer wrong. We must help our students believe that their deepest learning can stem from their mistakes." Indeed, the opportunity to celebrate mistakes and learn from them is deeply rooted in the not-yet approach and a vital part of a growth mindset.

The movement around growth mindsets monopolized much of education as teachers created opportunities to help students learn to believe that they can overcome learning challenges. Unfortunately, this effort is compromised if well-meaning teachers don't fully understand or misinterpret the application of a growth mindset (Canonica, 2019). As a result, students work frantically to achieve success yet continue to struggle because they don't yet realize that a growth mindset means something more, something deeper. Paolo Canonica (2019), a chartered psychologist and associate fellow of the British Psychological Society, says:

> In my years of teaching and counselling pupils I have come across a problem linked to growth mindset: pupils who try very hard indeed, but still do not achieve. Often these pupils have embraced the growth mindset message that intelligence, talent and ability can be grown through effort and determination.

In a conversation with *The Atlantic*, Dweck discusses the *false-growth mindset*, explaining that some teachers simply praise students' effort without any awareness of whether students made an *effective* effort (as cited in Gross-Loh, 2016). Dweck says:

> But students know that if they didn't make progress and you're praising them, it's a consolation prize . . . . Growth mindset's popularity was leading some educators to believe that it was simpler than it was, that it was only about putting forth effort or that a teacher could foster growth mindset merely by telling kids to try hard. (as cited in Gross-Loh, 2016)

The phrase *try hard* is counterproductive and hurtful. The inference is that the student hasn't tried and wants to fail *purposefully* or that simply trying automatically leads to success. For example, I once attended an aerial yoga class with a friend. The instructor wanted us to hold onto the ropes and, with our core muscles, flip ourselves over. I tried several times and couldn't lift my legs up high enough to flip myself over. When I asked the instructor for help, she told me to *keep trying*. I did try, again and again and again, until I grew frustrated and sat next to my mat. The instructor asked why I had given up. I explained I didn't have the core strength to lift myself up. Her advice—*keep trying*. If you've guessed that I never went back to the class, you're right.

In attempting to build students' growth mindsets, teachers have to be wary of using empty language that doesn't support students and the work they are doing. When the aerial yoga instructor told me to keep trying, she was using empty language. The struggle I experienced wasn't productive in that my attempts weren't building any skills that would lead me to eventual success. What I needed was specific coaching (scaffolds) about what I was getting wrong. Imagine if the instructor had looked at my attempt and helped me adjust my form or explained how to shift my balance, and how that might've helped me succeed.

While language is certainly important, developing worthwhile habits and purposeful strategies is necessary to a growth mindset. Author James Anderson (2021) explains teachers are most successful when they utilize a growth mindset as a pedagogical tool with "an increasing focus on growth and the process of learning" (p. 45). In essence, fostering growth mindsets in students is about supporting them in establishing accessible habits and strategies that support the learning process and use resulting products to achieve progress.

One habit that teachers can model for students is the value of being open to trying new things, thinking outside the box, and making repeated attempts to overcome challenges. Give your students permission to be courageous risk-takers by designing a classroom that highlights wonder and curiosity and encourages questions and what-ifs. If you don't already do this, start simple. Perhaps add some inspirational posters to your walls or ask your students to create posters that exemplify the habits of risk-takers. Or, start each morning with a question: "What problem did you encounter recently, and how are you facing that challenge?" Don't ask students how they "fixed" the problem. Not all problems are fixable, nor is the purpose of the question to focus students on failed attempts from a deficit perspective. Instead, encourage them to explain the setbacks and obstacles they encountered or are encountering and how they are progressing or hope to progress regarding that problem. As part of this exercise, ensure participation is voluntary (students don't have to share) but emphasize that simply sharing a problem with others often creates an opportunity to try a new way to solve it or a new way to think about it.

When considering how to best support student implementation of purposeful habits that reflect a growth mindset, consider that "Important achievements require a clear focus, all-out effort, and a bottomless trunkful of strategies" (Dweck, 2016, p. 67). Model for students how to move beyond being a passive consumer of information and instead be an active producer (Ward, 2017). As an example, teachers often ask students to research topics and concepts. But students with a fixed mindset may be unwilling to research, read, or analyze information they disagree with or information that goes against their belief systems. To be active producers, students need access to all sides of an issue or situation. Give your students the time and space to read controversial subjects, with you as their guide, and ensure they have the opportunity to pose questions and dig deeper. Become the facilitator as students become researchers of their own learning.

Helping students develop their *metacognition* (their ability to think about their own thinking) also helps build a growth mindset. Encourage students to be aware and in control of their own thought process. When they face setbacks, give them a chance to reflect on their thought process and what they might do differently next time (Busch, 2015). As an example, when student groups are working on difficult mathematics problems, applying productive struggle as they try various problem-solving techniques, ask them to record video or audio of their conversations. As students play back those conversations, they will hear themselves think out loud, ask questions of each other, abandon possible answers, and try again. Giving students time to hear themselves as thinkers is a powerful tool in the metacognitive thought process. When teachers provide the necessary supports for empowering students to develop needed skills, embrace creativity and originality, and eventually succeed in meeting their learning goals, *then* teachers can focus on the language of success.

Jim Taylor (2009) reminds adults that the phrase *good job* is lazy, worthless praise that is, in fact, harmful. The words *good job* offer no specifics. What is it the student is doing well, and what has the student learned from it? "In helping students develop a growth mindset, praise should be all about the learning, not about the learner. Take the opportunity to praise the work students are doing, but be careful of praising the individual" (Grafwallner, 2020, p. 51). Instead of generically saying, "Good job," consider using thoughtful praise that benefits the process and helps build students' confidence. Consider the following examples.

- "I know that took a lot of time and work, but you stuck to it and got it done."

- "What strategy have you already used? How did it help you? Which one should we try now?"

- "This approach didn't seem to work for you. Let's look together at what went wrong and what we can learn from it."

- "You seem frustrated about the amount of feedback I provided on your assessment. What can we do to look at the feedback as support and not as mistakes?"

- "I noticed the results improved from your last test. What did you do differently this time?"

- "I noticed you stayed at your desk and kept working on this problem even though it was challenging. I appreciate you sticking with it."

With this understanding, consider how a growth mindset fits into the not-yet approach. Thoughtful praise encourages the strategies, approaches, and habits that help students concentrate on the work. When teachers provide guidance and scaffolds that lead to productive struggle, using supportive growth-focused language with students, it's not about whether the student is good at a task or whether the student is trying. Rather, it reminds students to understand that the work of learning is challenging; there will be setbacks and obstacles, but students can overcome them and meet their learning goals. It's also about the teachers' mindset. By implementing the not-yet approach in the classroom, teachers never give up on students' willingness to tackle that hard work head on. As a result, students aren't allowed to give up on themselves.

Grit

Besides establishing a growth mindset, teachers need to help their students develop perseverance, the ability and desire to stay with a project or task until completion.

We know that it can be difficult for students to stay focused, particularly during whole-group direct instruction (The Hechinger Report, 2017). Off-task behavior can characterize itself in many different ways, such as daydreaming, walking around the room, or talking with peers. Often, students themselves don't know how to control their focus or have legitimate challenges doing so, such as attention-deficit/hyperactivity disorder (ADHD; Barnett, 2017). How can teachers help students develop perseverance when they struggle or find their minds easily distracted?

Angela Duckworth's (2016) *New York Times* bestseller, *Grit: The Power of Passion and Perseverance*, profiles highly successful individuals who possess "a kind of ferocious determination" (p. 8). Duckworth (2016) lists two traits common to these individuals: (1) they are unusually resilient and hardworking, and (2) "They knew in a very, very deep way what it was they wanted" (p. 8). Duckworth's (2016) theory of grit began when, as a teacher, she noticed that intelligence wasn't the only "factor separating successful students from those who struggled, and that grit—holding steadfast to a goal through time—was highly predictive of success" (as cited in Fessler, 2018). She eventually developed a *grit scale*, a self-reported questionnaire used to evaluate focused effort and interest over time (Duckworth, n.d.a).

Grit and the grit scale took the educational world by storm, encouraging teachers to teach grit to their students (Duckworth, n.d.a, n.d.b, n.d.c, 2009). Educator and consultant Eric Jensen (2019) classifies grit as an essential component of his achievement mindset for better supporting students who live in poverty. Author and former teacher Vicki Davis (2015) explains ways she teaches grit to her students, such as talking about grit, reading books about grit, and sharing examples that model grit. However, like teaching growth mindsets, instilling grit in your students as part of a comprehensive not-yet approach requires more than a slogan. Author, middle school teacher, and project-based learning coach Heather Wolpert-Gawron (2017) writes about the difficulty of teaching grit:

> I would argue that without passion or interest in a topic, grit is difficult to cultivate in oneself, and even harder to teach. . . . It can feel nearly impossible to convince students who haven't been on this planet very long, who haven't been around life's block often, that the effort of persistence is worth it. To do so, we need to ensure that our teaching taps into topics or processes that students genuinely feel.

Like Dweck (2016), Duckworth (2016) has also revised her approach to and thinking about grit based on how she's seen people apply it. In an interview with NPR reporter Anya Kamenetz (2016), Duckworth says of grit, "The enthusiasm is getting ahead of the science." Much like the growth mindset, educators had interpreted grit in their own way and taught their method to their students, not necessarily adhering to Duckworth's concept.

Duckworth (2016) stands by the science of her research on grit, which finds that self-confident students with strong worth ethics, impulse control, and an ability to take and reflect on feedback are likely to live happier, healthier, and more productive lives. The open question is how teachers can best cultivate those qualities among highly diverse classrooms of students. Or, as Fort Lewis College visiting assistant professor Paige Gray (2016) puts it, "So how can students have—or learn—grit when all kids face different realities—different struggles, different dreams and different social structures?"

Gray's (2016) question is one most educators ask about the one-size-fits-all educational system that remains the foundation of learning. In a classroom of thirty-plus students, there are thirty-plus stories. To get to know students, teachers must get to know their stories. Here are some ideas.

- **Ask questions:** Student voice is a powerful component of the not-yet classroom. Ask students, perhaps in a survey, what their interests are. What topics would they like to discuss, research, and analyze? Ask them what it is about the topic ideas they propose that they find interesting.

- **Use experts:** Teachers are experts in learning, but they can't be experts in everything. Bring in guest speakers with expertise in local government, repertory theater, restaurants, health care, manufacturing, or skilled trades to complement a unit or course of study. Create opportunities for students to ask questions, shadow, or even intern with professionals, and gather information.

- **Tap into families and neighborhoods:** Ask students to interview their family members or other relatives who might have lived through a significant time in history. Or, ask students to interview their neighbors to learn more about their neighborhood and how the neighborhood might have changed (Grafwallner, 2018a). Create research time for students to share that information with the class. Ask students to host their neighbors or family members as guest speakers.

These and similar ideas run counter to one-and-done approaches because they provide opportunities for students to dig deep and take their time. For example, students might begin interviewing family members with a specific intention or topic in mind, such as learning about the history of their community, only to realize there isn't enough there to meet specific learning goals. Maybe the student's family only recently moved in and doesn't yet have deep roots in the community, but the next-door neighbor runs a local restaurant and can talk to the student about how the community has evolved. The keys to these processes are time and determination, which almost always lead to something beneficial for learning.

A not-yet classroom culture must ultimately focus on flexibility as a way of demonstrating that teachers not only tolerate but encourage setbacks and obstacles. Being flexible does not mean giving in or making things easier, but rather listening to students, hearing their stories, and working together to walk a path toward progress. It's about helping students persevere through assignments, projects, and deadlines with work they can be proud of and work that is satisfying. Educators must teach students that even if they are determined, resilient, and hardworking (traits of a growth mindset), they could still fall down. Grit, then, is all about how to get back up again, demonstrating the necessary flexibility to try a new approach. Jensen (2019) posits five specific ways teachers can help their students develop grit.

1. Help students continually value their goals.

2. Show examples of what grit looks like, such as from movie or book characters, real-world figures, and so on.

3. Foster conditions for grit with a celebratory and positive classroom culture.

4. Make grit real by modeling gritty behavior.

5. Reinforce grit in action by calling it out when students display it.

While these strategies offer a foundation for building grit, remember that simply encouraging students to show grit isn't enough. You have to give students the time and space to share their stories and how they persevered. If a student doesn't feel he or she has a story to share or his or her story doesn't show grit, do not judge or evaluate his or her perseverance. Instead, remind all students that simply sharing their personal narrative is itself courageous and valuable. Reading about grit and talking about grit are important, but empower students to share their own gritty stories of their own reality and applaud their honesty in sharing those stories.

The Abolitionist Teacher

Although a growth mindset and grit are essential components of classroom culture, do not be quick to assume that an apparent lack of either in your students means they don't have it. In particular, teachers should *never* assume an apparent lack of grit or perseverance in a student means he or she lacks it. Always be mindful that students' grit reservoir may be tapped long before they step foot in the classroom.

Worse, teachers can do real damage if they imply to overtaxed students that they simply lack grit. This can be especially true of your students of color. Love (2019b), an associate professor of educational theory and practice at the University of Georgia, warns teachers against seeing grit, in particular, as a quick fix, noting that students of color already have plenty of it:

> If teachers knew how enslaved Africans made it to the United States and how we as African-Americans fight every day to matter in this country, I believe they would understand why questioning whether African-American kids have grit is not only trivial but also deeply hurtful.

The hurt Love (2019b) describes is indicative of a lack of awareness that many teachers unintentionally have of who their students of color are as individuals, the lives they lead outside of school, and what their unique needs are. Much as this is true of all students, it's especially important that White teachers, including myself as a White woman, not pretend to know the lived experiences of their Black and Brown students. However, as educators, we can teach with a focus on equity and understanding by adopting and modeling a mindset that is flexible, reflecting a willingness to listen and adapt to change.

Love (2019a) encourages educators to adopt *abolitionist teaching*, which means encouraging all educators to "fight with the creativity, imagination, urgency, boldness, ingenuity, and rebellious spirit of abolitionists to advocate for an education system where all Black and Brown children are thriving." That limitless spirit can become part of all educators' teaching by showing all students their teacher will tirelessly advocate for them to thrive in a system they are actively helping to change.

Unfortunately, the education system is a slow behemoth that takes its time in making any significant change, even at the schoolwide and districtwide levels. But you can create, right here and right now, an authentic classroom of change where you are willing to adopt an abolitionist mindset to move beyond previously accepted practice and instead imagine what's possible. To begin, be intentional in conversations regarding race, and don't be afraid to have them. Create safe spaces where students can share their feelings without being "wrong" or without being judged. Teach for America (www.teachforamerica.org) and the Southern Poverty Law Center (www.splcenter.org) are valuable places to begin that conversational journey. For example, the Southern Poverty Law Center (n.d.) offers various resources for teachers, administrators, and counselors at all grade levels to begin or continue the ongoing journey to abolitionist teaching.

Work with your students as a team to create change now for the good of all. Part of that work involves not making assumptions about student behavior. When faced with a student who seems to show disregard for his or her own education, the not-yet approach dictates how critical it is for teachers to ask *Why?* For example, when I was an alternative education English teacher, one of my students was continually late to my first-hour class. He would come to school frazzled, often without his book, paper, or pencil, and often agitated with himself for being late. Giving the student a classroom text, paper, and a pencil, and doing so without judgment, was easy; I wanted to know *why* he was always late to my class.

Initially, when I asked him why he was late, he would tell me he accidentally missed the bus. Another time, he told me his mom wasn't able to drive him because she got off work late. At this point, it's very easy for educators to assume the student is being lazy or careless, or to adopt some other deficit-driven mindset. But after more and more conversations and phone calls home (which went unanswered), he confided that he was responsible for getting his siblings off to school. But it was more than just getting his siblings on the bus—it was getting them up in the morning and helping them get dressed, combing their hair, and brushing their teeth. His mother worked third shift and trusted him to get everyone off to school. I explained his situation to his guidance counselor and our assistant principal, and I asked if they would change his schedule so he would have a first-hour study hall. As a result, the school's staff modified his schedule to accommodate his home responsibilities.

This student didn't need a stronger growth mindset, and he didn't need more grit. He illustrated his determination, resiliency, and hardworking spirit every morning as he cared for his family. What he needed most was for the school's teachers and leaders to adopt a nonjudgmental abolitionist mindset about his behavior, a mindset devoid of assumptions and focused on gathering information, so they could support him with a respectful way to retain the trust of his mother and also be a focused learner. After the change to his schedule, for the rest of the year, he was on time and able to balance his learning responsibilities with his home responsibilities.

As you look for ways to incorporate abolitionist teaching practices into your lessons and units, consider the following actions derived from guidance Love expressed in an interview with the Association for Supervision and Curriculum Development (ASCD) about her approach to abolitionist teaching (as cited in Stoltzfus, 2019).

- Create growth-focused discussions around racist, homophobic, or Islamophobic behaviors wherever you see them.

- If you're a White teacher and you have a classroom of White kids, talk to them about their privilege.

- Support local, state or province, and even national efforts to promote equity and equality in education.

- Always put love at the center of what you do.

In contemplating these actions, don't be afraid to challenge the status quo of your school, district, or community, particularly in cases where a toxic culture stands in opposition to equity and equality. However, do be mindful of school or district guidelines regarding such conversations, approaching conversations with a productive, growth-building mindset and grit.

Conclusion

The foundation for the not-yet approach is all about designing and creating a classroom culture that encourages the process of learning while accepting that setbacks and obstacles are part of that process. When students take risks and see those risks as normal, they can rise above what they knew yesterday and apply it toward tomorrow. Research from Dweck, Duckworth, and Love offers educators ways to support students in adopting a not-yet mindset. Utilize their research as a way to help your students realize that setbacks and obstacles don't define them but propel them to a new beginning of success. The not-yet approach is not easy; it's about creating a new way of understanding process, products, and progress, where students are willing to start over to begin again.

Ruminate and Respond

Consider what you've learned in this chapter, and individually or with your team, answer the following questions.

1. What is the cultural mindset in your classroom? How do you know? How could you strengthen it?

2. After reading Dweck (2016), Duckworth (2016), and Love (2019a, 2019b), what are your thoughts on their interpretation of a growth mindset, grit, and abolitionist teaching?

3. How can you incorporate examples of growth mindsets, grit, and abolitionist teaching in your classroom?

4. How is the not-yet approach evident in a growth mindset, grit, and abolitionist teaching?

5. What are some ways you could collaborate with your colleagues in creating interdisciplinary units that reflect a growth mindset, grit, and abolitionist teaching?

Vigorous Learning Intentions and Scaffolded Success Criteria

Your classroom is the hub of the not-yet approach. It is where you will have the most impact moving students beyond learning setbacks and obstacles and toward authentic understanding and achievement. As you'll read about in part 2 (page 79), there are many characteristics of the not-yet classroom, but creating vigorous learning intentions and scaffolded success criteria is the cornerstone that supports everything that follows. These are well-known and researched concepts (Hattie, 2012), but if you are unfamiliar with them, it's critical that you understand the following.

- **Learning intentions:** These are "what you want your students to know and be able to do by the end of one or more lessons" (Fisher & Frey, 2018, p. 82). Think of learning intentions as the essential goals you want students to achieve in a comprehensive unit.

- **Success criteria:** These are "a means for teachers and students to utilize feedback specifically oriented to the learning intentions. They clarify how a task or assignment will be judged" (Fisher & Frey, 2018, p. 83). Think of the success criteria as the milestones or learning targets you have determined that will enable students to meet the goals represented in their learning intentions.

Having vigorous learning intentions and scaffolded success criteria ensures students have clarity about what they are supposed to know and be able to do. Without such clarity, negative behavior (along with a negative mindset) becomes the norm. Fisher and Frey (2018) contend that without purposeful learning intentions and success criteria, "lessons wander and students become confused and frustrated." To avoid this outcome, it's vital that learning intentions be vigorous and success criteria be scaffolded. In this context, *vigorous* means something that students will *do*. Direct instruction has a role in setting students up for success with achieving learning intentions, but students will not meet them from a purely sit-and-get experience. Vigorous learning intentions engage and motivate students by giving them one or more questions to solve (Grafwallner, 2020). *Scaffolded* success criteria, then, are a means to break the learning up into chunks that each use a supporting tool or structure, such as a learning progression for students to achieve the specific criterion (Alber, 2014).

In essence, students complete a learning progression to achieve a success criterion, and they complete success criteria to achieve a learning intention (Grafwallner, 2020). By ensuring students have access to vigorous learning intentions and scaffolded success criteria, you give them the road map they need to self-assess their own learning journey, which aids students in engaging in and persevering through productive struggle.

However, no matter how well thought out or well written a learning intention is, and no matter how aimed toward student progress the success criteria are, if teachers don't ensure they are part of a classroom routine then, unfortunately, none of it will matter. For example, teachers should write learning intentions for a daily lesson the day before students walk into the classroom, not at the same time. Learning intentions need to be well planned and thought out to be vigorous. They can't be hashed out at the last minute. In addition, keep the daily lesson's learning intention and success criteria where students can see them and make sure they're in the same place every day. For example, use an easel at the front of the room or a prominently placed whiteboard where students can reference it at a glance. Discuss the learning intention and success criteria at the beginning of class. Give students opportunities to ask about them and analyze what they will have to do to be successful. When the learning intention and success criteria become part of the class routine, students will understand what they must know and be able to do.

In this chapter, you will learn about using pedagogical approaches to vigorous learning intentions and scaffolded success criteria to initiate the not-yet approach in your classroom. From this foundation, I further detail the purpose behind vigorous learning intentions and scaffolded success criteria and provide the knowledge you will need to write and apply them in the classroom. Finally, I show how you can use feedback from classroom experiences as data to iterate on and improve your learning intentions and success criteria.

Initiating the Not-Yet Approach in Your Classroom

Sometimes, teachers believe students show they've achieved their learning at the end of the lesson or unit, usually via a summative assessment. The thinking goes, for example, if a student has memorized multiplication tables, then he or she has learned multiplication skills. But that is not necessarily true. It's entirely possible for students to memorize the content of a multiplication table without understanding how the numbers relate to each other (number sense). It's the process of learning multiplication and how and when to use it that aligns with most state and provincial standards, making it important knowledge for students to understand. So, while a student may have memorized multiplication tables, the real work of productive struggle might actually take place as he or she works to understand how the numbers in multiplication tables relate to each other. Teachers use the not-yet approach in the classroom when they give students opportunities to work toward that understanding, such as by issuing activities and resources to help students define what multiplication means, offering visual supports to make the mathematics of multiplication concrete, breaking up multiplication tables into more manageable chunks, and providing time to practice. Utilize the language examples in chapter 3 (page 37) to gain a sense of students' process and provide supports where needed. Remember, there is always more to students' thinking and attitudes toward their learning than what they convey in a written test or capture in an essay.

It's easy for educators to get locked into the practice of doing what they've always done. However, it's important for teachers to focus on continuous pedagogical improvements (ways to improve how you teach) that give students the chance to engage in learning processes and then support them in meeting learning goals. According to Mike Fisher (2019), education author and blogger, teachers should "be critically aware of the traditional aspects of instruction and what is timeless and what is mindless. Educator comfort with past learning modalities should not be a factor for defending their use in the modern classroom."

By *mindless*, Fisher (2019) means the patterns and methods of instruction many teachers use simply because that's what they learned in their teaching programs, from a mentor, or from years of ingrained teaching habits. When teachers don't reflect on, research, and update their teaching methods or pedagogy, their classrooms don't progress. In such environments, it's impossible for teachers to establish and sustain vigorous learning intentions and scaffolded success criteria.

Successfully initiating the not-yet approach requires teachers to help students self-reflect on and self-assess their learning journey. To do that, teachers must determine if students have mastered a learning intention. Writing scaffolded success criteria then helps students self-assess whether they've achieved that intention. If a student has not mastered the learning intention, he or she can use their success criteria (on their own or with teacher support, as needed) to determine what kind of reforms he or she should embrace to achieve mastery. In some cases, students may implicitly know what changes they need to make just from reviewing what went wrong with a specific success criterion. Author and veteran teacher Patrice Bain (2018) explains that "the relationship between a student's understanding of their own learning, compared with their actual learning, has significant long-term impacts on study habits, motivation and overall learning." The not-yet approach emphasizes this sort of meta-cognition and growth mindset to engage in productive struggle. In addition, students apply what they *have* learned while engaging in productive struggle to support their high-level thinking, problem solving, and self-assessment. Acquiring new knowledge will happen most often with students who have attained these learn-to-learn skills (Sawchuk, 2017b), which are usually those students who are older or who have built experience with the not-yet approach. Elementary students or students new to the not-yet approach (students who need to build up their growth mindsets and grit) require teacher support to reform their approach.

In addition to the numerous actions I suggest in part 2 (page 79) for building a not-yet classroom, modeling actions and learning for students using explicit visual resources and other exemplars is critical for supporting students of all ages in productive struggle and learning to learn. Sometimes, students will seek out your support for reforms by requesting more precise feedback or reteaching. The most critical part of developing a not-yet approach in your classroom is understanding the importance of supporting students to learn to self-evaluate what they've done and how they can use that reflection (possibly, along with some reteaching or other supports) to do even better in the future.

Crafting Vigorous Learning Intentions and Scaffolded Success Criteria

In my book, *Ready to Learn* (Grafwallner, 2020), I explain the value of a well-written learning intention: "Learning intentions should engage and motivate by giving students one or more questions they want to solve. These questions are more likely to engage students in introspection if they are real, relevant, and relatable to the student" (p. 14). Let the words *engage* and *motivate* guide your efforts, as these are the traits that make learning intentions vigorous. For example, if you hand students a worksheet packet without introducing the packet or explaining its purpose, most students will quickly lose interest. Learning tools and aids, such as worksheets, graphic organizers, and mind maps work best when teachers provide and model them as supports to keep students on track, take notes, or organize their reflective thoughts. If worksheets or other support tools become simply a hoop to jump through before moving on to more interesting things, they will not engage students and support their learning. It's much harder to establish a not-yet classroom—one based on accepting challenges and striving to move forward—if the learning intentions don't motivate students to engage with complex tasks to solve.

Just as having engaging and motivating learning intentions is critical, it's equally important that your success criteria offer students clarity about the steps (scaffolds) needed to reach their goals. You must write them using student-friendly language, and they must be *achievable*. If students don't see themselves as being able to (eventually) master the success criteria, they will become disheartened very quickly, losing interest in undertaking challenges and learning from them. Writing for *Educational Leadership*, Connie M. Moss, Susan M. Brookhart, and Beverly A. Long (2011) explain that success criteria are "developmentally appropriate descriptions and concrete examples" of what success looks like. The key here is *developmentally appropriate*. If you are writing scaffolded success criteria that are too difficult for your students, they will not see themselves as learners with the possibility of success. They will view their lack of understanding as a personal failing.

When determining your success criteria, consider the goal of your learning intention and how your students will, via the milestones you have determined, demonstrate, apply, prove, or synthesize what they have learned to meet that goal (Grafwallner, 2020). Students want to know they can master those milestones. As I detail in *Ready to Learn* (Grafwallner, 2020), you can use the following specific guidelines when crafting vigorous learning intentions and scaffolded success criteria that will motivate, engage, and guide students to overcome challenges and achieve success.

- **Use intentional language:** Beginning learning intentions with *I can* statements implies a sense of knowing and doing, conveying confidence in a student's ability as a learner.

- **Focus on quality:** If students perceive a lesson to be busywork or lack relevance, they may choose not to fully engage in it or even participate at all. When writing a learning intention, keep it relevant and relatable. Students may not immediately see the relevance of the learning intention, so it is up to you to show them its significance.

- **Ensure clarity:** It is imperative you write a learning intention and success criteria in student-friendly language. Using teacher jargon or the jargon common to learning standards to write learning intentions and success criteria baffles students; student-friendly language helps students understand their goals, why they're important, and how they will achieve the expectations you have created for them.

- **Offer students choices:** Offering students choices in how they demonstrate what they know and can do that are based on their interests and learning styles *and* aligned with a learning intention and success criteria helps immerse them in the learning.

By aligning your learning intentions and success criteria with these characteristics, you begin to establish a not-yet classroom where challenges are part of the norm and where students self-assess what they have mastered and when they still need more practice. The following sections detail the processes you can use to write vigorous learning intentions and scaffolded success criteria.

Write a Vigorous Learning Intention

Writing learning intentions in concise, student-friendly language requires practice. Too much wordy teacher jargon (*teacherese*) will cause students to disengage because they will have no idea what the lesson will be about or what they are supposed to do. Further, if learning intentions aren't vigorous, that is, if they're too easy or seem impossible, students won't have the motivation they need to engage in productive struggle.

When writing a learning intention, also make sure you use productive verbs that demonstrate what the student is supposed to know and be able to do. If your learning intention is passive, students will not understand what to do with it, and the intention will be meaningless. Following are exemplary learning intentions for a range of K–12 classrooms.

- **Second-grade writing:**
  - *Learning intention*— I can introduce and explain my book using my opinion and linking words.

- **Fourth-grade reading:**
  - *Learning intention*—I can describe the character, setting, and event in my story using details.

- **Sixth- to eighth-grade science:**

    ○ *Learning intention*—I can define, demonstrate, and locate the differences among *superstition*, *pseudoscience*, and *science*.

- **Eighth-grade U.S. history:**

    ○ *Learning intention*—I can discuss, explain, and research the events leading to the American Revolution and their influence on the formation of the U.S. Constitution.

- **Ninth- and tenth-grade algebra:**

    ○ *Learning intention*—I can model the coordinate plane.

- **Eleventh-grade science:**

    ○ *Learning intention*— I can recognize the history, interactions, and trends of climate change.

Notice the use of *I can* statements in each of these learning intentions, which put the focus on students. *I can* statements make for strong prompts in learning intentions because they convey self-confidence in students' ability to be learners. They tell students they can meet the goal but put the responsibility on them to do so. This focus on what teacher and instructional coach Marine Freibrun (2019) refers to as *future success* supports the not-yet approach because, as you know, success may not come right away for your students. In the not-yet approach, teachers support students to develop a growth mindset and know that productive struggle is part of the learning process. *I can* statements give students approval to work through success criteria knowing that supports are available to them.

In addition, all of the learning intentions listed in this section have robust verbs, which tell the student exactly what he or she will be doing. For example, in the eighth-grade U. S. history lesson, the student will *discuss*, *explain*, and *research*. The student knows what he or she will be doing—there are no surprises in this lesson. Very likely, verbs such as these will stand out to you when reviewing national, state, or provincial standards, such as the CCSS. For example, when reading the grades 9–10 CCSS for reading informational texts, you will notice specific verbs under each anchor standard, such as *cite*, *determine*, and *analyze* (NGA & CCSSO, 2010). When writing your learning intentions, consider reviewing curriculum-connected national, state, or provincial standards for your curriculum to revise or modify the robust verbs to achieve the learning intention you want to write. In addition, consider using the action verbs that are part of Bloom's taxonomy (Anderson & Krathwohl, 2001) when you write your learning intentions. The list of robust verbs is scaffolded from low-level thinking (such as *remembering*) to high-level thinking (such as *creating*), thereby giving your students steps toward a natural thinking progression. Teachers may be tempted to simply utilize the full language of a learning standard as a learning intention. Avoid this. Writing learning intentions in student-friendly language makes them relevant to students, omitting teacher and education jargon so the task is clear.

Fortunately, you can use a simple template to help you craft vigorous learning intentions. Figure 4.1 shows an example of this template again utilizing the eighth-grade U.S. history example from this section. (See page 76 for a reproducible version of this figure.) Use this template as a working document as you flesh out what you want your students to know and be able to do. In the left column is what you want your students to know—the big picture. In the right column are the various components that make up the big picture. You will notice in the example that I want my students to know about the events leading up to the American Revolution and how these events formed the U.S. Constitution. In the right column, I've written down six events that meet this criterion. Consider this column a place where you can brainstorm ideas and possible suggestions about how you might want to teach these events and any supplemental resources you might use. You could use this template as a lesson plan or unit plan to capture all of your pedagogical resources, or you could use it as a template to jot down the basics. How you utilize this template is up to you and what you want to gain from it.

Write Scaffolded Success Criteria

As established earlier in this chapter, scaffolded success criteria offer students a way to self-assess if they have mastered what they are supposed to know and be able to do. By scaffolding the success criteria, students can see the milestones they must meet to reach mastery of a learning intention instead of relying on the teacher to tell them if they have learned the material. Mark Anderson (2017), a special education and ELA instructional specialist and author, writes about scaffolding, "Each step provides practice and feedback on a component skill that requires mastery before moving on." With scaffolding, students can determine if they have met a particular success criterion. If not, they can ask for assistance and, with teacher support, continue working to overcome that particular obstacle, then moving on to the next success criterion. By establishing milestones leading up to the ultimate goals, teachers make the work students must do feel achievable (Rollins, 2015). Further, within scaffolding lie opportunities for productive struggle that, because it occurs during classroom time, teachers are there to support.

Just like learning intentions, teachers must write success criteria in student-friendly language; after all, you are writing them for the students, so you want to be clear

Class: Eighth-grade U.S. history

Unit and Lesson: The American Revolution and the U.S. Constitution

What do you want your students to know?	I want my students to know:
The events leading to the American Revolution and how these events and their influence formed the Constitution	The following are the six events leading to the American Revolution. • The Stamp Act (1765) • The Townshend Act (1767) • The Boston Massacre (1770) • The Boston Tea Party (1773) • The Coercive Acts (1774) • British attacks on coastal towns (1776)
What do you want your students to be able to do with that information?	In the interest of time, I will combine the Coercive Acts and British attacks on coastal towns into one event.
Discuss, explain, and research the events and their influence.	Check the History Channel for videos and resources.
List possible verbs.	**I want my students to do:**
• **Knowledge:** *Define, recall, list* • **Understand:** *Explain, describe, predict* • **Apply:** *Solve, illustrate, produce* • **Analyze:** *Compare, calculate, deduce* • **Evaluate:** *Judge, convince, critique* • **Create:** *Design, construct, arrange*	I want my students to discuss each of these events, explain them, and research their influence. Possible ideas include: • Students, in small groups, pick an event, research the event, and discuss the importance of that event. Students share that information with the class by creating a video, a newscast, an original rap, or an original script to act out. (Allow for student ideas.) • Students evaluate their chosen events versus other events they didn't include. Were their events more important or less important? What was the influence of their events in forming the Constitution compared to the other events? Student groups could debate this issue with other groups to determine an event's influence.

Write your vigorous learning intention:

I can . . . discuss, explain, and research the events leading to the American Revolution and their influence on the formation of the U.S. Constitution.

Figure 4.1: Not-yet learning intention template.

and omit any kind of jargon that may be inherent in, for example, national, state, or provincial standards that learning intentions may be derived from. As with learning intentions, teachers should continue to use *I can* statements when writing each individual criterion, which again emphasizes student confidence in mastering key milestones. Writing each criterion using robust verbs demonstrates something the student must do. As a result, the learning is not passive but focused and specific. Table 4.1 highlights some dos and don'ts of effectively written success criteria.

Table 4.1: Dos and Don'ts of Scaffolded Success Criteria

Do . . .	Don't . . .
Create a list, using bullets or numbers so students can, if they want, cross off what they mastered; crossing off listed items gives students a sense of accomplishment and momentum, which aids in productivity (Oregon State University, n.d.).	Create a paragraph of success criteria or separate success criteria using a series of *ands*; a paragraph of stuff to do can be very difficult for students to visualize and use to self-assess when determining if they've achieved proficiency.
Keep the number of success criteria appropriate; there should be multiple criteria per learning intention, but don't overwhelm them. Consider the age and skill level of your students and the complexity of the task when determining the appropriate number (Freibrun, 2019).	Provide so many success criteria that students are overwhelmed or may not be able to complete them and achieve the learning intention as part of the lesson.
Design the success criteria based on *specific descriptors* that students need to complete (Ainsworth, 2017); the success criteria should reflect a progression of skills.	Write success criteria that are too big for students to accomplish; remember, these are smaller components that reflect achievable progression.
Use *I can* statements; *I can* statements show confidence in being a learner and focus students on future success (Freibrun, 2019).	Use *I will* statements; *I will* statements imply that the learning may happen or may not. *I will* doesn't offer the confidence that the student can learn the information and move forward.

Let's take a look at the success criteria for each of the learning intentions from the previous section.

- **Second-grade writing:**
  - *Learning intention*—I can introduce and explain my book using my opinion and linking words.
  - *Success criteria*—I know I am successful because . . .
    1. I can write a topic sentence introducing my book

2.   I can explain my opinion about my book, giving three reasons

3.   I can use linking words to connect my opinion and reasons

- **Fourth-grade reading:**

  o   *Learning intention*—I can describe the character, setting, and event in my story using details.

  o   *Success criteria*—I know I am successful because . . .

  1.   I can describe the character in my story using details (thoughts, words, or actions)

  2.   I can illustrate the setting in my story drawing three details and sharing those details with my reading partner

  3.   I can explain one event in my story to my reading partner, sharing three details

- **Sixth- to eighth-grade science:**

  o   *Learning intention*— I can define, demonstrate, and locate the differences among *superstition*, *pseudoscience*, and *science*.

  o   *Success criteria*—I know I am successful because . . .

  1.   I can define *superstition*, *pseudoscience*, and *science*

  2.   I can demonstrate the differences using a graphic organizer

  3.   I can find real-life examples of *superstition*, *pseudoscience*, and *science* and share them with the class

- **Eighth-grade U.S. history:**

  o   *Learning intention*—I can discuss, explain, and research the events leading to the American Revolution and their influence on the formation of the U.S. Constitution.

  o   *Success criteria*—I know I am successful because . . .

  1.   I can create a timeline of the events leading to the American Revolution

  2.   I can explain the impact of these events to a partner, keeping track of my thinking with a graphic organizer

  3.   I can show the connection among these important events and how they helped create the U.S. Constitution using a graphic organizer

- **Ninth- and tenth-grade algebra:**
  - *Learning intention*—I can model the coordinate plane.
  - *Success criteria*—I know I am successful because . . .
    1. I can plot points on the coordinate plane
    2. I can explain the power of the coordinate plane
    3. I can graph the coordinate plane
- **Eleventh-grade science:**
  - *Learning intention*— I can recognize the history, interactions, and trends of climate change.
  - *Success criteria*—I know I am successful because . . .
    1. I can read about the history of climate change
    2. I can research the causes and effects of climate change in my state
    3. I can create a graph showing the trends of climate change in the area where I live

Notice that by scaffolding the success criteria, students can self-assess their understanding. For example, if an eighth-grade student successfully creates *a timeline of the events leading to the American Revolution* that he or she believes the teacher will assess positively, the student can check that criterion off the list and move on to the next criterion. However, what if the student is struggling with the timeline? As an eighth-grade student, he or she may be able to self-reflect to determine or research solutions him- or herself. The student might also decide to meet with the teacher for some guided help, or he or she might ask a peer or study group for support. In any case, the student continues to work toward mastery, self-assessing as needed to determine if his or her work demonstrates mastery. In this way, students aren't wholly reliant on their teacher, instead taking a leadership role in their own learning.

At this point, you may be thinking, "This is great, but how will students know when they've met my expectations of their work?" One way is to provide students with a rubric describing what qualities demonstrate each success criterion. Teacher and instructional coach Marine Freibrun (2019) explains, "Success criteria can also include rubrics or teacher/student co-constructed rubrics. The rubrics need to be written with descriptive and strong language so students can monitor their own learning." Using rubrics in this way supports students in staying on track while eliminating common questions they may have (freeing time for more intricate or specific questions about achieving the learning). The late Grant Wiggins (2015), author and education consultant, agrees: "[A rubric] summarizes what a range of concrete works looks like as reflections of a complex performance goal."

Another way to model such complex performance goals to students is through various student exemplars. For example, to support student understanding of the eleventh-grade science success criteria in this section, the teacher could show various websites to their students that discuss the history of climate change. Next, the teacher can offer examples of previous student work, such as graphic organizers, T-charts, and mind maps that depict the causes and effects of climate change in that state. Writing for the Online Learning Consortium, Heather Garcia (2018) explains, "Sharing student work is a wonderful way to showcase the efforts and talents of your students as well as your pedagogical approach as an educator." However, prior to sharing the work, always ask for permission from the students to show their work to their peers or anonymize the work of previous students such that it isn't identifiable.

Finally, offer students feedback about their progress toward success criteria. This can include having informal conversations with students, conducting one-on-one mini-conferences, issuing surveys, or requesting written feedback. When offering feedback, be detailed but still concise enough that students can internalize and implement it (The Graide Network, n.d.). Further, remember to link your feedback to the specific expectations you laid out in your success criteria and any supporting materials, such as rubrics (The Graide Network, n.d.).

When offering feedback, it's also useful to get feedback back from students. This can be as formal as asking direct questions or seeking comments about the success criteria or observational notes based on how students reacted to those criteria. For example, say a teacher is giving student feedback about a graph the student created when working toward the third criterion in the eleventh-grade science example from this section (*I can create a graph showing the trends of climate change in the area where I live*). The teacher suggests the student uses a bar graph to show his or her findings instead of a pie chart, but the teacher also notes the success criterion could easily have stipulated the type of graph students should use.

With this knowledge in mind, see figure 4.2 (page 64) for an example of a template you can use when crafting success criteria. Note that this figure builds off of the template from figure 4.1 (page 59), so it's important that this template reflect the language you previously used (such as the action verbs *discuss*, *explain*, and *research* specified here). Similar to the learning intention template in figure 4.1 (page 59), this figure offers an opportunity to jot down your ideas on how you might want to teach these specific success criteria. Use it as a working document to flesh out your ideas so you can be

Class: Eighth-grade U.S. history

Unit and Lesson: The American Revolution and the U.S. Constitution

Learning Intention: I can discuss, explain, and research the events leading to the American Revolution and their influence on the formation of the U.S. Constitution.

How will students demonstrate what they know about the learning intention?	
List what you want students to be able to do (robust verbs), and determine essential questions about this learning intention.	**Using your robust verbs from your learning intention and the essential questions you associate with them, explain how your students can demonstrate they have mastered the full scope of the learning intention.**
Discuss: How will students demonstrate they know about the events leading to the American Revolution?	**Draft success criterion:** I can *create* a timeline of events. **Student actions:** • Students create a timeline listing the important events and their dates. • When students have completed their timeline, they can discuss the events with their partner to determine if they need to add anything else.
Explain: How will students demonstrate they understand these events?	**Draft success criterion:** I can *explain* the impact of these events to a partner. **Student actions:** • With a partner, students explain the impact of each event with their partner, taking notes or using a concept map to capture their thinking.
Research: How will students demonstrate these connections?	**Draft success criterion:** I can *research* to show the connection among these important events and how they helped create the U.S. Constitution. **Student actions:** • Students research various websites and use a graphic organizer to show the connection among these events. • Students use their graphic organizer to explain to their peers how these connections helped to create the U.S. Constitution.

Write your final scaffolded success criteria:

I know I am successful because . . .

1. I can *create* a timeline of the events leading to the American Revolution
2. I can *explain* the impact of these events to a partner, keeping track of my thinking with a graphic organizer
3. I can *show* the connection among these important events and how they helped create the U.S. Constitution using a graphic organizer

Figure 4.2: Not-yet success criteria template.

clear and concise in your language. You will notice that the example in figure 4.2 keeps the same language—*discuss*, *explain*, and *research*. (See page 77 for a reproducible version of this figure.) Use that language as your guide when determining what you want your students to do. As an example, how will students demonstrate that they know about the events leading to the American Revolution? In this case, I've determined that my students will create a timeline of those critical events, share that timeline with their peers, and discuss it in small groups, adding more information or removing unnecessary information based on that collaboration.

Applying Vigorous Learning Intentions and Scaffolded Success Criteria

Writing effective vigorous learning intentions and scaffolded success criteria is a vital step, but so is ensuring students have easy access to them. For example, because teachers use vigorous learning intentions and scaffolded success criteria as a road map to what they want students to know and be able to do, they often display them prominently in the front of the classroom. This ensures students can see them and enables teachers to refer directly to them during lessons. While this provides both students and teachers an easily accessible point of reference for their goals and their progress in meeting them, if the learning intentions and success criteria do not become authentic, then they will remain just words on the whiteboard.

To make learning progressions and success criteria authentic, teachers and students have to know in detail the progress they are making through the use of rubrics, student exemplars, and feedback. Sharing the rubrics with the students and asking for their feedback can certainly help eliminate any confusion later. TeachersFirst (n.d.) explains, "Students who are involved in the process of creating a rubric have a better understanding of the standards, gradations, and expectations of the assignment. Students also feel as if they have a 'voice' within the classroom." In addition, student exemplars are a visual reminder of what the student needs to do and that students just like them have been able to do it (Rashid-Doubell, O'Farrell, & Fredericks, 2018). Ongoing feedback throughout this process eliminates confusion, anxiety, and frustration.

Remember, applying the learning intentions and success criteria takes time, patience, and support from all involved. In my role as an instructional coach and reading specialist, I also support teachers in creating vigorous learning intentions and scaffolded success criteria. However, without an overall purpose or goal, in the classroom or schoolwide, learning intentions and success criteria could seem like busywork for teachers. That purpose or goal must be clear to all stakeholders: the students in the classroom, the teacher creating the learning intentions and success criteria, and even school leadership if their use is a schoolwide effort.

In 2014, my principal at Ronald W. Reagan College Preparatory High School in Milwaukee, Wisconsin, asked our school's literacy committee to develop a set of literacy skills members believed all students needed to learn to be successful in the four domains of reading, writing, speaking, and listening (Peterson, 2020). As literacy committee members, we reviewed a huge array of sources. We reviewed the reading skills on the ACT (n.d.) College and Career Readiness Standards (specifically the 16–28 score band) and the 6–12 informational reading skills of the Common Core College and Career Readiness Standards (NGA & CCSSO, 2010). We sent out a needs assessment asking teachers what skills they felt their students lacked. This wasn't a scientific survey; rather, it was just the teachers' own anecdotal data about what skills their students were missing. Last, we looked at our ACT Aspire data (the freshman or sophomore standardized test that students take several times a year to help predict their ACT score) to determine the types of questions students inaccurately answered. Based on the data, we determined the following six skills would represent the school's core proficiency skills.

1. Annotation and inquiry

2. Main idea, detail, and summary

3. Compare and contrast, cause and effect

4. Inference

5. Evaluation and critique

6. Vocabulary

After creating this list, the committee designed professional development sessions to introduce these skills to the remainder of the faculty. While many teachers were already teaching these skills, we wanted to meet with our colleagues and share ways they could teach skills explicitly within their content area. However, some teachers, who didn't necessarily consider themselves literacy teachers, didn't make the critical-skills connection right away. For example, members of the physical education department had some initial trepidation that the integration of reading skills might diminish students' time to move in class. These teachers shared their concern about having to be both reading teachers and physical education teachers.

To address their concerns, I offered to meet with all academic departments individually to illustrate how to explicitly incorporate these critical-thinking skills into their discipline's learning intentions and success criteria. I stressed that doing so would support students in transferring literacy to all disciplines. For example, students would be able to see the concept of a *main idea*, while frequently taught in ELA and social studies, is also a skill used in reading word problems in mathematics. Giving students an opportunity to see these connections and transfer these skills encourages students to practice transfer, which also encourages them to more willingly engage in a lesson (Poorvu Center for Teaching and Learning, 2021). We wanted students to be able to recognize those skills and see that they were, indeed, able to transfer them.

During my first meeting with the physical education department, I wanted to help the teachers realize they were already using various literacy proficiencies in their classes; as such, they were *already* teachers of disciplinary literacy in their content area. The next unit in their freshman physical education course was *ultimate* (the team sport featuring thrown discs). Before we created a lesson utilizing the proficiency skills, we created a thinking chart, making notes on what we wanted students to know about ultimate and do with ultimate. I asked the department teachers to jot down their ideas about what they wanted their students to know and be able to do. They came up with the following.

- To define the terms associated with ultimate

- To define the rules of the game and apply them

- To stand on the field and practice throwing the disc

We then designed the thinking chart in figure 4.3, based on what the physical education teachers wanted their students to know and be able to do.

What do I want my students to know? (Learning intention)	How to play ultimate
What do I want my students to do? (Success criteria)	1. Define the terms associated with ultimate. 2. Define the rules of ultimate and apply them. 3. Stand on the field and practice throwing the disc.

Figure 4.3: Sample thinking chart for playing ultimate.

You will notice that defining the terms associated with ultimate and defining the rules of ultimate are vocabulary skills, which I made sure to highlight to the physical education teachers. Next, I asked them, "What are some methods or techniques students could use to learn the terms associated with ultimate? What are some methods or techniques students could use to define the rules of the game and apply them? Lastly, what are some methods or techniques students could use to stand on the field and practice throwing the disc?" We brainstormed some ideas and created the chart in figure 4.4.

Learning Intention:	
I can learn to play ultimate.	
Success Criteria: I know I am successful because . . .	**Learning Methods and Techniques**
1. I can define the terms associated with ultimate	a. Create flashcards using 3 × 5 note cards. Write the term on one side and the definition on the other.
	b. Practice the definitions with peers.
	c. Match the objects used in ultimate to the corresponding note cards.
2. I can define the rules of the game and apply them	a. Read the rules of the game.
	b. Watch an ultimate game and apply the rules.
	c. With a partner, study the rules of the game.
3. I can stand on the field and practice throwing the disc	a. Practice a playing stance on the field.
	b. Practice holding the disc on the field.
	c. Practice a game of ultimate with peers.
	d. Observe other peers playing to study self-refereeing and to acquire knowledge of the rules.

Figure 4.4: Sample learning methods and techniques for playing ultimate.

Our next step was to identify where the students use the new methods and techniques to determine what they revealed about needed student proficiencies. One example, of course, was the use of content-specific vocabulary when playing ultimate. Without knowing and understanding the sport's language, it would be difficult to play the game. While brainstorming the learning methods and techniques, we realized another proficiency students needed to successfully complete this lesson: since students would be observing their peers to study self-refereeing, they would be offering feedback to their peers. Therefore, students would be using evaluation and critique during this lesson.

Through this process, the physical education teachers successfully fashioned a learning intention and success criteria, along with learning methods and techniques, for the next freshman unit. In addition, as we created our learning intention and success criteria, we determined that we had crafted two proficiency skills based on what the teachers wanted their students to know and be able to do.

During the first several weeks of introducing the proficiencies, I met with each department and used a similar process to review how to write vigorous learning intentions and scaffolded success criteria using the thinking chart pictured in figure 4.3 (page 67), highlighting the learning methods and techniques. I found that all departments, from art and music to world languages, benefitted from using thinking charts as a way to brainstorm how to write vigorous learning intentions and scaffolded success criteria. In addition, I also showed departments how to incorporate the proficiencies into what they were already teaching. Many teachers were already employing these critical-thinking skills in their classrooms; however, now we were simply asking them to explicitly announce these skills to their students and clearly show students how they were using them. As a result of the work our committee did moving students toward mastery of these critical-thinking skills, our ACT scores continue to rise above the Wisconsin state average (Wisconsin Policy Forum, 2020).

But test scores are just part of the real story. We know that real learning comes when students are able to show us what they know and are able to do (DuFour et al., 2016). The proficiencies gave us a set of skills that were doable in all content areas. Further, with support and practice, all teachers were able to write vigorous learning intentions and scaffolded success criteria for their lessons without omitting or compromising on their individual content standards.

Using Data to Personalize Learning Intentions and Success Criteria

As teachers, we know that not every vigorous learning intention or every scaffolded success criterion we write will connect with every student. While we do the best we can to write engaging and motivating learning intentions and success criteria meant for every student, we know that sometimes we must customize the learning intention and success criteria for a specific student or students to be successful. Such personalization does not compromise the spirit or purpose of students engaging in productive struggle. Put simply, sometimes teachers need to rewrite a learning intention and success criteria with an individual student in mind. So, while assessments and data tell one part of the educational story, a customized learning intention and success criteria explain the other part—applying equity and empathy to students who need what the not-yet approach offers (a growth mindset and support toward individualized success).

More important than the improved benchmark data from the improvements we tried at Ronald W. Reagan College Preparatory High School are the hidden struggles that led to achievement. Everyone at the school is certainly proud of the rise in standardized test scores, but they're just one part of the story. According to *Psychology Today* writer Cody Kommers (2019):

> The only thing that standardized tests *can* measure is whether or
> not a student falls short. They're designed to poke and prod until a

soft spot is found. Once the weakness is exposed, the shortcoming is cataloged and the process continues until another is identified.

It's important that teachers understand it's the soft spots that can be frustrating for students who have not had academic successes or have not yet gained the knowledge necessary for success on a standardized test. Even those who experience success are bound to notice and focus on what they haven't learned *yet* as opposed to what they achieved.

Educators should look for and emphasize to students how they've grown as they've engaged in the hard work of productive struggle. Progress, no matter how small, shows a student that success is coming, that they should stick with their learning and continue to move forward.

In the classroom, it is the application of a vigorous learning intention and scaffolded success criteria that gives students an opportunity to show teachers what they know and are able to do; but more important, by applying success criteria in the class, students know if they have mastered those criteria. When evidence suggests students haven't met them, teachers and students can partner together to determine what is missing for mastery.

In some cases, the teacher may find that the success criteria are inadequate and require revision or redesign. However, in many cases, teachers may just need a more customized set of scaffolded success criteria to meet the needs of specific students or groups of students facing particular challenges. For example, my daughter, Ani, is autistic and cognitively impaired. The success criteria in all her classes were far different than those of her peers. Nonetheless, Ani was still able to achieve the essence of the learning intention based on her own specific set of success criteria. While Ani's scores on standardized tests were always dismal, my husband and I knew, despite what the tests told us, that she was making gains based on those success criteria. As a result, Ani's ultimate success was highly personalized and highly effective.

As an example, let's take a look at the sixth- to eighth-grade science and technical subjects learning intention that I had shared earlier in this chapter and illustrate how a teacher might rewrite it to support a student similar to Ani: *I can define, demonstrate, and locate the differences among* superstition, pseudoscience, *and* science.

By sixth grade, Ani was in a self-contained class with peers similar in ability to her. This learning intention, as written, would have been exceptionally challenging for Ani. Ani is a linear thinker, and a conceptual learning intention like this would have caused her unnecessary anxiety. More important, her teachers, my husband, and I had a shared goal to make learning relevant for her. Does she need to learn about superstition and pseudoscience? No, those concepts aren't necessary for her life. But to be self-sufficient, she does need to understand the very basics and fundamentals of science and how science affects her. So, I asked her teacher about using science as a way to determine expiration dates on foods. Typically, one looks at the date on the package or container, and if the food product has expired, we know to throw the food away. However, in Ani's case, she didn't understand the concept of expiration dates and might eat something she shouldn't.

We quickly realized this particular opportunity could cover a myriad of topics: learning that numbers align to months, dates, and years; using a calendar to determine dates; and creating experiments that showed what happened if the food was "bad" (think about the smell of a rotten egg). Based on this thinking, Ani's teacher created two vigorous learning intentions and corresponding scaffolded success criteria to give Ani the opportunity to learn something real, relevant, and relatable to her own life.

Here is the first learning intention and its success criteria.

- **Learning intention:** I can read expiration dates of foods to figure out which foods are "good" or "bad."

- **Success criteria:** I know I am successful because . . .

    1. I can match the dates on the calendar to the numbers
       (1 = January, 2 = February, and so on)

    2. I can use a calendar to figure out if the date is sooner or later

Following is the second learning intention and its success criteria.

- **Learning intention:** I can use my senses to figure out which foods are "good" or "bad."

- **Success criteria:** I know I am successful because . . .

    1. I can do an experiment using my favorite food, oatmeal, to see if the oatmeal is "good" or "bad"

    2. I can do an experiment using my favorite food, oatmeal, and smell it to figure out if the oatmeal is "good" or "bad"

    3. I can do an experiment using my favorite food, oatmeal, and touch it to figure out if the oatmeal is "good" or "bad"

You will notice the learning intentions and success criteria, while still vigorous and still scaffolded, were uniquely written for Ani and still utilized the building blocks of a not-yet approach to achieve the desired learning outcome. No, Ani didn't learn about *superstition* and *pseudoscience* like her peers in a traditional classroom that year;

instead, she learned the very basics of *science* and how it affected her life every day—a worthwhile lesson, to be sure. Throughout Ani's academic career, learning intentions and success criteria like these further required her to engage in productive struggle, trying different methods and strategies to be successful. The learning intentions and success criteria simply needed to be tailored to work for her, and I'm proud to say she was successful in meeting the learning intention for both lessons and always checks expiration dates before she eats.

Whether your students are simply struggling with a specific aspect of grade- or course-level learning or require more foundational knowledge based on what learning they most need to acquire, the thinking behind how you personalize learning intentions and success criteria is the same. What is the source of student struggles? What do they need to know and do? What scaffolds and supports do they need to achieve that learning?

Conclusion

The not-yet approach is all about designing and creating a classroom culture that encourages the learning process while accepting that setbacks and obstacles are part of that process. Vigorous learning intentions and scaffolded success criteria support the not-yet approach because the goal is to create a classroom culture that encourages reform. They give students a clear road map for what they must know and be able to do and provide opportunities for self-assessment, so they become successful learners of process and progression. Even if it might take a student a little longer to master the success criteria, the student knows (due to the classroom culture the teacher creates and upholds) that the setbacks and obstacles he or she experiences are part of learning and success.

When determining what critical-thinking skills to teach, it is important to look at student data and standardized test scores to establish schoolwide or grade-level proficiency skills. It is also significant to choose skills that *all* disciplines can embrace, not just the core subjects. Teachers are more apt to support skills they deem significant to the mastery of their subject and vital in producing critical readers. Much as standardized test scores are important to a school's enrollment, culture, and appearance, it is more important to capture the progress all students are making throughout their academic careers and celebrate those milestones together.

A Look Inside

by Teri Knight, Language Acquisition Teacher

I am a National Board Certified language acquisition and French teacher at Ronald W. Reagan College Preparatory High School in Milwaukee, Wisconsin. I created a classroom that thrives on reform, and I'm always striving to improve my teaching for the sake of my students by reforming classroom structure and processes, classroom language, or academic content. I have never taught a lesson the same way, whether it's two different classes or two different years. This willingness to reflect and revise is what makes my French classes so successful.

Vigorous learning intentions and scaffolded success criteria are the cornerstones of my classroom and have fostered a trusting classroom culture between myself and my students. As part of my process, I always explain to students that the *learning intention* is where we want to end up, and the success criteria tell us what it looks like when we've gotten there—the lesson comes from the journey, not the destination.

The following example highlights a learning intention and success criteria from my French 3 class.

- **Learning intention:** I can learn how to explore, discuss, and write about social organizations in various French-speaking cultures.

- **Success criteria:** I know I am successful because . . .

  ○ I can explore social organizations in various French-speaking cultures

  ○ I can discuss social organizations in various French-speaking cultures

  ○ I can write about social organizations in various French-speaking cultures

Notice how the learning intention and success criteria are concise and use student-friendly *I can* language. In addition, the learning intention utilizes three productive verbs—*explore*, *discuss*, and *write*—demonstrating what the student is supposed to know and be able to do. I scaffold the success criteria so students can self-assess their own mastery of the skills as they begin by exploring, then discussing, and finally, writing. I also tier the success criteria from remembering to understanding to analyzing.

Students in my class move beyond just learning the French language by diving deep into the French culture. I have embedded not-yet processes into my class and reformed my classroom content by offering students a choice—selecting a francophone country that interests them. I have offered students authentic ways of demonstrating what they have learned and encouraged an authentic classroom experience where students are able to talk with and present to their peers, create an engaging presentation, or write an engrossing blog. The learning intentions and success criteria I design engage, motivate, and entertain students.

Part of ensuring students persevere through productive struggle involves ensuring I have positive, trusting relationships with them. This doesn't mean that they confide their deepest, darkest secrets to me, but they do know I will never mock them when they struggle and that I value them all as human beings and enjoy being with them. When students struggle, I find that if I ask them to talk with me outside of the classroom (away from the eyes and the ears of their peers) and ask them how I can help them—whether it's to figure out a time or space to study or if they need a new seat with less distractions—students will almost always respond positively. Part of this process, and a reform I had to make, means refraining from using ultimatums, which only cause pain all around and never leads to positive learning experiences.

Finally, my classroom is successful because I created an atmosphere where the process of learning, growing, and adapting is shared by the students and me. The successes my students experience as they persevere through the notable curriculum challenges I issue to them lie in the acknowledgment that we all make progress together as a team instead of me acting as the pedagogue imparting wisdom to my pupils.

Ruminate and Respond

Consider what you've learned in this chapter, and individually or with your team, answer the following questions.

1. How do you know if the learning intentions and success criteria you create contribute to a successful classroom?

2. What processes are you currently using in your classroom? How do you know they are successful?

3. How might you integrate current successful practices with a not-yet approach based on using vigorous learning intentions and scaffolded success criteria?

4. How have you determined what skills or standards you are teaching in your classroom?

5. How do you align your learning intentions and success criteria with learning standards?

Not-Yet Learning Intention Template

Class: _____

Unit and Lesson: _____

What do you want your students to know?	**I want my students to know:**
What do you want your students to be able to do with that information?	**I want my students to do:**
List possible verbs.	

Write your vigorous learning intention:

Not-Yet Success Criteria Template

Class: _____

Unit and Lesson: _____

Learning Intention: _____

_____

How will students demonstrate what they *know* about the learning intention?	
List what you want students to be able to do (up to five robust verbs), and determine essential questions about this learning intention.	Using your robust verbs from your learning intention and the essential questions you associate with them, explain how your students can demonstrate they have mastered the full scope of the learning intention.
Verb: _____ Essential question:	Draft success criterion: _____ _____ Student actions:
Verb: _____ Essential question:	Draft success criterion: _____ _____ Student actions:
Verb: _____ Essential question:	Draft success criterion: _____ _____ Student actions:

page 1 of 2

Verb: _____ Essential question:	Draft success criterion: _____ _____ Student actions:
Verb: _____ Essential question:	Draft success criterion: Student actions: _____ _____

Write your final scaffolded success criteria:

I know I am successful because . . .

PART 2

The Not-Yet Classrooms

The Practical Classroom

As a certified ELA teacher in Wisconsin, I love words—how they're used, how they make others feel, what they mean. One of my favorite quotes is from Mark Twain (BrainyQuote, n.d.): "The difference between the almost right word and the right word is really a large matter—'tis the difference between the lightning-bug and the lightning." The words we use matter, especially in the classroom and especially when the learning gets hard.

When I was student teaching, I shared with my professor that one of my sophomore ELA classes was really tough—the students didn't listen, didn't finish the work, didn't respect me, and so on. Lots of *didn'ts*. After listening to me complain, she said the true mettle of a teacher comes from working with students that didn't. What was *I* going to do to get them to *did*? Moving to did takes a change in language, language that is useful to students, language that is explicit in what you want your students to know and be able to do. The right language makes your classroom practical; it moves students from unclear in their learning goals to clarity about what they want to achieve.

In this chapter, we look at three ways you can examine, reflect on, and refine the language you use with students to align it with a practical not-yet culture and approach. First, I explain the concept of a practical classroom and its place within the not-yet approach. Second, I provide guidance specifically geared to avoiding deficit-minded language while engaging in disciplinary instruction. Third, I focus on the not-yet language of a practical classroom focused on engaging students in productive struggle and meeting learning goals.

The Not-Yet Approach in the Practical Classroom

A *practical classroom* grounded in the not-yet approach focuses on specific language that is useful to students—language that is explicit and focused. Useful language tells students what they need to know and what to do. Think of the robust verbs emphasized in chapter 4 (page 51) for writing learning intentions and success criteria. Another example of useful language is the feedback teachers give students. You want your feedback to be pointed and specific, such as by using explicit examples to guide students' learning efforts. Such practical language is authentic and relevant, and it offers students hope and empowerment while reminding them to move beyond the setbacks and obstacles they face.

How often do you consider the language you use in the classroom? According to coauthors and experts in education practice Amy J. Heineke and Jay McTighe (2018), teachers often "don't stop to critically consider [their] use of language in the classroom and how it deters or promotes student learning and achievement." I like to think of this in terms of *right* words and *almost right* words. Right words get students to *did*. Almost right words may not always provoke students to *didn't*, but they could because they are often deficit-driven and can carry various messaging, particularly when teachers are discouraged, overstretched, or impatient. Even when used with good intentions, these words may cause students to shut down or otherwise disengage and feel disenfranchised.

Sometimes teachers choose words they think will build up a student's esteem or foster a growth mindset, only to realize later that the words they thought were inspiring actually came across as condescending or belittling. Right words use robust verbs as part of explicit feedback and positive, growth-minded language that focuses on the process instead of the product. The right words, as in scaffolded success criteria, give students a clear road map to success. These words are the opposite of deficit-driven and ineffective language; they build up students' confidence, and they encourage students to use productive struggle to be successful learners.

There are also *never right* words. Sometimes teachers may use inefficient or unreasonable language toward a student personally, citing a student's lack of engagement, motivation, respect, or responsibility toward anything the teacher deems as missing from the student's character. Or teachers use some of these deficit words toward the student academically, citing a student's lack of mathematics (or any other subject) skills, critical-thinking skills, collaborative skills, or research skills. Remember, avoid using any language with students that might deem them as having qualities absent from their academic toolbox. Every student has the tools; they just need the right supports to learn to use them.

In a practical classroom, teachers modify their language from a deficit model to the not-yet approach, which focuses on language that is explicit and empowering and language that is useful in showing students how to move forward versus language that chastises where they have been. ELA, mathematics, and special education teacher Alyssa Nucaro (2017) explains how practical language empowers students and enhances classroom productivity: "Communicating to students that you believe in them and their abilities gives students the confidence they need to collaborate with others, become respectful learners, and work competently by reiterating positive behaviors and encouraging all students to do the same." In this context, practical language expresses belief in students and their abilities, the confidence to collaborate with them around their learning efforts, and the value of a growth mindset.

See Not-Yet Language for Learning Success (page 86), in this chapter, to explore more examples of empowering language.

Deficit Language in Disciplinary Instruction

Although simply building a general vocabulary for a practical classroom is important, teachers must further reflect on the language they use when engaging in disciplinary instruction. Education author and consultant Rick Wormeli (2020) cautions, "Judgement and evaluation tend to invoke ego and self-preservation, not useful reflection and personal growth." As students confront skill deficits specific to particular content areas, it's very easy to inadvertently adopt deficit-minded thinking and language that are contrary to the ideas you learned about in chapter 3 (page 37) regarding a growth mindset, grit, and abolitionist teaching.

When teachers see a student struggling in ELA but not mathematics, or in chemistry but not physics, there can be a tendency to believe the student lacks skills in these specific areas. This leads to acceptance of student struggles ("He just can't do _____.") and causes lasting harm. Judgment and evaluation reflect fixed-mindset thinking, which discourages students from engaging in productive struggle as they endeavor to stick with it through problems and try new strategies to overcome a setback or roadblock. Wormeli (2020) reminds us that "the goal is for children themselves to see the errors and how to fix them." That goal aligns with the not-yet approach—helping students to build their capacity for growth and understand they can overcome struggles in a particular content area if they have time and the right supports.

For example, when I was a sophomore in high school, I took geometry. For as long as I could remember, I wasn't "good" at mathematics. I didn't see mathematics as practical or useful in my life. Geometry was a painful struggle; if it weren't for my neighborhood friend, I'm sure I wouldn't have passed. I received a D–, which you could argue I didn't even earn given that my friend let me copy her mathematics homework. I turned in all my homework and received satisfactory grades, but I miserably failed every test. Obviously, there are many pedagogical things wrong with this scenario, not the least of which was the feedback I received from my teacher, who encouraged me *not* to take any more mathematics! He said I "clearly wasn't a mathematician," and since I didn't need any more mathematics to graduate, why take something I would most likely fail? Truthfully, I was thrilled with the prospect of being done with mathematics. However, Responsive Classroom (2012) reminds us how deeply problematic this guidance was: "With our words, we convey our assumptions and expectations about children, which, in turn, influence children's assumptions and expectations about themselves." The teacher had conveyed to me I was never going to get any better in mathematics, and I believed him. To call such language *almost right* is being charitable, and it certainly wasn't productive.

The insidious component to this scenario is that I'm sure this teacher thought he was giving me sage advice meant to be useful to me and my future (after all, my mathematics career *was* over). However, it's telling that the conversation happened in 1975, and I still remember it, highlighting the long-term effects of failure I wrote about in chapter 1 (page 11). A *teacher* told me I would never get better at mathematics, and I needed to accept that fate. While my teacher never specifically mentioned my lack of engagement, motivation, respect, or responsibility, he certainly inferred I didn't have any motivation to continue in mathematics since I would never be a mathematician. In addition, while he didn't explicitly mention my lack of academic knowledge, my absence of mathematics skills was obvious. The language he gave me wasn't language I could use because it wasn't practical for me. Instead, it was deficit language that magnified every mathematical gap I ever had.

Consider for a moment your students' past experiences, no matter what age they are. Maybe they're high school students who've had an experience similar to mine. Maybe you teach U.S. history and have a student for whom a previous social studies teacher said, "It might be best if you stuck to science." Maybe you're a sixth-grade ELA teacher with a student whose elementary teachers passed him or her up—grade to grade, without an intervention—because the student is exceptional at mathematics while still lacking essential grade-level language skills. Or maybe you have a first-grade student who simply doesn't believe he or she can learn due to never receiving positive reinforcement or scaffolded supports at home for basic number and letter skills. Also, think back to the story of Willie in chapter 1. I had asked him who told him he wasn't a good reader or a good writer. When asked, he merely shook his head. Perhaps no one teacher had outright said anything specific to him, but there is clearly a reason Willie didn't believe he could learn how to read and write "good." As your students' *current* teacher, you must understand how to use not-yet language to help students engage in the right kind of struggle so they believe they can make up learning gaps regardless of the content area to achieve learning goals.

To illustrate, let's fast forward from my high school experience in geometry to my senior year in college. Six months before I was to graduate with my English certification, the dean called me and explained that after studying my transcript, it was noticed that I lacked a mathematics class. The only class available that summer was Elementary Math Methods (K–4); fortunately, it fulfilled the missing credit. I wasn't excited about returning to a mathematics classroom, but at least I would learn how to teach mathematics to elementary students. At the time, I had no idea how this class would change my outlook.

My professor was excited about teaching and excited about mathematics. In the class, I learned how to use patterns, arrange manipulatives, and apply mathematics language for elementary students. But the most exciting part of the class was when I learned how to add, subtract, multiply, and divide fractions. This was something I never did with proficiency during my primary and secondary learning, and much of my mathematics learning had involved me being anxious if there was any semblance of fractions. Yet there I was with a teacher who created excitement and engagement (not to mention patience and a practical, not-yet attitude), and suddenly, that anxiety was gone.

For the first time in my mathematics career, I did my own homework. It made sense, and I came to appreciate the practicality and usefulness of mathematics. Looking back, it's easy to say that I simply shouldn't have skipped mathematics after my sophomore year, and instead should have jumped into that next course with both feet. But without a teacher to patiently push me through productive struggle, using scaffolds appropriate to *me* and practical, growth-minded language, it's not a given that anything would have been different for me in the next course. To this day, I can't help but wonder about my mathematical journey had I received the supports that would've enabled me to pursue mathematics.

I share this story because it is an example of a deficit-language model in a school where teachers never considered creating a practical classroom and regarded students' disciplinary abilities with a fixed mindset. There was no encouragement to unlock students' potential; rather, just a shove out the mathematics door. Think back to chapter 4 (page 51) and the importance of clear and vigorous learning intentions and scaffolded success criteria. Embedding productive struggle into your classroom requires identifying specific sources of students' struggles so they *can* acquire the curriculum knowledge and skills within each academic discipline.

Not-Yet Language for Learning Success

Consider the harm teachers can inadvertently do when using almost-right and similar deficit-driven language, particularly with regard to assessing students' disciplinary abilities. Often your students need supports not because they can't understand your curriculum content but because they *currently* lack specific foundational skills or perhaps the mindset to get beyond mental setbacks of feeling like they're "bad" at something. Had my geometry teacher adopted a not-yet approach, he and I would have met once he noticed the disparity between my homework scores and test scores. How could I possibly have earned As on homework and still failed my tests? Simple data observations, such as this, can lay the groundwork for conversations with students that help them create and apply new mindsets about their learning, conversations focused not on the grades but on learning. Such conversations also help students understand the practicality of any content area and how knowledge of curriculum standards can be useful in everyday life far beyond test taking.

As you reflect on the language you use in your classroom, is it almost right, or do you consistently use practical, not-yet language? Is the language you use authentic and relevant, and do you use it in ways students can apply both personally and academically for their own hope, growth, and empowerment? Yes, you want to keep the language you use with students real. Practical language does not ignore struggle or offer meaningless platitudes and encouragement. Practical language also conveys that students must still do the heavy lifting when it comes to struggling productively. When you use growth-minded language focused on process, not necessarily product, you can feel confident you're using a practical approach. Table 5.1 shows examples of deficit language and not-yet language that focus on creating a practical classroom.

As you reflect on the deficit language, don't feel embarrassed or ill at ease if you see terms you sometimes or regularly use. I can share this chart with you, in part, because I've also used such language with my students. Most teachers do. As I look back on some of the language I've used in the past, I realize that much of it centered on blame instead of assistance. I encourage you to reflect on your own language and begin moving toward practical examples of support. Just as you want your students to reflect and grow from productive struggle, recognizing when you use language

Table 5.1: Deficit Language Versus Not-Yet Language

Examples of Deficit Language in the Classroom	Practical Examples of Not-Yet Language in the Classroom
"I read your response paper. Did you read the text?"	"I read your response paper. From what I read, you seemed uncertain in your response. Let's talk about how I can help make your response more convincing."
"I'm not going to say it again. You need to listen next time."	"If you are unclear, can you tell me where the confusion began?"
"This should be easy for you. You've been studying this since you were in elementary school."	"It seems this particular concept is challenging for you. Let's figure out where the concept becomes challenging and try again."
"I never give As in my class because an A means perfect, and no one is perfect."	"I want my grading to be fair and authentic. I'll be grading your work according to the standards and using rubrics so you will always know the grading expectations."
"Any late work is a zero. You will fail the assignment or assessment if the work is not turned in on time."	"I realize that sometimes it might be difficult to turn in your work on time. Let's discuss due dates, why they're important, and how to adhere to them as best as possible."

that isn't useful or practical will help you engage in productive struggle to become more effective in your practice.

Shifting from deficit language to not-yet language may take time, but it is well worth it. According to author Josh Kaufman's (2013) best-seller *The First 20 Hours: How to Learn Anything . . . Fast,* it can take as much as ten thousand hours to develop a new skill or mastery, and this learning is hardest and most frustrating at the beginning. You likely see this in your students, which is why productive struggle is necessary. Ensure your students understand that, practically speaking, frustration about learning something new and challenging is normal and expected. Explain to those who are struggling that no one picks up every new skill immediately, but that doesn't mean they can't do it. Productive struggle builds in that opportunity to think through, wonder, and reflect on what is working in the learning and what is not.

Also, be mindful that students sometimes get frustrated because they're so focused on achieving mastery that they lose sight of the intermediate steps that lead to it. In an interview, Kaufman is careful to write, "The idea of 'mastering' a skill when you're just getting started is counterproductive: it can be a significant barrier to exploring a new skill in the first place'" (as cited in Schawbel, 2013). That is why process is so vital in the not-yet approach. Instead of telling students they must "master" a task, subject, or language, explain that it is about getting started with their success criteria and staying with it to the end. Remind them of the common proverb that the only way to eat an elephant is one bite at a time (Fournier, 2018).

Students respond when they are part of the learning process—when they explicitly see that the work they are doing is practical and has use inside and outside the classroom. In addition, "Our words and tone of voice have a profound effect on children. By tuning in to the language we use with children, day in and day out, everywhere in school, we can empower our students" (Responsive Classroom, 2012). Applying not-yet language in the classroom is necessary to help students learn practical skills and become successful learners.

Conclusion

In this chapter, I asked you to confront whether you are using a deficit approach to classroom language or an approach rooted firmly in a not-yet mindset. The language you use in the classroom must be *practical*—language that is of use to your students. That's why the not-yet approach to classroom language focuses on building and empowering engaging student-teacher relationships that emphasize growth. When the language teachers use is deficit minded, it creates barriers to learning and saps students' confidence that they can achieve through productive struggle; as a result, your relationships with them may fail. Further, changing your language also changes your mindset about students' struggles, enabling you to see the potential in your students rather than any temporary shortcomings.

A Look Inside

by April Nagel, Special Education Teacher

I am a special education teacher, and I am a co-teacher in the ELA department (Diploma Programme level) at Ronald W. Reagan College Preparatory High School. All classes in the Diploma Programme are inclusive; therefore, my students are learning right alongside general education learners. During my career, I have written hundreds of Individualized Education Plans, counseled thousands of students, and advocated for hundreds more. My philosophy centers on inclusion and self-advocacy. While I believe all students can achieve growth, I am also realistic. I know that setbacks and obstacles present themselves to all learners in various ways. I apply not-yet language and thinking in all aspects of my conversations with students, parents, colleagues, and administrators.

In my practice, I often reflect not only on the language I use in the classroom but also the language I hear from students. For example, during an ELA class, I spoke with a student about the difficulty level of an upcoming assignment. After speaking with this particular student, I could tell from his mannerisms and tone of voice that he was worried, and I wondered if perhaps many more students were also feeling anxious about the assignment. When my students worry about assignments, I know it's time to reflect on my scaffolded success criteria, often breaking components down to make the learning more tangible. Often the ways I am asking them to think are new, and I've found that comparing something new to something that is already in their experience helps.

In this case, I asked how many students were feeling overwhelmed just thinking about the upcoming assignment. Several hands went up, but I could still see a few faces that just weren't sure. I knew I needed to break down the assignment into more manageable chunks (clearer scaffolded success criteria), so I decided to pull those students into a small group.

Once in a small group, I explained to my students that I was getting the feeling they were worried, putting the onus of their worry on myself. I didn't blame the students for their fear; instead, I immediately explained that it was *my feeling* that something was amiss. I then asked the small group how many of them ever played video games. Of course, all the students nodded their heads, so I asked them how many felt as comfortable and skilled at a game when they started versus after they had spent a dozen or even a hundred or more hours playing it. Most said it took time for them to get comfortable and build their skills, so I posed another question, "When you struggled, did you just quit playing?" They each agreed that they didn't and instead focused on how they could make changes that would move them forward. One student even commented, "You could also lower the difficulty level to help you make it to the next level and eventually win the game." One by one, the students proceeded to share how they had met the challenge to succeed. None of their stories involved giving up but instead engaging themselves in ways to get to the next level. Even the student who changed the difficulty was, in essence, putting scaffolds in place to achieve the goal. Ultimately, they each realized they felt motivated when they achieved success at each level and accepted responsibility when they made a mistake and needed to try again.

I explained to my small group that learning course content was no different from overcoming video game challenges. I explained that it's not easy to understand something the first time you read it, and many times I have to read something more than once to get it. I then said, "Let's go over the most difficult part again, and we'll figure it out together."

Ruminate and Respond

Consider what you've learned in this chapter, and individually or with your team, answer the following questions.

1. Why is classroom language so vital to learning?

2. Think about the language you use in your classroom. Does it reflect a not-yet approach? If not, why not? If so, how do you know?

3. How do you help your students understand the value of a practical classroom?

4. What are some things you could do to remove deficit-focused language in your disciplinary instruction?

5. If you were to add two more examples to table 5.1 (page 87), what might they be?

The Transformational Classroom

In our role as educators, we know the value of communicating with all stakeholders involved in a student's education: the student's family, other classroom teachers, administrators, anyone whom we know can help us facilitate learning. In a transformational classroom, data are a big part of those communications—test scores, observational data, anecdotal data, and so on— but teachers must be wary of those conversations becoming one sided, with teachers primarily communicating *out* results. It is just as important for teachers to listen to the data coming *in* from the stakeholders with whom they partner. What can you learn from your students, their parents, your colleagues, and your administrators that will help you embed and sustain your not-yet approach? What can they share that will help you design successful experiences, rooted in productive struggle, for students?

One way all stakeholders can work together to students' benefit is to think and communicate through the lens of the whole child approach. According to the ASCD (n.d.), "a whole child approach, which ensures that each student is healthy, safe, engaged, supported, and challenged, sets the standard for comprehensive, sustainable school improvement and provides for long-term student success." Communication around student growth, academically, socially, and emotionally, is central to the whole child approach. When applying this to the not-yet approach, teachers create safe classrooms where they use verbal and body language to ensure students feel academically healthy, engaged, supported, and challenged. They provide opportunities for students to use new and different learning strategies, explore a variety of resources, and engage in the learning process as a journey to learn. The transformational classroom values communication, feedback, and the goal of whole child success.

Thankfully, communication with parents and guardians (going forward, I use *parent* to encompass any family members or guardians who take care of and support children) has evolved from the obligatory twice-a-year face-to-face parent-teacher conferences to phone calls, newsletters, emails, texts, and even communication through app platforms such as Remind (https://remind.com), Seesaw (https://web .seesaw.me), and Weebly (https://education.weebly.com). All of these options will help you connect with parents to learn more about your students and, ultimately, support students' academic and personal progress, particularly with respect to your grading practices.

Communicating with parents to inform and collaborate is vital in creating a respectful partnership. But, it seems, many teachers worry about the upcoming phone call or parent-teacher meeting, wondering if the communication will be negative (Rosser, 2016). Communicating with parents, even about difficult topics related to students' learning, should not cause fear or distress for you, your students, or students' parents. Rather, as you will read in this chapter, the student-parent-teacher relationship is all about creating two or three common goals and adhering to those goals throughout the school year.

In this chapter, you'll explore the not-yet approach for the transformational classroom and ways of ensuring you build student-parent-teacher relationships focused on crafting a necessary feedback loop to support students through productive struggle. I further share some additional best practices for offering feedback. By amassing data about your teaching and your students' essential needs, you will have what you need to transform your grading practices with a focus on students' mastery of learning standards.

The Not-Yet Approach in the Transformational Classroom

A *transformational classroom* is a classroom of change that focuses on designing new ways of partnering with parents and students to support the whole student. In a transformational classroom, the teacher and parents are sharing information and looking for ways to support a student's learning process. Think of the transformational classroom as a place that embraces whole child thinking while giving students the opportunity to use the not-yet approach for long-term development and success. Note that it's the focus on long-term development that is indicative of the not-yet approach as students use a growth mindset paired with learning strategies and resources to gain new insights. Thinking long term also gives students the time they need to work through productive struggle and achieve. As Kaufman (2013) explains, anything less than that is counterproductive. By pairing long-term thinking with parent-student-teacher communication, all stakeholders have the opportunity to be a meaningful part of the learning and assessment processes.

Like the whole child approach, the transformational classroom also recognizes the impacts of factors outside the classroom in how students approach learning (ASCD, n.d.). Students face change and unknowns in many aspects of their lives that their teachers may not know anything about, and because change often presages uncertain outcomes, that uncertainty can make students (or anyone) fearful (Razzetti, 2018). Most adults have dealt with change in their life experiences and have developed certain coping skills they use to handle change. But many students haven't had as much experience dealing with change, or they have had such enormous change throughout their lives, they are unsure how to manage it or their anxiety about change. This anxiety impacts students' approach to learning in different ways.

The American Academy of Child and Adolescent Psychiatry (n.d.) explains, "When flooded with anxiety, adolescents may appear extremely shy. They may avoid their usual activities or refuse to engage in new experiences." However, other students might manage change by ignoring it and rejecting their anxiety. Those students who "deny their fears and worries . . . may engage in risky behaviors, drug experimentation, or impulsive sexual behavior" (American Academy of Child and Adolescent Psychiatry, n.d.). Therefore, educators must help students accept and utilize change as part of an encouraging classroom culture. To create a transformational not-yet classroom, you must support students in understanding how change can be a positive opportunity to learn from the setbacks and obstacles that are part of the learning process. In addition, it is important to share that message with parents. Help parents understand that change can be paralyzing to students and accepting change takes time, patience, and communication.

But understanding how to cope with change is complicated. Gustavo Razzetti (2018), the CEO of Fearless Culture, which is dedicated to helping organizations manage uncertainty, states, "On one hand, we are hardwired to resist uncertainty—our brain prefers a predictable, negative outcome over an uncertain one. On the other hand, our mind is flexible and adaptive—it can be trained to thrive in change." Many students thrive on procedure and structure (Kise, 2021). Other students might complain about a routine schedule, but even they will appreciate knowing what comes next. For example, chapter 4 (page 51) explains the value of vigorous learning intentions and scaffolded success criteria. Part of the reason these are effective is that they create certainty. Students know what their goals are and the milestones they must hit to achieve them (what they must know and be able to do). This offers predictability and helps eliminate the anxiety of uncertainty while still offering opportunities to differentiate approaches for different learning styles.

The differentiated approach encourages stakeholders to help students of all ages take control of their learning process:

> This can be done by talking with children about the best approach to a particular task and having them describe the strategy they intend to test or asking a child to consider what could go wrong and how they might improve a task if completing it again. (Thomsen & Ackermann, 2015)

In this way, student voice is also a key component of a transformational classroom because students have the opportunity to share concerns about their learning, themselves as learners, and how those concerns might impact other parts of their life. Enabling students to be avid participants in their educational journey, where teachers are open to hearing their voice and ideas and accept them with respect and empathy, is vital to the transformational classroom. In addition, encouraging students to reflect on their learning and ruminate on how to enhance their process for subsequent learning, as Thomsen and Ackermann (2015) suggest, is one of the key concepts within productive struggle. It gives students a voice and a responsibility to make purposeful and meaningful change centering on what they want and need to feel successful.

Razzetti (2018) asserts the human mind can "be trained to thrive in change." In chapter 3 (page 37), you learned about growth mindsets (Dweck, 2016), grit (Duckworth, 2016), and abolitionist teaching (Love, 2019a, 2019b). All three of these mindsets illustrate the significance of flexibility and the value of being adaptive by anticipating and allowing for setbacks in the classroom with the understanding that transformation is a part of learning. When communicating with parents who may not be well-versed in these concepts or the research underpinning them, you can still encourage them to support change and be flexible in the face of it.

As an example, I noted in chapter 5 (page 81) my struggles with secondary-level mathematics. My geometry teacher didn't communicate with my mom about my difficulties. Their only communication was through a report card. Imagine the difference it might have made had my teacher called home or offered to meet with my parents as my grade started to dip. A teacher communicating with parents can use the data they each have available to them about the student to indicate if a dip merely reflects engagement with productive struggle that will lead to success with learning goals or a need for different scaffolds or other intervention. When teachers encourage communications among themselves, students, and parents, giving all stakeholders the chance to share their concerns about the learning, students come to know they have a support system in place that reflects the whole of who they are (the whole child).

Ensuring Feedback for Academic Transformation and Personal Success

Transformation in classroom culture is not about change for the sake of change; rather, it is change based on gaining understanding about what students need to be successful. But even the definition of *success* can vary depending on who sets that definition: students, parents, or teachers. Part of building a transformational classroom requires all stakeholders to share a common understanding of what standards students must achieve for the curriculum and what students' individual goals are based on where they currently are in their learning. Accomplishing those goals during the school year requires frequent communication and feedback.

We've touched on the importance of feedback in various contexts in previous chapters and will continue to throughout this book. When it comes to students and their families, feedback is essential in building a trusting and collaborative relationship aligned with the not-yet approach. Trust holds special emphasis in this dynamic, as experts consistently emphasize its critical role in student-teacher relationships (Brendtro, Brokenleg, & Van Bockern, 2019; Colburn & Beggs, 2021; Jensen, 2019). One way to build that trust is to make sure feedback is positive and genuine. Researcher Trynia Kaufman (n.d.) writes, "When you authentically praise a student or have a positive interaction, the student's brain releases dopamine." The key word here is *authentic*. In the not-yet classroom, one that is built on productive struggle, teachers encourage students to apply a growth mindset to setbacks and challenges. Don't merely praise for the sake of praise; focus instead on process and the specific actions students take to move themselves toward progress and academic transformation. Kaufman (n.d.) continues, "The student feels good and is motivated to feel that way again. With this increased motivation, students spend more time and attention working on a skill."

As trust builds, it unlocks the power of feedback that allows it to act as a loop (Meredith, 2015). When establishing a student-driven *feedback loop*, educator Taylor Meredith writes, "The teacher supports the students by clearly defining a structure for feedback, modeling effective feedback, highlighting critical student feedback, and participating when necessary." When teachers ensure students have the opportunity to listen to *and* offer feedback, they encourage student voice, which has benefits for individual and collaborative growth. Meredith (2015) goes on to state, "Throughout the process, students may identify areas of growth in their own work, find peer examples as models, and take ownership over their work."

Finally, according to The Graide Network (n.d.), "feedback is something that every student [and every teacher] can benefit from," and that benefit can be a transformative process for all stakeholders. When students are able to work together or when students are able to collaborate with their teachers, learning becomes an opportunity for growth and change, academically and personally. By including families in the feedback loops, teachers can increase the likelihood of students extending their ability to engage in productive struggle both in the classroom and at home.

To aid you in this process, and either before the school year even begins or on the first day, I suggest teachers share with students and their parents the academic transformation and personal success feedback form illustrated in figure 6.1. (See page 108 for a reproducible version of this form.) This form offers an opportunity for teachers to partner with students and parents to learn what supports may help the student be successful and establish a foundation for ongoing communication throughout the semester or school year. It also gives parents and students a chance to think about how teachers can best meet a student's needs.

To use this form, ask parents to sit down with their child and complete the form together. In addition to helping build a bridge for communication between you and parents, this form also facilitates communication between students and parents. When sending out the form, emphasize there are no right answers for parents and students to provide and that parents should support students who require it (such as young students who lack foundational writing skills) in answering questions as needed. You want students and parents to reflect on what students need and how everyone (you, students, and parents) can collectively support those needs. Let parents know this form is meant to be an ongoing opportunity for communication; therefore, when they want to update the form or even start a new one, encourage them to do so. In keeping this feedback loop ongoing, teachers, parents, and students will have a running record of supportive communication and student progress through productive struggle. For example, over the course of a year, this form (or a small set of these forms) will come to reflect the full range of academic challenges the student faced, how the student overcame those challenges, and the challenges still to overcome. As students progress, emphasize that this record of real growth should be a point of pride to both students and families.

When getting started, you have a few options for distributing the form. The most direct method is to send the form directly to parents electronically; however, you could mail it home or provide it with start-of-year book and resource distribution or as part of some other schoolwide function where parents might attend. If you prefer, you can make this form part of your classroom introduction during the first week of

Work with your child to fill in the following two boxes, and return the form.	
What's Working? (List one or more items.) My teacher last year gave us time at the end of class to start my homework. I liked that, in case I needed any help from my teacher or was confused.	**Challenge (List one item.)** Writing is hard for me.

As your teacher, I will take the following steps to help support you.
• I will ask to see your writing during class and offer writing suggestions. • I will ask you to come in for extra writing help, as needed. • I will have you add to this form when you come in for writing help.

Review the teacher-provided feedback, and use the following two boxes to determine next steps.	
Student's Next Step I will come in for extra help with writing.	**Parent or Guardian's Next Step** I will ensure my child comes in for writing help.

Indicate your follow-up plan (email, phone call, or meetings).	
Parent or Guardian's Follow-Up Plan *I will contact the teacher each month (or as needed) to learn about my child's progress in writing.*	**Teacher's Follow-Up Plan** • I will contact the parent if the student does not come in for writing support. • I will discuss the student's writing progress with the student and his or her parent or guardian, as needed.

Additional follow-up notes (for teachers, students, or parents or guardians)
9/26: I conferenced with my teacher in class today to talk about my first writing assignment. 10/8: I came in after school today to get help with using basic punctuation.

Figure 6.1: The academic transformation and personal success feedback form.

the school year. Simply distribute the template to students during class, and provide directions as needed. Students then take the form home to fill out with their parents.

The following sections explain the different parts of the academic transformation and personal success feedback form in more detail.

What's Working? and Challenge Sections

One advantage of introducing this form in class is that you can explain to students both the purpose of the form and how students should complete it with their parents. For example, you might ask students to share some of their ideas for *what's working* items and their *challenges*. The teacher could write these on the board as examples. Of course, if students are feeling anxious, they certainly don't have to share their challenges. However, in sharing, some students might realize they are not the only ones who feel anxiety over learning curriculum skills or other challenges.

Start students with the What's Working? section. To get the conversation moving and model for students how to think about answering the form's questions, you might write on the board what worked for you in school. As part of doing so, explain to students that those who are visual learners often benefit from being able to literally see what they need to do (Kise, 2021), asking which students in your class believe they are visual learners. Follow this by asking which students feel like they learn best in ways other than use of visuals, such as written directions. As students share what works for them, have them choose one strategy that could be especially helpful to their success during the upcoming school year. For example, in figure 6.1 (page 97), the student wrote that he liked that his previous teacher gave him time at the end of class to work on his homework because it gave him time to try out specific problem-solving strategies in class, with the teacher there to support him, before attempting them at home. As students share their ideas, encourage them to write down, separately or on the back of the form, anything that resonates with them, whether it's to do with classroom norms, specific learning strategies, or so on. Such ideas may be valuable to them in the future as they engage in productive struggle, revise existing goals, or set new goals.

You can engage in this same way to show students how to think about the form's Challenge section. For example, you might share with students how you felt shy or had social anxiety when you were younger and were afraid to raise your hand in the classroom because you thought you might say something incorrect. You could then ask students to share what they think challenges them. This has the advantage of vocalizing lots of different challenges that some students might otherwise struggle to describe. (Again, be cognizant and respectful of those students who prefer not to share their challenges with the class.) As different challenges come to light, encourage students to choose just one to write down on their own form to work on during the upcoming school year. In addition to providing clear modeling, this approach may help students feel less alone as they see that other students have the same fears or challenges.

When engaging in modeling, class activities, and discussion about the form, don't lose sight that part of this process is about having parents reflect together about their child's learning. Encourage students to regard anything they write down in class as a way to initiate a conversation with their parents, but ensure they know they can change their answer when they get home. As you explain directions to students about what's working, remember to ask them and their parents to reflect on the student's previous school year when providing final answers. If a previous teacher always built in time during class to begin homework practice, perhaps that's something you can continue. Here, the student and parent can also list several things that worked during the previous school year.

When providing direction about listing challenges, emphasize that the challenges students list don't need to be detailed. The example in figure 6.1 simply emphasizes that writing has been a challenge. While such descriptions are vague, they still alert you to an aspect of the student's learning that might require extra support. Again, students should list only *one challenge*—too many challenges may overwhelm them and cause them to wonder why they should bother given how many challenges they have to overcome (Willis, 2016). When students are able to focus on a single challenge and eventually conquer it, there is a true sense of accomplishment and mastery.

Next Steps Section

The Next Steps component of the form is intended for students, parents, and teachers to each share what they think will best support the student in overcoming the challenge the student listed. For example, maybe the student decides that his or her next step will be to come in for extra help in writing when needed; the parent's next step will be to ensure he or she will provide the needed support (such as transportation to or from the school) to facilitate that action.

At this point, the student or his or her parents return the form to you. You'll review the information they provided and consider and detail the steps you will take to support the student. In the example in figure 6.1, the teacher wrote, "I will ask to see your writing during class and offer writing suggestions." The teacher also noted that every time the student comes in for extra writing help, the teacher will note the date and time on the feedback form as described in the next section. This creates a visual record that reflects the student's desire for support.

Follow-Up Section

The final section of the form ensures there is a plan for follow up. As the form is now with you, you will be the first to complete it by noting what further communication you believe should take place among the student, parents, and yourself. Then make a copy of the feedback form, either returning it to the student to take home or sending it electronically to both the student and his or her parents. Remember, while this might be the first communication among students, parents, and teacher, it is by no means the last! For this reason, there is a final box for additional notes that anyone (teachers, students, or parents) can fill out. This can serve as a log of teacher-student interactions, observations about learning progress or challenges, and so on.

Depending on the nature of the feedback loop you build with each student and their family, you may find that a single copy of this form will serve its purpose for a full semester or school year. Based on how students progress, the amount of detail documented, and whether there is a single year-long goal or a progression of new goals as each are met, you may use multiple copies of this form to reflect year-long progress. Or, you might create an all-digital version of the form that all parties can access and update online. Remember, the ultimate purpose is the building of a productive feedback loop to support student learning and help students see the connection between their personal habits and their academic habits by setting specific goals and utilizing learning strategies to attain goals, which *will* impact academic performance (Schippers et al., 2020).

Using Best Practices for Feedback

The academic transformation and personal success feedback form isn't meant to be a quick fix. It might take an entire school year for students to meet or overcome a challenge. For that reason, don't use it for evaluative purposes or as an accountability measure to determine if everyone is doing their job. On the contrary, this form is simply a communication device for partnering with students and parents to work cohesively toward student progress as students engage in productive struggle. If students aren't meeting goals, that's an indication to review your process in conjunction with students' progress, including your learning intentions and success criteria, to determine how you can provide more effective supports.

The key component to measuring progress is ensuring all stakeholders have a common language about what defines *success*. In the figure 6.1 (page 97) example, building in extra time at the end of the class and accepting writing support define success for the student, parents, and teacher. When convenient, the student, parents, and teacher can determine when they should consider a new *what's working* or a new *challenge*. That means, depending on the student, the form could go home weekly, monthly, or some other duration. Don't worry about dates or times. Think about engaging students in productive struggle to overcome challenges.

When determining how to best make use of a feedback form (whether it's the one included in this chapter or one of your own creation), consider whether you prefer to use handouts or distribute them digitally. While you can utilize either method, you might also consider letting students and parents use the format most comfortable for them. Sometimes students prefer when ideas and goals are on paper—involving the physical act of writing something—because they seem more permanent and are, thus, more likely to be taken seriously. Other times, students might prefer a digital format because it helps them stay more organized than having one more piece of paper to put in a backpack. In either case, you can always scan physical forms or print electronic forms to keep a record of them in your preferred format.

Remember, feedback forms are part of the not-yet approach in a transformational classroom because they improve communication and support students in moving beyond the setbacks and obstacles they will undoubtedly encounter with the challenges they reveal. When all stakeholders work together toward commonly defined success criteria, students are more likely to have the clarity and support they need to ensure any struggles they experience are productive and will lead to growth (Schippers et al., 2020).

However, as you know, parents are often very busy and sometimes don't have time to complete paperwork; in some households, the parents expect the child to "do" school solo. If you find that parents aren't filling out or returning feedback forms, you can gently remind and encourage the parents and students through a phone call, an email, or both to complete the feedback forms. If the feedback forms are still not returned or parents directly refuse to participate, instead make a special effort to miniconference with those students and support them in completing the feedback forms. Assure these students that lack of parental feedback is not a problem and will not hold them back. Tell them you will partner with them to help them be successful.

As the year progresses, you will build a library of feedback based on student performance. You can then use feedback forms whenever you, the student, or a parent deems necessary, which might include before midterm assessments, as part of parent-teacher conferences, or just at regular intervals throughout the school year. In addition, consider feedback forms as another way to communicate with students and parents about grading and assessments. As an example, in the academic transformation and personal success feedback form in figure 6.1 (page 97), the student needs help with writing. The teacher could share on the form the grades the student has earned in recent writing assessments. As a result, the parent can stay apprised of how their child is doing, and if warranted, meet with the teacher to discuss the writing strategies that are working or new strategies to try. Finally, as with all examples, you might find it necessary, depending on the student, to revise the language of the form or change the format. As previously stated, the feedback form might be your first means of communication with the student and parent; therefore, as the year progresses, you might change the form to illustrate changes in process and progress.

Transforming Grading Practices

As noted in the preceding section, feedback loops include information about grading practices and grading, so it's important to understand how grading practices impact your transformational classroom. *Transformative grading* is grading that embraces change but not for the sake of change. As education technology specialist Ryan L. Schaaf (n.d.) writes, teachers cannot accept the "mundane and find comfort in the status quo rather than head towards the undiscovered country on the unknown." That undiscovered country could be your not-yet classroom where a growth mindset, grit, and abolitionist teaching are the norm; or it could be creating productive struggle experiences for your students, where students "learn to persist in the face of challenge" (Blackburn, 2018).

When I began teaching freshman English in 1994, it wasn't unusual for me to have a gradebook full of grades. As previously mentioned, I graded everything—homework, formative assessments, and participation. As an instructional coach and reading specialist, I collaborate with teachers in building literacy into their content area without disrupting their classroom objectives. I no longer have a classroom of my own and am not responsible for communicating with parents or grading students. However, I often work with teachers on how to create truly transformational grading practices. The following are four ways you can revise your grading practice to create a transformational classroom culture and support parents in becoming an integral part of the assessment process.

Change Your Language

Do not use the words *quiz* and *test* when discussing evaluation. Students and parents think of quizzes and tests as things with permanent outcomes in which, if students fail, the entire experience is a waste and failure. When I was a classroom teacher, I liked to frame assessments to my students and their families as *check-ups*, a way for me to learn more about students' understanding of the material we had covered (Grafwallner, 2017b).

Giving students formative check-ups allows teachers to determine if students can synthesize their learning to their teacher or someone else. If not, teachers can use the data they gather to determine what might help students learn the material, what students might need to do differently to be successful, and so on.

In my experience, this simple change of language and approach alleviates most student and parent concerns and fears. In addition, the idea of assessing learning as *check-ups* helps students expect and anticipate feedback about their learning. Students become eager to learn how they could better prepare for the next check-up to demonstrate their understanding, which sustains the feedback loop.

Send Check-Ups Home

Sometimes students do not always tell their parents about an upcoming assessment or their grade on an assessment. While many school districts use software that allows parents to monitor their child's grades, just seeing a grade doesn't explain what a check-up is testing or measuring. Encourage students to share check-ups with their parents, and discuss the purpose and value of the information you're assessing (the learning standards as outlined by your learning intentions and success criteria). Check-ups are an opportunity for conversation among teachers, parents, and students as they work together to support learning.

As part of this process, consider sending home a check-up's directions and an example of it *before* conducting the check-up. As an example, if you are a social studies teacher and you expect students to write a cause-and-effect analysis, it would be beneficial to students and parents to actually see the directions for and an example of the assessment prior to assigning it. When paired with the "Academic Transformation and Personal Success Feedback Form" (page 108), students and parents can build awareness of what supports the student might benefit from before an assessment occurs.

Of course, parents are naturally most interested in knowing how their child fared in a check-up. Therefore, continue to involve parents by sharing an example of that graded paper or a recent check-up. Again, use your learning intentions and success criteria to help students and parents focus on the learning students have achieved or haven't achieved *yet*. Use check-ups not as a tool for judgment but as an opportunity for conversation to support students' learning efforts.

Explain Your Grading Practice

During those first several weeks of school, explain your grading practice to students and parents. Most teachers distribute a syllabus and have this information on the internet. However, sometimes the syllabus doesn't make it home, and sometimes parents are unable to access the teacher's or school's website.

Therefore, I suggest offering a virtual group meeting explaining your grading practice to parents, giving them the opportunity to pose questions and offer possible scenarios. Give students the date and time of the virtual meeting, and ask them to share it with their parents. Send an email or a Remind (https://remind.com) of the meeting to parents. Also, be mindful of district, state or province, and national guidelines regarding teacher communications and language barriers. For example, the U.S. Department of Justice Civil Rights Division and the U.S. Department of Education Office for Civil Rights (n.d.) state, "Schools must respond to a parent's request for language assistance and remember that parents can be limited English proficient even if their child is proficient in English" (p. 1). Most likely, your school has translation services available to help you communicate, so always make sure you are aware of any non-native language speakers in your class.

Of course, not every parent will be able to participate in a virtual meeting, but you could record it and make it available online as a download, a link on a school or class website, or so on. Parents are important partners; you want them to feel involved in all aspects of their child's learning.

In any case, emphasize that the language you use to describe how you assess students (be it *check-ups* or any other descriptors) doesn't change that you will be evaluating and grading student work. Using terminology like *check-ups* is about changing mindsets to reduce anxiety and frame the real purpose for your assessments (to measure learning and determine next steps).

Clarify Equity *and* Equality *in Grading*

In the not-yet classroom, grading for equity and equality is all about our unwavering belief in students' abilities and treating students with sincere integrity. According to Crescendo Education Group (https://crescendoedgroup.org) CEO Joe Feldman (2017), *grading for equity* means grading "in ways that demonstrate our unflagging belief that every student can meet our academic expectations, regardless of their privileges or previous experiences" (p. 10).

Equality in grading means treating students fairly in the classroom (Thought Leaders, 2018). Therefore, offer the same type of homework and assessments to students, but give students what they need to be successful on that homework and assessments. As previously stated, ask students and parents to complete the "Academic Transformation and Personal Success Feedback Form" (page 108). While all students will be completing the same form (equality), the What's Working? and Challenge components will be unique to each individual student, enabling teachers to know what unique supports that student might need (equity).

When you grade for both equity and equality, you are applying the not-yet approach in support of your students and their learning process, products, and progress. As an example, when grading for equity, teachers are mindful of teaching techniques that incorporate the whole child and his or her long-term development. We know that learning must be a constant and that learning time is a variable (DuFour et al., 2016); therefore, when grading for equity, offer differentiated strategies and resources for success. In addition, when grading for equality, be fair toward all students, but think back to my example in chapter 3 (page 37) about the student who was continuously late to school because he was responsible for his siblings at home. In this case, being fair meant adjusting his start time based on what was right for him, not adhering to the district-prescribed start time.

Finally, understanding how to grade equitably and equally is important for teachers, but it's also important to explain the difference between equity and equality in grading to your students and parents. Ask them what they think grading for equity and equality means and, as part of your ongoing communication (feedback loop), help clarify differences of perception that align their expectations with your grading practices. To help reinforce this for students, consider posting in your classroom accurate definitions of equity and equality in grading that you will adhere to.

Conclusion

In this chapter, you gained insight into the whole child approach, how students often feel anxiety about change, and how you can best communicate with students and parents to obtain feedback about students' needs and ensure that each students' instructional supports meet those needs. Including students and parents in a feedback loop that highlights what's working for students in the classroom (and what isn't) and what challenges students need to overcome enables students and their families to become advocates for students' learning process. In this way, you focus on respect for and inclusion of all stakeholders and transform the culture of learning in your classroom. Further, by transforming grading practices and concentrating on authentic change that moves your classroom culture forward, students become owners of their learning and, ultimately, owners of their own success.

A Look Inside

by Robert Ward, English Language Arts Teacher

I always endeavor to meet the needs of the whole child (socially, emotionally, soulfully, and academically) in my middle school English language arts classroom. For example, in a telephone appointment with a parent of one of my students, the parent seemed upset, and I braced myself for a difficult conversation. This particular student had a learning disability that affects his executive-functioning skills. Much to my surprise, the parent wanted to know why, in eight years of school, my class was the only one that her son ever enjoyed and was successful in! I took a relieved breath and explained to her my approach to teaching (and, by extension, parenting): leadership, love, laughter, and learning.

I told her that I run a very tight ship. Respect, responsibility, and cooperation are character traits that I model implicitly and teach explicitly. I regularly employ specific, personal praise to capitalize on good choices and improvements each student is making. This emphasis on self-regulation and common courtesy is the first tenet of my transformational classroom.

Next, I explained how by creating a warm and welcoming learning environment, I see my students come out of their shells and begin to express themselves passionately and intelligently. No one is willing to change unless they're sure others notice it, so I listen carefully to what my students say and write. A strong sense of belonging is created when students know that their ideas and opinions are heard and valued.

I went on to suggest ways to tap into her son's capacity for engagement with any lesson. I encouraged her to use what she knows about her son's interests to give him direction whenever a teacher offers him voice and choice on assignments. Perhaps a certain topic may not interest her son, but what inner passions could *he* bring to that assignment to make it meaningful to *him*? Transformation is a two-way street, and parents and teachers can share in encouraging students to guide their own transformations.

Last, I explained how I break down complex topics and assignments into more-manageable chunks and build from there. One sure way a teacher knows that transformation is taking place is when the students themselves tell you they "got it" and are hungry for the next step forward or level deeper!

After this conversation, I realized that because I did my job well in the classroom, her child himself spontaneously sung my praises to his mother. By discovering that this parent was actually on my side from the get-go, we were able to strategize together the ways to continue to move her son forward.

Ruminate and Respond

Consider what you've learned in this chapter, and individually or with your team, answer the following questions.

1. What are some examples of successful communication you have had with parents?

2. What are some classroom techniques you use to support anxious students?

3. Do you currently encourage parents and students to be a part of the assessment process? If not, why not? If so, how?

4. After reading this chapter, how do your practices reflect a transformational classroom?

5. What can you do to enhance the feedback loop between yourself, your students, and their parents?

Academic Transformation and Personal Success Feedback Form

Work with your child to fill in the following two boxes, and return the form.	
What's Working? (List one or more items.)	**Challenge (List one item.)**

As your teacher, I will take the following steps to help support you.

Review the teacher-provided feedback, and use the following two boxes to determine next steps.	
Student's Next Step	**Parent or Guardian's Next Step**

Indicate your follow-up plan (email, phone call, or meetings).	
Parent or Guardian's Follow-Up Plan	**Teacher's Follow-Up Plan**

Additional follow-up notes (for teachers, students, or parents or guardians)

The Productive Classroom

The not-yet approach depends on classrooms providing students with environments that ensure they can engage in productive struggle when facing learning challenges. Part of ensuring students persevere through those struggles is to prepare them to expect to encounter and approach struggles with a sense of joy and creativity as a norm. Steven Wolk (2008), a professor of teacher education at Northeastern Illinois University, writes, "As educators, we have the responsibility to educate and inspire the whole child—mind, heart, and soul. . . . we can put more joy into students' experience of going to school and get more joy out of working inside one."

A productive classroom culture emphasizes to students that the act of learning is a joyous one, rife with opportunities for creativity. Researchers Nader Ofoghi, Abbas Sadeghi, and Maryam Babaei (2016), explain, "In attractive classes there is a positive and active relationship along with respect, cooperation and inner satisfaction" (p. 1646) that surely inspire joy and creativity. When a student or teacher feels inner satisfaction, their needs are being taken seriously and being taken care of. As a result, the student and teacher are more likely to experience joy and creativity in a classroom where they are feeling positive and alive!

On the contrary, a negative classroom adversely impacts student learning. Renee Kauffmann (2020), from the School of Information Science at the University of Kentucky, explains some of the implications of a negative classroom culture: "When students perceive the instructor's communication as confrontational, biased, unfair, and unequitable, they are more likely to report the learning environment is unhelpful, not conducive to their welfare, unhealthy, and not engaging" (Kaufmann, 2020). This type of learning environment can make students feel unsafe, especially when it comes time to share their voice (Kaufmann, 2020). Students are most joyful and creative (their most productive) when they have the chance to share who they are and what they know with those around them (Jensen, 2019).

In this chapter, I explain how you can implement productive classroom practices and assign tasks that differentiate learning and foster your students' creativity in the learning process. You will also learn about how to instill the joy of learning in your students that will buoy them when encountering roadblocks and obstacles.

The Not-Yet Approach in the Productive Classroom

A *productive classroom* is a classroom where joy and creativity meet alongside lessons, resources, and assessments as students engage in productive struggle as a norm. Creativity is essential within the not-yet approach because it gives students the opportunity to show what they know and are able to do in a personal and authentic way as they reframe setbacks and obstacles as integral to their personal learning journey. However, as a concept, joy is a bit more nebulous.

Most resources define *joy* as some combination of feeling extreme pleasure, delight, and happiness (Joy, n.d.). But what does that mean, and what does that look like in the classroom? Some teachers consider their career a job, while others think of teaching as a passion or being a part of the greater good. Timothy D. Kanold (2017), author of *HEART! Fully Forming Your Professional Life as a Teacher and Leader*, writes, "Teaching, when properly understood as a career of positive emotion and action, is such a wonderful gift you can give—a gift of your heart and your life to others" (p. xi). It is this outlook on joy in the classroom that helps foster productive learning. Finding joy in the classroom begins with giving students the opportunity to be creative, find their own positive action, and share it with you and their peers.

From this perspective, joy is what makes the whole learning experience satisfying. Wabisabi Learning (n.d.), an organization spearheaded by mindfulness expert Lee Watanabe-Crockett, explains it this way:

> When it comes to classroom productivity, the ideal classroom is a happy one. It means students are creating solutions and projects that have meaning and purpose. They gladly take initiatives and assume responsible ownership of class time. Above all, it means students are loving their learning.

In the not-yet classroom, one where students experience productive struggle, there can be occasional bouts of frustration as students plow through an especially challenging task or project. But when students are able to apply the strategies they've gathered with a growth mindset, accept supports they've received from their teacher or peers, and ultimately realize they have the power to move forward without a crushing sense of self-doubt, they experience a sense of self-satisfaction that is uniquely their own.

As you've come to know, the not-yet approach is all about designing and creating an authentic classroom culture in which teachers don't give up on students who've already given up on themselves. Students know when teachers are doing everything they can to support them and their learning; that desire to be a part of a student's learning journey can be a joyful experience. While joy may not be evident right then and there, once a student has successfully applied a growth mindset and grit to productive learning, he or she will experience the joy inherent in overcoming setbacks and moving forward. But while students must do the heavy lifting, they need teachers to create meaningful, purposeful, and creative learning tasks meant to support and empower students through productive struggle.

Sometimes, teachers can find meaningful, purposeful, and creative learning tasks online. Such resources offer students learning supplements that might open their mind to new ways of thinking or inspire them to dig deeper into a topic. Giving students the chance to learn about a new concept or offering them the chance to delve into a passion project can bring them personal joy and encourage their creativity.

Teachers and students alike have opportunities to utilize current online resources, technology, and personal passions so that, when setbacks and obstacles occur, all stakeholders are focused on achieving the growth necessary to overcome them. Consider the following.

- **Current online resources:** Online resources such as Khan Academy (www.khanacademy.org) offer numerous courses and lessons to help students meet grade- or course-level standards. Another way to stir students' imagination and creativity is to explore cultural and historical resources through virtual field trips like those available through Smithsonian Open Access (www.si.edu/openaccess), about which Common Sense Education (n.d.) writes, "This high-quality collection of museum resources—ranging from artifacts to full-blown exhibits— provides unlimited exploration for students, [and] reliable primary sources for teachers." Also consider other online learning packets and toolkits like the Digital Civics Toolkit (www.digitalcivicstoolkit.org), which provides educators with resources to support students in exploring and recognizing the civic potential for a digital world.

- **Technology:** While online content and resources can help drive creativity and a joy for learning, also consider the tools you might use to facilitate those explorations. For example, Flipgrid (https://flipgrid .com) is a video-based platform that enables teachers to "post discussion topics to which students respond via video, creating a social learning environment that provides every student an equal voice and increases engagement" (Bellow, 2020). Padlet (https://padlet.com) can facilitate real-time online discussions that empower students to share videos, photos, documents, and more for collaborative purposes. Finally, there is Buncee (https://app.edu.buncee.com), which helps facilitate personalized and differentiated learning across a range of content areas and grade levels.

- **Personal passions:** Give students the opportunity to share their heritage, culture, ethnicity, and belief systems in productive ways that empower and inspire. For example, the Milwaukee's Finest Scholarship Foundation (www.mfsf.org) and the University of Wisconsin– Milwaukee host poetry slams throughout the year that encourage students to embrace their creativity by performing poetry they've written in front of an audience with judges. Such explorations break tired stereotypes that often convey topic areas like poetry as elitist or rigid ("Poetry Slam," n.d.). Another opportunity for students to share their creativity is by getting involved in their local government or participating in a social cause that educates students about their rights and how to protect them. As an example, the American Civil Liberties Union (ACLU) of Wisconsin (2020) organizes the Youth Social Justice Forum where the ACLU teaches "essential leadership and social justice issues, skills and techniques for civic engagement." Self-care activities can also be inspiring for students. For example, you set aside time to engage them in brief breathing exercises or physical activity to clear their heads and reduce anxiety, or emphasize the benefits of pets they have at home as a source for reducing anxiety and loneliness.

All together, activities like those described here encourage students to productively engage in a creative process with their learning in which the products they create are personal to them. During the creative process, teachers encourage missteps as a method of nurturing productivity. In an interview with Es Devlin, artist and stage designer, writer Rebecca Fulleylove (n.d.) asks, "How do you feel about making mistakes in your work?" Devlin replies:

Mistakes are pretty much things that don't work, aren't they? We're always making prototypes and there's never any guarantee that any of it will work, you just have a hunch, and what I tend to do is I'm very flexible as I go. If something isn't working, I change it. It's a process of learning from the material. (as cited in Fulleylove, n.d.)

As students engage in curriculum content and the learning process, think of them as also creating prototypes of their work (essay drafts, science mock-ups, and preliminary arguments) and model this thinking about the learning process to them. The purpose of thinking about the learning process as prototyping is to help students embrace creativity and the idea that achievement with vigorous learning intentions doesn't come all at once but in a progression (the scaffolded success criteria).

In a productive classroom, teachers can help students apply this prototyping mindset by sharing with students examples of the creative process. Show students videos of famous people who did not achieve success overnight but rather worked at their creative process for years. For example, MasterClass (www.masterclass.com) offers a series of videos (for a subscription fee) where actors, writers, designers, and more share their creative process. Another example of prototyping is giving students fewer rules, directions, and rubrics when in the brainstorming stage of an activity and instead asking them to be as organic as possible as they conceive of new ideas. Perhaps you want students to come up with a new game or sport in a physical education class, for students to compose a new piece of music in a music class, or see if students can think of ways to reinvent common household items—the possibilities are endless, and they all encourage both joyous creativity and productive struggle.

As Benjamin Earl Evans (2017), director of product inclusion for PayPal, writes, "A lot of people give up in frustration when they're trying to complete a project because they think it's a block in their creative road. Wrong! Frustration is an essential part of the creative process." Within that frustration, it can be difficult to find the joy. But that creative process, while challenging, is unleashing all kinds of great ideas, thoughts, and out-of-the-box thinking students haven't thought of before. By sticking with students and encouraging them to stick with it through struggle, eventually, they will find joy in the learning process and in themselves as determined individuals who are moving forward.

Differentiation and Creativity in the Learning Process

When I was an ELA teacher, especially when I was just starting out, many of the learning products (assignments) I issued were more traditional—the students would read a whole-class novel and write an essay as their assessment, and I would grade their essays. Lather, rinse, repeat. It was boring for both myself and my students, and the one-size-fits-all tasks I assigned stimulated neither their creativity nor joy. However, as I gained more confidence as a teacher and gained a deeper understanding of pedagogy, I began to design assignments and activities based on what author and educator Douglas Reeves (2011) refers to as *differentiated assessment*, which he describes as a "strategy to encourage every student to meet the same rigorous standards in different ways." Not only did Reeves (2011) stir my own creativity as I began to think about new ways to allow students to show what they had learned, his work emphasized to me how important it is to get my students involved in coming up with creative ways to demonstrate their learning.

It's also important to emphasize that, although Reeves (2011) focuses on assessment as a means for differentiation, your approach to differentiation and classroom creativity need not. The learning process encompasses every aspect of the curriculum your students engage in, from direct instruction to group lab work to independent writing and beyond. In *Doable Differentiation*, instructional coach and leadership expert Jane A. G. Kise (2021) identifies the following four cognitive processing styles students connect with and prefer.

1. **Structure and certainty:** This processing style describes students who prefer when teachers tell them what to do. They tend to prefer clear expectations and goals, concrete examples, feedback, and few surprises.

2. **Vision and interpretation:** Students who tend toward this style like to follow their own lead. They like to focus intently on what most interests them, have choices around how to accomplish their learning, and work independently with free rein to explore their creativity and curiosity.

3. **Experience and movement:** This style describes students who like to *do* something as part of their learning. As you might expect, they tend to prefer hands-on activities with steps to follow, chances to move around and work in groups, and clear, realistic deadlines.

4. **Question and connection**: This style describes students who like to lead as they learn. These are students who aren't concerned with minute details, preferring to focus on big-picture ideas and concepts. They tend to gravitate toward experimentation, guiding and teaching others, and working in groups.

Kise (2021) recommends that, when developing lesson plans, teachers provide instruction, activities, and assignments that collectively align with at least one of each of these tendencies. In this way, all students get to experience some component of learning aligned with how they think while still stretching themselves to accomplish learning aligned to their non-preferred styles.

An example of this kind of approach to differentiation comes from one of my ELA units, which was based on Homer's (750 BC/1999) *The Odyssey*. Students read excerpts I assigned of the translated version in class, but I purposely didn't have them read excerpts of Books Six through Ten because I wanted students to present those books to the class in their own way. Students could choose their presentation groups (approximately five or six students per group) and then choose a book that interested them. After reading and discussing the book, the groups presented it to their peers based on what most appealed to them. The presentations were engaging and exciting. One group—dressed as a news team complete with anchor, weather person, sports enthusiast, and human-interest reporter—told the story of the Cyclops; another group sang the story of Odysseus traveling to the underworld in an indie goth band, all dressed in black and sporting fake tattoos and body piercings.

What made these presentations so authentic was the students' desire to show what they knew and were able to do in their own way. They still all had to meet the same rigorous standards; I simply empowered them with the means to learn and present the evidence of their learning in a highly personalized way. While I provided a solid foundation and guidance along the way, which was especially appealing for students who crave clear direction, it also wasn't just me simply assigning work all students had to then accomplish in the exact same way. As a result, students were personally invested and individually productive. Reading *The Odyssey* (Homer, 750 BC/1999) could have become what Reeves (2011) calls boring, inappropriate, or excessively challenging. Instead, by applying a differentiated approach to the learning process, students enthusiastically applied a not-yet mindset as they struggled through group setbacks and obstacles to produce presentations that were courageous, contemporary, comprehensible, and—most of all—creative.

The Joy of Learning

When people think of joy, they tend to think of specific, in-the-moment events that brought them happiness. But there are several types of joy. In *Poor Students, Rich Teaching*, Jensen (2019) details three types of joy: (1) spontaneous (in-the-moment happiness), (2) hedonic (pursued happiness), and (3) eudaimonic (long-term happiness). While there is always a place for the unexpected, moment-to-moment joys, and there is nothing wrong with temporary, joyous pursuits (think of video game rewards or the short-lived pleasure of sugary treats), eudaimonic happiness concerns the joy found from achieving long-term goals, developing new skills, and so on. This is the brand of joy most aligned with the not-yet approach and what you should pursue in earnest as part of your productive classroom.

The question becomes, How do teachers provide the right kind of work for facilitating long-term successes that produce a love of learning? Wolk (2008) writes:

> According to Mihaly Csikszentmihalyi (1990), such learning is an example of *flow*, which he defines as "the state in which people are so involved in an activity that nothing else seems to matter; the experience itself is so enjoyable that people will do it at even great cost, for the sheer sake of doing it.

Flow is the key to that love of learning. Wolk (2008) argues that when teachers want students to experience the kind of joyful embrace of learning that leads to flow, they need to rethink how and what they teach. That rethinking begins with giving students real, relevant, and relatable work that is meaningful to them and their lives.

Begin by asking students what they enjoy, what their passions are, and how they want to make an impact. Giving students opportunities to share what they think (giving them voice) creates shared interest among the sharing student, yourself, and other students. Through your knowledge of students' interests, you can then offer them choices and curriculum-aligned avenues for exploration that lead to joy in their learning. Further, students might want to work in groups, collaborating on shared experiences that support their interests and, hopefully, their flow.

Another way to keep learning real and relevant is to make it relatable. For example, in the late 1960s and early 1970s, my mother was a waitress at a swanky supper club in Milwaukee, Wisconsin. Dave, one of the bus boys she worked with, was drafted into the conflict in Vietnam. My mother and Dave corresponded for several years, and when she passed away, I found the letters Dave wrote her bundled at the bottom of a drawer. They had yellowed, but they were readable and fascinating, so I uploaded them to a flash drive and shared them with the ELA and social studies teachers I collaborate with, giving them permission to use the letters as primary documents in their lessons. As colleagues, we agreed that we had students with family members who had served, some in conflict, and, used correctly, the letters could serve as a point of connection between them and curriculum content.

Two of our English teachers and social studies teachers created an interdisciplinary unit titled Power, Authority, and Governance. In ELA, the letters served as prereading activities for Tim O'Brien's (2009) novel, *The Things They Carried*. In social studies, teachers used the letters as supplemental resources as students studied the causes, effects, and consequences of the Vietnam conflict. They asked their students to keep a journal and write down their questions or comments as they read Dave's letters and their reactions to the novel. This learning was real, and when I read a couple of the letters aloud to students, they were riveted as Dave described life-changing and life-threatening events and worries over whether his girlfriend would still be there for him when he returned home. Many of the concepts discussed in Dave's letters and the novel remain relevant: race, xenophobia, culture, politics, and power.

In developing the unit, I suggested the ELA and social studies teachers ask students how *they* wanted to demonstrate their learning through a final project. Did students want to dig more deeply into the Vietnam conflict or some other historical event and perhaps write from the perspective of those involved (like Dave)? Did students want to interview family members who served in wars or conflicts and share their stories with us? Did students want to share their social justice concerns with the class and discuss how they could make changes in their neighborhood? In developing our unit with real-world connections of relevance to our students, we offered them standards- and curriculum-aligned opportunities for exploration that would inspire, influence, and illuminate them and their peers.

This example is representative of the kind of creativity teachers can apply to their lessons and units to build engagement with the learning process. Very often these endeavors come from the most unexpected places. As a final example, I once created a lesson with a biology teacher who wanted her students to practice their speaking skills prior to giving group presentations. First, we asked students to create a list of the speaking skills people need to be good speakers. Several students commented that speakers must be loud, clear, stand still, and not fidget. In addition, several commented that speakers should be confident and, if necessary, take pauses to make sure they can process the information. Students also stressed that speakers need to be interesting and engaging, and avoid speaking in a monotone by using inflection to help the presentation feel more motivating. Finally, students stressed that the information presented should focus on the theme of the presentation. In other words, stick to the presentation and don't include any unnecessary information.

Next, I showed a video clip of a teenager answering a question for a nationally tele-vised audience. I asked students to use the list they had created and jot down what they saw in the video. Many students commented that the speaker was loud, clear, and didn't fidget. But they also stated that her speech did not make any sense and she was boring. Several students pointed out that she never answered the question, instead going off on a tangent. Last, students commented that she didn't ask for the question to be repeated, which gave the impression she answered without taking the time to process what she was asked or how to respond.

Then, I spread out nearly a dozen Dr. Seuss books on a table—classics like *Green Eggs and Ham* (Dr. Seuss, 1960) and *The Cat in the Hat* (Dr. Seuss, 1957). I asked students to create pairs and then choose their favorite children's book. Students were giddy with excitement in choosing a book that many remembered fondly as younger children. After the pairs had chosen their favorite book, I explained that I wanted them to practice their speaking skills using Dr. Seuss as the text. I demonstrated confident speaking skills using *Green Eggs and Ham*. As I read, I used inflection and gestured, and I was loud, clear, and didn't fidget—modeling examples of a positive and confident speaker.

As students began practicing their speaking skills using the texts, several shared their memories of having their parents read the same texts to them. Many began laughing at the tongue-twisting language indicative of Dr. Seuss. After a few minutes, students paired up and began to focus and practice the skills associated with being a good speaker. Each student in the pair practiced for ten minutes and then switched places with their partner. After each student practiced, we gathered back in the classroom and debriefed on the lesson. Students commented on how much fun they had reading Dr. Seuss and practicing their speaking skills. Several asked if we would be doing this lesson again, and if could we use *Arthur* books (http://marc brownstudios.com/arthur/books), *Berenstain Bears* books (https://berenstainbears.com/kids.html), or another set of books they fondly remembered.

At this point, you may wonder what reading Dr. Seuss has to do with biology learning. In truth, nothing. But literacy is an interdisciplinary skill, and this classroom activity helped students practice their speaking skills as preparation for upcoming group presentations directly connected to the curriculum, and it created new excitement for the disciplinary content as students considered how they could apply the activity to what they were learning about biology. In effect, the biology teacher and I had created joy, enthusiasm, and flow within a productive classroom where we encouraged missteps as students practiced their speaking skills in preparation for the core activity that would let them show what they knew and were able to do in a personal and authentic way. With a little creativity and joy, the biology teacher made the students' learning personal and exciting, which helped the students persevere when they engaged in the curriculum content.

Conclusion

Creativity and joy are not necessarily elements that come to mind when thinking about education. Rather, standardized assignments and assessments, district mandates, negative national press, and more seem to be what teachers hear when community and online talk turns to students and teachers. But that doesn't have to be the case in your classroom. You can design a productive classroom where joy and creativity are the foundation of a purposeful, worthwhile learning process that leads to academic achievement. Differentiate the instruction and learning tasks you provide to empower students and bring out their creativity, and emphasize the joy that comes from them successfully overcoming obstacles as they demonstrate what they know and are able to do in creative and engaging ways.

A Look Inside

by Aubrey Lynn, Special Education Teacher

While looking for ways to foster students' creativity and joy for learning, I found that games can be an innovative way to engage students while working on skills they haven't yet fully developed. They also serve instructional value. For example, a guessing game can help anxious students learn to navigate friendships more easily by promoting structured opportunities for exchanges. In my fourth-grade classroom, with students of varying intellectual and language skills, I created an assignment where my students could turn a book they chose into a board game, which I thought might help my developing readers (who struggled to relate to the magic of literature) make connections to their selected book.

When introducing students to ways they could integrate board games with their selections, I began with the basics. I used the gameboards from Candy Land, Monopoly, and Chutes and Ladders as models. It is essential to model for students what they need to produce, especially for new skills or activities. My students had a strong belief that they could accomplish creating a fun board game if they followed one of the game models.

Next, my students chose their groups. Groups were flexible in number, but no one could work alone. Each group had to choose or agree on a favorite book as the basis of their game. The only supplies I gave them were dice, a file folder, tape, markers, glue, and paper.

There were specific non-negotiables for the game: there had to be a way to move around the board; there had to be a path in the game; there had to be a game piece or pieces; and the groups had to use fifteen questions or facts from the book they selected. The game must also have clear and detailed instructions. I gave the groups limited instructions and materials but encouraged maximum creativity. Across two weeks, I gave the students time each day to work on their games as a fun way to break from other learning content.

At the end of the two weeks, I decided to host a game day in my room. Once the students created the games, the class partnered with a neighboring fourth-grade class to play the games. I wanted this to be a fun and engaging experience, so I provided snacks and gave students opportunities to show off what they had created.

The creators of each game explained the rules and helped facilitate playing the game. The game creators (or "experts") subdivided among the other groups, so each group playing the games had an expert. The expert explained the game and facilitated play. The expert was responsible for answering questions and troubleshooting. Sometimes, the experts became lifelines to help answer the trickier questions from the book. Everyone got a turn to play each game. It was a joyful day, full of laughter, connections, support, and engagement that followed weeks of problem solving and critical thinking. These students came together despite language barriers, learning differences, and cultural disagreements to form a joyful, productive classroom community.

When teachers think creatively about how to integrate games and game-like activities into their productive classroom, they quickly see how games can play a vital role in language-learning classrooms. They are a great way to practice new vocabulary, even helping students overcome inhibitions when learning a new language. In my experience, games also increase students' motivation and encourage them to get involved in the class and continue working.

Ruminate and Respond

Consider what you've learned in this chapter, and individually or with your team, answer the following questions.

1. What do creativity and joy mean to you?

2. Creativity is hard. How do you support your students in implementing their growth mindset when they are creative?

3. How would you describe the various ways you have designed a productive classroom and its impact on students?

4. What is the impact of a productive classroom on you and your teaching life?

5. What do you do to encourage your colleagues to build productive classrooms?

The Supportive Classroom

Sometimes it can be difficult for educators to resist the urge to jump in and help a developing student rather than take a step back and give him or her the time and space to develop autonomy. As an example, I became an English teacher because I loved Shakespeare, Dickens, and Kesey. But, I also wanted to bring my love of these authors to students. As a novice teacher, I remember doing many things for my students ("Let me help you with that thesis," which I then basically wrote for them). Looking back, I've come to realize that offering students help and offering them support are two different things, and I've integrated that realization into the not-yet approach.

Educators often use the terms *help* and *support* interchangeably. Most teachers become teachers precisely because they want to help students become better readers, writers, mathematicians, scientists, historians, or musicians. Even the definitions for *help* and *support* overlap in several respects, with phrasing such as "to give assistance or support to" (Help, n.d.) and, literally, "ASSIST, HELP" (Support, n.d.). However, the connotations for *help* people conjure tend to frame around the ideas of *rescuing, saving, making easier,* and so on. *Help* implies that the onus is on the teacher to spoon-feed information to the student, a passive recipient of that information. If teachers think of their students as needing rescue, where and when does the learning take place? If you make everything easy, will you be able to teach your students how to be critical thinkers and problem solvers who are comfortable independently assessing and overcoming setbacks and obstacles—key components of the not-yet approach? As teachers, we want to provide *support* for our students as they develop their growth mindset and learn to accept setbacks and obstacles as a natural part of learning.

In this chapter, you will learn about using the not-yet approach to develop a supportive classroom. In particular, you learn several ways to issue flexible supports that provide the right amount of productive struggle for students to grow.

The Not-Yet Approach in the Supportive Classroom

In a *supportive classroom* rooted in the not-yet approach, teachers avoid spoon-feeding information to students. A sit-and-get or sage-on-stage classroom mentality is anathema to the supportive classroom, which instead involves students, parents, and the teacher as invested stakeholders guiding students toward success.

According to associate professor in the School of Public Affairs at American University Seth Gershenson (2020b), teachers must "guard against the 'easy A' and work together to enforce higher grading standards." When a class is construed as easy, Gershenson (2020b) argues, students "may become complacent and fail to reach their full potential." In receiving that "easy A," students have failed to master standards-derived learning intentions but have still received a passing grade. Rather than make the learning easier, teachers must ensure students have access to the instruction and resources that will support them as they engage in productive struggle to achieve the vigorous learning intentions and scaffolded success criteria that reflect what they know and are able to do.

Scaffolds are an integral part of an authentic not-yet classroom because they serve as opportunities for students to overcome setbacks and challenges. As I am fond of saying, scaffolding a lesson is just good teaching (Grafwallner, 2017e). They provide opportunities for all students to be successful, and because teachers can use them in response to student struggles with learning, teachers can tailor them to specific student needs based on the learning intention.

Scaffolds are most effective when they help students break down learning "into manageable chunks as they progress toward stronger understanding and ultimately greater independence" (Mulvahill, 2018). When teachers scaffold large tasks into smaller pieces, students can make sense of each individual part and can take advantage of supports in the form of teacher explanation and modeling, practice, and practical application to put the pieces together into a whole that signifies understanding. However, as I wrote for *Edutopia*, "Too much lecturing, too thick a packet, or too many directions can cause anxiety and disquiet. One small step at a time usually works best" (Grafwallner, 2017e). When scaffolding, EducationCorner contributor Becton Loveless (n.d.) explains that teachers should place emphasis "on connecting old concepts to new ones to set a foundation for learning." As you continually help students connect familiar concepts (background knowledge) to new ones, the learning doesn't seem so overwhelming. Students are already familiar with certain concepts, and as they learn more, they will retain more (Loveless, n.d.).

According to education researcher Linda Darling-Hammond (2016), there are many scaffolds that teachers can put in place to help students be successful. She explains:

> [Teachers] scaffold a process of successive conversations, steps, and learning experiences that take students from their very different starting points to a proficient performance—including many opportunities for approximation and practice, debriefing and conversing, sharing work in progress, and continual revision.

In scaffolding, teachers can offer many different opportunities to students based on ability and grade level. In addition, teachers can revise and modify these scaffolding methods based on the work that students are able to do and if they need more scaffolding or less. The following list explains five specific scaffolding methods you might use.

1. **Activate prior knowledge:** Loveless (n.d.) encourages teachers, when scaffolding, to connect prior knowledge to new learning. When activating prior knowledge, students are making connections to both old concepts and new learning. As an example, consider the sixth- to eighth-grade learning intention for a science class from chapter 4 (page 51). Instead of just diving into the definitions of *superstition*, *pseudoscience*, and *science*, teachers can support students with scaffolds that activate their prior knowledge. Ask students to draw three columns on their paper; at the top of each column, write one of the words: *superstition*, *pseudoscience*, and *science*. Then, ask students to write down what they already know about each of these words. They might write down their definitions, how they use the word (if they use it yet), or how they've heard or seen others use the words.

2. **Front-load concept-specific vocabulary:** Let's stick with the previous item's science-based learning intention. New science vocabulary, in particular, can be very intimidating to students. To mitigate this, design a lesson where you break down the words so students know the prefixes, roots, and suffixes of vocabulary words (Herrmann, 2018). As an example, *super* means *over* or *above* in Latin. Can students think of other words that begin with *super*? Next, *pseudo* is a Greek prefix that means

false. Can students think of other words that start with *pseudo*? Finally, *sci* is a Latin prefix that means *to know*. Can students think of other words that start with *sci*?

When front-loading content-specific vocabulary, students can take what they've learned and connect those prefixes to other words, thereby extending their vocabulary. According to consultant and English learner specialist Erick Herrmann (2018), "As [students] learn these word parts, it helps them to analyze specific unknown words they encounter, and it helps them to determine the meaning of these words."

3. **Get students talking:** Creating opportunities for talk gives students the chance to "discuss tasks or ideas and question one another, negotiate meaning, clarify their own understanding, and make their ideas comprehensible to their partners" (Fisher, Frey, & Rothenberg, 2008, p. 17). When students share their ideas, they are able to process out loud, hearing their own thoughts and their peers' views. After students have read a brief piece of text, ask them to create groups of three to four students. Then, ask three critical-thinking questions that focus on *how* and *why*. Ask students to jot down the most important themes of their content-specific conversation to share with the class. By giving students the chance to talk in this way, they are able to make meaning and process information.

4. **Get students writing:** Consider creating journal time in your class. Students can answer an engaging warm-up question at the start of class or can respond to reflection prompts after reading. Researchers Mary-Ann Jarvis and Olivia B. Baloyi (2020) explain, "[Reflective journaling] requires the learner writing connected entries that spiral from the preceding entry. Such spiraling involves newly constructing knowledge and skills built on learning from the previous journal entry and avoids a journal with disconnected stand-alone entries." Teachers can then collect students' journals and offer comments and feedback based on students' evidence of learning. Students can also use the journals as examples of content-specific growth since the journals build on skills from entry to entry.

5. **Use graphic organizers:** There are limitless designs and styles of graphic organizers available online to support all sorts of subject areas, academic abilities, and grade levels. When searching for a graphic organizer, don't just use what you find. Instead, think about how you might use

its strengths to adapt it for your curriculum and daily lessons. When you create, modify, or revise a graphic organizer, you can build in individualized scaffolds to help specific students who might need a little extra support.

One of my favorite graphic organizers is the concept map or mind map because it is so easy to use (Kise, 2021), and students can draw map elements right on their paper, which means teachers don't have to search for templates. Students can create their own concept map, like the magnet summary I explain in chapter 10 (page 167), or they can create cause-and-effect maps where one column is the cause, and the next column is the effect. Then offer students some cause-and-effect linking words, such as *because, therefore, so, consequently*, and *as a result*. The possibilities are endless.

Scaffolding supports such as these are an important part of the not-yet classroom because they break down the learning into manageable pieces. As a result, students can struggle productively through setbacks and obstacles that are part of any academic task and develop a mindset that focuses on overcoming barriers to achieve learning intentions.

Supportive Check-Ups

Graded or ungraded, formative or summative, remember that the purpose of using assignments, essays, labs, check-ups, and so on is to assess student learning. A supportive classroom gives students the opportunity to demonstrate what they know and are able to do, giving you information about essential learnings students have or haven't acquired yet. It's not uncommon for teachers, students, and families alike to misunderstand that the purpose of assessments is to *inform* instead of viewing assessments as the end of a learning journey regardless of whether that learning was successful. For students, graded assessments are also a frequent source of fear and anxiety. If that anxiety becomes overpowering, the opportunity to use assessments as a support tool is lost.

Recall from chapter 6 (page 91) that one effective way to pull the anxiety from graded work and put the emphasis on learning is to refer to it as a *check-up*. One way the supportive classroom ensures students see check-ups not as objects of fear but as feedback measurements about what they know and can do is to offer choice-focused supports that offer flexibility in the way students show their learning. Like the individual steps of scaffolded success criteria, the supports you put in place with the check-ups you issue aren't permanent structures. You add or remove them as needed, based on what scaffolds support students in overcoming obstacles to learning and then showing that learning.

The following sections explore two aspects of choice: (1) choice in classroom culture and (2) choice in approaches to learning.

Choice in Classroom Culture

Scaffolded supports that utilize choice are a vital part of any successful lesson in a not-yet classroom because choice instills ownership in a classroom's culture. Teacher, consultant, and curriculum and instruction specialist Lauren Gehr (2020) explains, "Many students' day-to-day activities are controlled by others, which may leave them feeling powerless." Being a facilitator and not an owner of student learning means eliminating that mindset of control. You want students to feel the classroom is also theirs and that they are the influencers of their learning. Education consultant John McCarthy (2015) clarifies, "Power and authority will ensure that lessons occur and classrooms are managed," but a managed classroom doesn't help students learn how to develop their growth mindset, and a managed classroom is not an indication of support within the not-yet approach. In a not-yet classroom where student choice is the norm, the struggles students engage in are productive in part because they have the opportunity to control their environment and culture without distractions. As a result, they focus on what they want to know and be able to do with that learning as directed by vigorous learning intentions and scaffolded success criteria. Veteran teacher, consultant, and author Mike Anderson (2016) asserts, "Students learn more when they are motivated. . . . when students have energy and passion for their work and are driven to excel, they can accomplish incredible feats" (p. 11).

The following examples highlight how teachers can create an environment of choice.

1. **Use flexible seating:** Give students a chance to choose where to sit, and provide various seating arrangements, such as tables, individual desks, standing desks, or podiums. You might be surprised at what extra furniture you can find in your school. Look around and talk to colleagues and facilities staff. Is there a table tucked in a closet that you can have or a podium a teacher isn't using? Be creative to build a choice-enabling environment.

2. **Post wall art:** If you have your own classroom, consider asking students to share their art on a designated wall, making it their own. Art could be pictures, photos, or inspirational messages. Give students a chance to make the classroom their own. If you are a secondary teacher with multiple classes, perhaps designate a space for each of your classes.

3. **Listen to music:** Allow students the opportunity to share their music during attendance or during warm-up. Music creates a vibe—it can be soft and low to calm us down or loud and thumping to amp us up. Ask for volunteer DJs who are willing to set up a peer's music and play it during the first five minutes of class. You can manage this choice by creating a sign-up sheet for students to share their music with the class. If a student wants to play his or her music, he or she must provide the lyrics to you ahead of time, ensuring they don't conflict with any class or school norms or guidelines.

4. **Determine words to live by:** Treating oneself and one's peers with respect creates an empathetic and equitable classroom culture. At the beginning of the school year, ask students to form small groups of four or five members and create a list of what they think creates a warm and respectful classroom environment. (In essence, behavioral norms for your class.) Then have the groups read each other's lists and eliminate the repetition. Finally, ask all students to create a final list that they can live by. If you have multiple classes, have each class create its own list.

5. **Ask your students:** What do your students want to see in your classroom? How do they want to set it up? Maybe younger (elementary) students want to bring in pictures of their pets and create a pet wall. Secondary students may want to see inspirational messaging focusing on social justice. Gather their voice about how their classroom environment reflects them as learners.

Don't overlook the physical environment and classroom culture when looking for ways to enhance student choice. Choice in their learning environment empowers students to determine an environment that motivates and empowers them to focus on the learning and not on distractions.

Choice in Approaches to Learning

When students receive a chance to choose their own text, topic, or task, they take ownership and pride in the work they are about to do (Wolpert-Gawron, 2018). With that investment, they are more apt to stick with it and learn it. In this way, student choice in the methods of their learning (not in the standards they acquire) can help eliminate apathy and disconnect, boost engagement and motivation, and focus on their strengths as they endeavor to achieve learning goals (Parker, Novak, & Bartell, 2017). Wolpert-Gawron (2018) affirms that "choice allows students to display their learning in the way that they feel best represents their knowledge."

Students are much more passionate and expressive when they can demonstrate their learning in their own way—a model they designed themselves, an original song, an original spoken word—anything that shows their level of expertise and their understanding with learning intentions and success criteria. For teachers, the opportunity to embed student choice doesn't have to be difficult or time-consuming (Kise, 2021). Even simple choices give students the opportunity to be in charge of their own learning journey, empowering them in that journey (Anderson, 2016).

Here are four examples of choice supports you can use with students.

1. **Lesson choice:** When designing a lesson, offer opportunities for students to demonstrate what they know in individualized ways. For example, while you might offer three or four exemplars for them to follow if they want, always leave the last option up to students (with your approval). This gives students the chance to tie in something they are invested in to the course curriculum and learning standards. So, if you have a student whose family members are Civil War re-creators, allow him or her to tap into that expertise and inspiration as part of his or her learning product.

2. **Digital tools:** Offer students the chance to show off their digital prowess. Robotics, engineering, and computer science classes all lend themselves particularly well to fascinating opportunities for choice in the classroom. As an example, when the pandemic started, one of our students recreated a Minecraft (www.minecraft.net) replica of our school building—every room, office, nook, and cranny. It was incredible!

3. **Self-differentiation:** Student choice encourages differentiation since students are able to individualize their assignments based on their own preferred way to learn. (See Differentiation and Creativity in the Learning Process, page 115.) As an example, if you've assigned students to individually read a novel, perhaps a small student group wants to read it together, taking turns speaking, listening, and discussing as a group. While you must determine if the classroom culture is strong enough that students will be able to focus on the reading and still achieve the learning goals, if you believe they can, then you've enabled them to advocate for themselves, thus making the experience that much more personal.

4. **Individualized inquiry:** Students are used to reading a text and answering questions about it. But instead of giving students

teacher-supplied questions, encourage them to create their own open-ended questions that focus on something they're interested in and perhaps something they want to research. As an example, if students have read an article about the Mars rover, what questions do they have or research do they want to do? This can unlock perspectives on the learning that might not be immediately obvious from your own conception of the assignment, like if students explore the rover's functions from the perspective of computer scientists rather than from the perspective of planetary explorers or geologists. Give them a wide path from which to start their inquiry journey.

The power of student choice in the means and method of learning is critical to the success of the not-yet classroom, as students adopt and develop mindsets that focus on overcoming challenges and use that growth mindset to craft an individualized learning journey.

Tools to Support Choice

As you reflect on ways to use this chapter's guidance to foster a supportive classroom grounded in student choice, consider how you will use classroom time and learning supports to enhance and support the learning experience for your students. I've included the following two sections—(1) character-trait charts and (2) choice reading—to help illustrate approaches I've used successfully in the past to offer students choice-driven supports.

Character-Trait Charts

In my freshman English class, I often use a modified version of the Education Oasis (2006) "Character Trait Chart" graphic organizer, which you can access online (https://bit.ly/2RxxDxw). This organizer has students choose a character from a reading, list traits associated with that character using a word bank found at the bottom of the organizer, and then provide evidence from the text that supports the listed trait. In my class, after students had read act 1 of Shakespeare's (1597/2004) *Romeo and Juliet*, I asked them to keep a record of the characters' traits. However, rather than simply give students one graphic organizer, I instead created several versions of it. All students would have to accomplish the same learning goals, but the different organizers provided choice and different supports in how they accomplished that learning.

Here is the lesson's vigorous learning intention and scaffolded success criteria.

- **Learning intention:** I can practice close-reading skills, inference skills, and Modern Language Association (MLA) citations using the character's traits.

- **Success criteria:** I know I am successful because . . .

    1. I can perform a close reading of act 1

    2. I can infer a trait that exemplifies the textual evidence

    3. I can write the textual evidence according to MLA citation style guidelines

For this check-up, I asked students to collaborate in groups of four, shuffling their desks to form pods, as they reflected on the main characters from their reading: Romeo, Juliet, Nurse, Lady Capulet, Lord Capulet, Benvolio, Tybalt, and Mercutio. Then, I asked students to choose a character-trait chart graphic organizer they would prefer to use. I explained the choice options as follows.

- **Choice support 1:** Students who chose this version were responsible for utilizing the word bank and showing proper MLA citation evidence where that particular trait was demonstrated in act 1.

- **Choice support 2:** Students who chose this version received a list of already-selected traits, but these groups were required to use a thesaurus to find a more sophisticated synonym for that trait. After writing down the new, more sophisticated word, students were responsible for showing proper MLA citation evidence where that particular trait was demonstrated in act 1. Figure 8.1 shows an excerpted example of this version (the word bank is omitted).

- **Choice support 3:** Students who chose this version were responsible for using a word they already knew (no word bank) or a sophisticated synonym, showing proper MLA citation evidence where that particular trait was demonstrated in act 1.

These supportive choice graphic organizers are the very basis of the not-yet classroom because while students have the opportunity to choose how they demonstrate their learning, they still have to achieve the same learning standard.

Remember, when considering how to implement choice in your learning activities and assessments, it's important not to lose sight of how they connect with your vigorous learning intentions and scaffolded success criteria. According to teacher resource specialist for curriculum and instruction Beth Pandolpho (2018), "We can empower

Directions: Using the Trait column as inspiration, write a synonym of the character you have chosen in the Thesaurus column. Then, list an example of textual evidence to demonstrate how the text reveals that trait. (Events, actions, words, thoughts, attitudes, and feelings can reveal traits.)

Character: _____

Trait	Thesaurus	Textual Evidence (using proper MLA citation style)
Curious		
Dishonest		
Empathetic		
Fearful		
Foolish		
Happy		
Imaginative		
Jealous		
Mysterious		
Quiet		
Responsible		
Sad		
Sympathetic		
Talented		
Unfriendly		
Wise		

Source: Adapted from Education Oasis, 2006.

Figure 8.1: Character-trait chart graphic organizer.

our students to be in charge of their own learning by creating interesting, open-ended tasks that target real-world skills . . . and enable students to make choices and then measure and reflect on their progress." Since I scaffolded the success criteria for this lesson, students also had the opportunity to self-assess. If they had done a successful close read of act 1, they could move on to connecting the trait, possibly from a word bank, to a piece of textual evidence. If the students had successfully found a piece of evidence that exemplified the trait, they could write the evidence using proper MLA citation style. The work students did always remained connected to the overall learning intention and success criteria.

In addition, students were able to discuss their findings in groups. During the discussion, students had the opportunity to share their inference examples, question one another about their evidence choices, and justify why they chose the trait evidence they did. In this way, students had the opportunity to critique and evaluate their peers' traits and evidence, and they had the chance to explain how and why an inference aligns to a particular piece of textual evidence. Finally, students had the chance to strengthen their vocabulary while utilizing individualized supports.

While this example is rooted in literature for a secondary ELA class, consider how you might adapt it for your curriculum.

Choice Reading

Just as you can offer choice in the tools that support students' learning, consider how you might unlock student choice through reading and research materials. For example, if you want students to explore themes related to science, technology, engineering, and mathematics (STEM), instead of assigning a specific reading, provide students with a menu of options to choose from along with the opportunity to suggest sources not on your list.

According to author, teacher, coach, and international speaker Laura Robb (2018), "When students self-select books to read, they have opportunities to read what interests them, what they care about, and at the same time, they discover what kinds of books they enjoy." Choice reading empowers students to choose *what* they want to read and *how* they want to read it. But, as Robb (2018) points out, teachers must give students time to get interested and time to care. Teachers can appeal to students' visual senses by showing them book trailers and then discussing why that particular book looks interesting to read. Teachers can give students purpose in reading for enjoyment—something that many of my students had not necessarily done before.

In addition, Robb (2018) writes:

> Reading is social. That's why students love talking about books with a partner or in a small group. Discussions reveal a range of interpretations supported with evidence from the text. In addition, students practice active listening as well as organizing their thoughts, so they can communicate their thinking to peers.

In my English skills class, I decided that choice reading would be an explicit part of my classroom curriculum. Choice reading was not an afterthought that students did when there was time at the end of the class; instead, I made it a top priority so students had the time and space to read books of their choice.

My choice-reading program had three distinct parts.

- **Choice support 1:** I created a two-week calendar (see figure 8.2, page 138) so students knew exactly when they would be reading. (See page 143 for a reproducible version of this figure that is applicable for any content area.) That reading time was never taken away from them, so they always knew they could count on it.

- **Choice support 2:** When students picked their choice-reading book, I gave them about ten to fifteen minutes to read. No discussion. No paper to complete. The next day, they read again for about ten to fifteen minutes, but this time I gave each student a note card to write down the one thing he or she thought was interesting from the reading that day— just one thing. Students shared their note cards with the class. This generated questions and predictions about each book.

- **Choice support 3:** I read with every student during choice-reading time. For example, I would sit next to a student and would read a page aloud. He or she would read the next page, and then we would discuss. Or I would sit next to a student, and we would read a page silently and then discuss. Or I would ask the student to summarize what was happening in his or her book for me. I didn't make accountability the main point of reading. I collected a reflection from students every other reading, and students hosted book chats once a month.

At the end of the book, students wrote a summary utilizing who, what, where, when, why, and how. For many students, this was very difficult since many just wanted to write a retelling of the story, not a summary. So, I taught students how to write a summary, and we practiced that skill during the two weeks.

Learning intentions and success criteria for Monday, October 5 through Friday, October 16

Vocabulary:

Learning intention—I can define, practice, and successfully demonstrate my comprehension of the vocabulary words.

Success criteria—I know I am successful because . . .

1. I can define five new vocabulary words every two weeks

2. I can practice the new and former vocabulary words

3. I can demonstrate my understanding of the vocabulary words

Skills:

Learning intention—I can create a summary based on who, what, where, when, why, and how and apply it to Martin Luther King Jr.'s (1963) "I Have a Dream" speech excerpt.

Success criteria—I know I am successful because . . .

1. I can define and explain the difference between a retelling and a summary

2. I can find the who, what, where, when, why, and how in a children's nursery rhyme

3. I can use who, what, where, when, why, and how to write a summary based on a children's nursery rhyme

Choice Reading:

Learning intention—I can choose a book, read the book, talk about it, and write a summary and review based on my book.

Success criteria—I know I am successful because . . .

1. I can choose a book and complete it

2. I can read my book and talk about it

3. I can successfully write a summary and review based on my book

Week One Calendar

Monday	Tuesday	Wednesday	Thursday	Friday
Vocabulary pretest	Recall and practice new vocabulary words.	Identify and practice all vocabulary words.	Application day	Vocabulary matching game
Introduce five new vocabulary words.	Introduce who, what, where, when, why, and how to find information.	Apply who, what, where, when, why, and how information to write a summary based on King's "I Have a Dream" speech excerpt.	(Utilizing the skill learned in class this week, students practice this skill on their homework.)	Sustained silent reading; complete a 3 × 5 note card summary of my book and share in my small group.
Sustained silent reading	Practice who, what, where, when, why, and how to find information in a nursery rhyme; get feedback from peers; revise for accuracy.	Sustained silent reading		

Week Two Calendar

Monday	Tuesday	Wednesday	Thursday	Friday
Vocabulary check-up of all words	Recall and practice vocabulary words.	Identify and practice all vocabulary words.	Application day	Vocabulary assessment of all words
Peer feedback of who, what, where, when, why, and how to write a summary graphic organizer about King's "I Have a Dream" speech	Revisions for who, what, where, when, why, and how to write a summary graphic organizer; miniconference with the teacher for feedback	Sustained silent reading	(Utilizing the skill learned in class this week, students practice this skill on their homework.)	Sustained silent reading; book chat
Sustained silent reading			Revisions for who, what, where, when, why, and how to write a summary graphic organizer based on teacher feedback; turn in to the teacher	

Figure 8.2: Two-week reading calendar example.

The final step was to email the summary and review to the school's media specialist, who then uploaded them to the library database so students could read their peers' summaries and reviews to get authentic, relevant book reviews from peers.

Through this multi-week exercise, I offered choice and structured supports that enabled students to choose what book they wanted to read, how they wanted to demonstrate their reading, and how they wanted their reading assessed. In addition, students had a chance to practice how to write a summary, a viable skill needed in all content areas. As Anderson (2016) explains, choice doesn't have to be complicated for teachers or students; it can be as simple as students choosing their own graphic organizer for a reading. As long as the choice options you provide still require students to engage in productive struggle as they achieve the goals in their learning intentions and success criteria, then you are meeting the needs of a supportive classroom.

Conclusion

Supportive classrooms understand the difference between offering supports to scaffold up students' learning and offering help that sidesteps the need for productive struggle. By building choice into your supports as you issue check-ups on student acquisition of learning intentions and success criteria, you empower, motivate, and engage your students. Supportive classroom environments built on choice permeate all aspects of learning, from the classroom's inherent culture to the tools and materials students use to learn. In this way, a supportive classroom gives all students a chance to determine success on their own terms, acknowledging that while challenges are part of the learning, students still have the opportunity to personalize what they are learning for better understanding.

A Look Inside

by Chey Cheney and Pav Wander, Creators of *The Staffroom Podcast*

Middle school students are notorious for shying away from seeking attention in academic settings unless it is absolutely necessary. This heightened insecurity in the tween and teen years often can pose problems when it comes to self-advocacy, especially in traditionally more challenging and intimidating subjects such as mathematics, where teachers often expect independent work.

In a setting where students are seeking support but are not speaking up, the onus is often left to the teacher in the room to identify where further assistance may be necessary. Start early by establishing a classroom culture that shows students everyone will be at different points on the spectrum of understanding mathematics concepts. By ensuring that understanding, the whole class can utilize the not-yet approach appropriately.

In middle school mathematics classrooms, teachers like to engage in regular one-to-one conferencing to establish how students are doing and where they might need further reinforcement. We divide the class into four groups, and each week endeavor to meet with one group. Students keep a mathematics journal beginning on the first day of class, and we encourage them to write in it each week. Ask them key guiding questions to help move the conversation and highlight the challenges. These questions could include the following.

1. "What topics did we cover this week?"
2. "What skills and concepts did you master?"
3. "Are there skills and concepts that you got stuck on?"

Teachers can use this information to guide their planning and to identify which students need additional supports to guide them along their mathematics journey. It's interesting to note that when the teacher normalizes a culture of individualized pacing, students open up more about where they are on the spectrum of understanding and, therefore, allow the teacher and potentially other students in the room to offer their expertise to scaffold and assist.

In a setting where it's usually much simpler for middle school students to suffer in silence rather than speak up about needing help, normalization of individualized pacing and regular conferencing are ways teachers can effectively keep students open about their challenges and help them along the way.

Ruminate and Respond

Consider what you've learned in this chapter, and individually or with your team, answer the following questions.

1. How do you differentiate between *help* and *support*? On reflection, do you help your students or support them? How do you know?

2. Do you offer students choices in their approach to learning? What do you do? How might you increase choice?

3. What can you do to enhance student participation in classroom culture, including the look and physical arrangement of the room?

4. What kind of scaffolding opportunities do you offer your students? Are they successful; how do you know?

5. What are some examples of choice supports you have given your students? What was their reaction to these opportunities?

Two-Week Instructional Calendar

List learning intentions and success criteria for _____.

List essential vocabulary:

List essential skills:

List learning materials (texts, graphic organizers, and so on):

Week One Calendar				
Monday	Tuesday	Wednesday	Thursday	Friday

Week Two Calendar				
Monday	Tuesday	Wednesday	Thursday	Friday

The Flexible Classroom

As teachers, individually or as part of a collaborative team, we devote considerable time and energy to designing, creating, implementing, and assessing lessons to deliver what researcher, speaker, trainer, and author Robert J. Marzano (2017) describes as *critical-input experiences*. About these, Marzano (2017) writes, "Critical-input experiences introduce important new content to students and are vital to enhancing student learning. The teacher takes special care in planning for these experiences" (p. 56). For teachers, part of constructing high-quality critical-input experiences is to offer students your very best teaching self. For example, when sharing critical-input experiences with students, I wanted them to be real, relevant, and relatable, and I wanted to share personal experiences, a piece of me, with the students in my class. I also wanted them to know that their comments mattered to me and that I took their suggestions and ideas to heart. So, I often asked them to evaluate and critique my lessons. Even though I had spent much time creating what I thought was an excellent lesson, I knew their voice and perspective could help me make them better.

For students, reflection is also a critical piece of ensuring they get the most out of their own critical-input experience, something teachers and students often forget to do (Hedberg, 2009). Associate dean of graduate business programs at the University of St. Thomas (St. Paul, Minnesota) Patricia Raber Hedberg (2009) further notes, "Reflection is a natural, and essential, part of the learning process" (p. 10). It helps make meaning for students and is vital to the learning process. However, due to the myriad of other demands on teachers' time, whether or not students are reflecting on their learning (successful or otherwise) is often the last thing on a teacher's mind. Researcher and adult-education expert Bo Chang (2019) comments:

> Many times, students complete their assignments without reflection. Reflection in learning is necessary for students to revisit what

they have learned for improvement and for in-depth learning. It gives students an opportunity to document their learning journey and provide references and suggestions for future students.

The learning process is a direct benefit of reflection. Students are able to take time and look back over the work they have completed and determine what they need to do to make necessary improvements. Because of this reflective process, students are more apt to share their work with peers and accept and offer suggestions. Through collaboration, students generate even more ideas and interpretations about how to improve their own learning.

In this chapter, you'll learn more about how establishing a flexible classroom built on critical-input experiences and reflection on those experiences is an important part of the not-yet approach. I introduce you to effective ways to approach both teacher- and student-focused reflection and provide guidance on how to seek student feedback on your instruction.

The Not-Yet Approach in the Flexible Classroom

A *flexible classroom* describes any classroom that is willing to accept evaluation and critique as part of its classroom structure. It is a classroom rooted in effective action that is crucial to the continuing growth of teachers and students. The key word, however, is *effective*. Without taking time to reflect and make adjustments, teachers cannot determine what instructional practices are effective and result in student growth, nor can students independently assess their own learning. However, for reflections to be beneficial, it's just as important that your reflective practices be as effective as your instructional practices. During my first year as an ELA teacher, I decided to keep a journal of my teaching experience as a way to self-reflect. My reflections consisted of merely summarizing my day; there was no digging deep to answer the *why* or *how*. I was only recapping the *what* of my day. I didn't sustain my journal writing for long because it just became one more thing to do, and the record didn't offer insight into the outcomes of my work with students. Also, I had my lesson plans to show what I was doing, so it felt like my summarizing was overkill. It was an ineffective form of reflection, and I let it go.

There is an axiom that people are their own worst critics, but self-criticism can quickly become toxic and damaging (Shahar, 2015). However, reflection isn't about engaging in self-criticism (or criticism and blame of others). Looking back on my journaling experience, I find a lot of negative self-talk often guided my writing.

According to coauthors Narelle Lemon and Sharon McDonough (2020), "When you engage in a reflective practice, it can be easy to slip into negative thinking and think you are to blame for things that didn't go well in the classroom environment" (p. 60). If a lesson went poorly or if I felt I didn't connect with a student, I would simply retell the event in my journal instead of addressing *why*. It wasn't until much later that I began to focus on meaningful reflection that focused on the *why* as a means to change and grow.

To get to your own *why*, consider using a concept map or brief table to capture your ideas or try using renowned Japanese industrialist Sakichi Toyoda's *five whys* (Tanner, 2020). This technique involves establishing an initial problem and then using the question *Why?* five times in succession to explore the cause-and-effect relationships to analyze the root source of an outcome. (Such outcomes can include both successes and failures, as understanding the reasons for both is instructive.) Figure 9.1 illustrates how this works.

Problem statement:	My lesson failed.
Why?	It failed because students were confused over my references about fairy tales.
Why?	I assumed students had more background knowledge in fairy tales.
Why?	Most parents read fairy tales to their children, and I assumed this was commonplace.
Why?	My parents always used to read fairy tales to me.
Why?	I cannot assume that my experiences and those of people I know or grew up with are the same as those of my students.

Figure 9.1: Using the five whys to reflect on instruction.

As you can see from figure 9.1, I had used fairy tales as a reference in a lesson, and several students were unaware of the fairy tales to which I alluded. When I began questioning, you'll notice I used the word *failed*. I began to reflect on the lesson right after I taught it. In truth, my entire lesson didn't fail; rather, I had one concept within the lesson that I would need to modify in the future. I either needed to incorporate more background knowledge into my instruction and modeling or ask students to share examples of fairy tales they remembered. I suggest jotting down some thought bullets about the lessons you teach after you teach them, but refrain from a paragraph being critical of yourself or your students (venting), which is not a productive use of your time or talent.

High school English teacher and instructional coach Grant Piros (2019) writes:

> In order to serve our students, we too must change and grow. As teachers, we need not frantically chase the next new thing in education, but we must improve the core of our craft as research, best practices, and the world evolve.

Teacher *and* student growth derived from reflection on learning experiences and outcomes, such as those described here, make a classroom flexible and feed a not-yet mindset. As you know, classroom time is at a premium, and lecturing to students for the entirety of a single lesson or course period, with students sitting and (you hope) listening passively, is a dead-end for the concept you are about to teach. According to researchers Louis Deslauriers, Logan S. McCarty, Kelly Miller, Kristina Callaghan, and Greg Kestin (2019), "Students learn more when they are actively engaged in the classroom than they do in a passive lecture environment." It's critical for teachers to enliven instruction by modifying their academic language (chapter 5, page 81), collecting feedback (see chapter 6, page 91), getting creative (chapter 7, page 111), incorporating choice (see chapter 8, page 125), and so on, especially when we know the benefits of active instruction and learning (Deslauriers et al., 2019).

While using strategies to produce engagement—for example, asking open-ended questions, facilitating student-centered discussions, or using curiosity creators (Kise, 2021)—can get students thinking, talking, and evaluating their own work, true reflection still requires a concerted and cognizant effort to implement and sustain. It requires flexibility. That's why flexible classrooms inspire students to engage in *metacognitive thinking* (thinking about their own thinking; Cohen, Opatosky, Savage, Stevens, & Darrah, 2021) as an effective way to reflect on the learning process. You'll learn more about this later in this chapter (see Student Reflection, page 154). But first, let's dig deeper into the reflection you do as a teacher with regard to your own practice.

Teacher Self-Reflection

Teachers often self-reflect sporadically, engaging in it when they have time to fit it in. Given how little extra time teachers have, this usually means reflection is among the first thing teachers cut from their process when looking to make extra time for other priorities. Brian Lane Stanley (2018), a Teach Plus Commonwealth Teaching Policy Fellow, notes:

Taking that time to reflect, not only about the lessons but about myself, does, in fact, benefit my students. That reflection is the key to feeling fully engaged in the work. But for this to occur, teachers like me need dedicated time and support.

Time and support are critical for moving from merely reflecting on *what* happened during a given day and instead focusing on the *why* and *how* for helping make real classroom change. Adult education scholar Stephen D. Brookfield (2017) explains a common pitfall in teacher reflections, "Our actions as teachers are based on assumptions we have about how best to help students learn" (p. 2). These teaching assumptions limit thinking about the *why* and *how* about students' learning (or lack thereof), hindering educators' growth and leaving untapped students' capacity to achieve. Teachers must be critical in their reflections, digging deep into their experiences, perceptions, and biases to support all students.

Remember, this isn't about engaging in destructive self-criticism. *Critical reflection*, according to Brookfield (2017), "is, quite simply, the sustained and intentional process of identifying and checking the accuracy and validity of our teaching assumptions" (p. 3). The journaling exercise I wrote about in the previous section was an attempt at reflection, but it wasn't sustained, and it certainly wasn't critical in the way Brookfield (2017) intends. For example, if a class of mine didn't do well on a check-up, I seldom thought that it could have been my fault. I chose interesting material, taught it well, and gave a worthwhile assessment. What could possibly go wrong? It never occurred to me that maybe students didn't do homework I assigned because they were overloaded, didn't understand it, or simply didn't want to do it. Instead, I complained about how uninterested my students were.

Critical reflection would have encouraged me to engage more deeply and break through my assumptions, such as thinking the material was engaging simply because I enjoyed it. I didn't survey my students, asking them what their interests were or what they might enjoy reading, using that feedback to design more inclusive and equitable instruction. Similarly, my assessments weren't as effective as measures of learning as they could have been because I didn't check the accuracy or validity of my teaching assumptions, asking why and then asking why again (and again). Flexible classrooms need student voice to be a part of the learning process, backed with authentic learning opportunities that enrich the learning and connect students to it in ways that are meaningful, motivating, and even fun.

To help accomplish this goal, Gonzalez (2014b) encourages teachers to engage in what she calls *gut talk* by doing the following five actions that encourage teachers to go beyond surface-level reflection.

1. **Look around or picture in your mind your classroom:** "What parts of the room make you feel tense, anxious, or exhausted? What parts make you feel calm, happy, or proud?" (Gonzalez, 2014b). Perhaps you hadn't thought of your environment as being something to reflect on, but really think about the pictures you display, the trinkets you have, and student work posted to walls that convey students' deep learning and achievement with challenging learning goals. Conversely, what causes you anxiety? Are there piles of ungraded student papers? Yes, you'll obviously have to deal with those, but for the moment, pick just two or three high-priority items that require your attention.

2. **Browse your plan book:** "Start browsing, paying attention to how you're feeling as your eyes meet certain events. What days and weeks give you a lift when you see them, a feeling of pride or satisfaction? Which ones make you feel disappointed, irritated or embarrassed?" (Gonzalez, 2014b). I always looked forward to student presentations or student projects. When I had set aside days for students to show or demonstrate what they had been working on, those were enjoyable opportunities to get to know my students in different ways. Conversely, I felt irritated during standardized testing; students were anxious, and I was expected to be a part of something I didn't believe in. So I supported students during standardized testing and tried to lift the mood for my students and myself.

3. **Review your student roster:** "What do you feel when you see each name? Which names make you feel relaxed, satisfied and proud, which ones make your chest tighten with regret, and which ones make your stomach tense?" (Gonzalez, 2014b). As teachers, we all know those feelings—the students we would want as our own children and the students whose behavior has us question our choice of profession. What are the commonalities? What *why* questions might you ask about your perceptions of your students, both positive and negative?

4. **Envision your colleagues:** "Mentally travel from classroom to classroom, picturing each teacher in the building. What are your feelings as you approach each one? Which coworkers give you a generally positive feeling, which ones are neutral, and which ones make you feel nervous, angry, or annoyed?" (Gonzalez, 2014b). Creating those sincere friendships with colleagues is one of the perks of teaching. For many teachers, it is what keeps them coming back every year. But also consider

the how and why of collegial relationships that aren't so collegial. What would mend those fences? What relationships would benefit from a little nurturing?

5. **Reflect on your buzz words:** Think about and write down all the words you use that are tied to your practice: *differentiation*, *Common Core*, *flipped learning*, *data analysis*, *culture*, and so on. Read them. "As you read each one, do you have positive, negative, or mixed feelings? What other words have you heard a lot this year that give you a strong feeling one way or the other?" (Gonzalez, 2014b). Education buzzwords strike a chord in all teachers, and you may feel like the list gets bigger every year. Limit your use of buzzwords, keeping your practice focused on what students really need—the tools to engage in struggle productively. For the words that do cause you negative or mixed feelings, take time to reflect on the why. How might you see the purpose and intent of those words from a growth-minded perspective?

About these questions, Gonzalez (2014b) explains, "while it's easy to find good questions for reviewing accomplishments and setbacks, I believe that to learn as much as possible from a reflection on your teaching, you have to let your gut talk, too." Having the gut talk means believing in the value of self-evaluation and critique as a means to be more flexible in your thinking and teaching and grow for the sake of your students. Whether positive, negative, or mixed, the emotions that emerge from engaging in gut talk are authentic and true. How you interpret them and what you do based on them are what matters.

Reflection, much like teaching, can also be an isolated experience; when you reflect on your own methodology through your own lens, you might be unable to determine the *how* and *why*. You might be stuck on the *what* of the lesson, foregoing pedagogy—the art and science of teaching. While teacher reflection is highly personal, sometimes teachers need to look beyond themselves to determine how to hone their practice and support students. Reach out to like-minded colleagues who want to continually ask the hard questions about themselves and their pedagogical practice. By working as a small group and supporting one another's practices, reflection can take on new meaning as something informative and altering—not forgotten or ignored.

However, even group reflection requires a focused and effective approach. According to consultant, writer, Cambridge examiner, and e-moderator Roseli Serra (2015), "If you spend all your time discussing the events of the lesson, it's possible to jump to abrupt conclusions about why things happened as they did." The professional-reflection form template (figure 9.2, page 152) and professional-observation form

List group members: 1. Peg 2. Sam 3. Luis 4. Brianna
List planned meeting dates: 1. Monday, September 13 2. Monday, September 27 3. Monday, October 11
Topic for today's meeting: Classroom management
My reflection: During my English 9 class (27 students), three students took the pass to the bathroom, another one walked several times to the wastebasket, and a third one didn't open her book (even when gently asked twice). I think I need help with classroom-management skills. What are some things I could do to keep everyone motivated and engaged?
Colleague comments: I read Peg's comments and am thinking that maybe her students need more movement during class. She could apply some activities or strategies that have students up and moving while still being responsible for the content. Maybe even changing from rows to pods or changing the environment (tables, desks, standing desks—flexible seating) might help. I'm including two websites that offer some ideas that could be easily modified for her grade level: (https://bit.ly/32qo3ie) and (https://bit.ly/2REEoO6). I would be happy to observe Peg's class when she applies one of these strategies and offer feedback.

Figure 9.2: Professional-reflection form template.

template (figure 9.3) provide two tools teachers can use to establish opportunities for the time and support they need for reflection. (See page 165 and page 166, respectively, for reproducible versions of these figures.)

To utilize the professional-reflection form, join with three or four collaborative team members or other like-minded teachers who also want to make professional reflection a priority. Decide to meet as a group during a specified time. Determine what works best for your group, but invest in the timeframe. Try to stick with the time you have agreed on, choosing just one topic the group wants to reflect on. Examples include classroom management, clarity of expectations, technology implementation, and social-emotional language. Then, for the first ten minutes of the meetings, each team member focuses explicitly on the topic and writes down their reflections on a specific class or unit, a specific grade level, or both. After ten more minutes, ask a colleague in the group to read and comment on your reflection for five

List group or team members:
1. Peg
2. Sam
3. Luis
4. Brianna
List observation dates:
1. Thursday, October 14
2. Thursday, October 21
Topic for observation: Clarity of instructions regarding a new sixth-grade science unit
My reflection:
I noticed that when I gave instructions for the new unit, there seemed to be a lot of questions from students and a lot of repetition from me. I created a packet with due dates and exemplars to keep students on track and give them a visual example of what they were to do. However, I'm wondering if the length of the packet (eight pages) seemed like too much. Even though many pages had bulleted directions or exemplars, I'm wondering if visually it was too much, or just being a new unit poses lots of questions anyway. Also, students asked me questions I hadn't thought of including in the packet (I jotted those down so I could revise the packet for next time).
Observer comments:
Peg asked if I wanted the handouts for her class ahead of time, and I said, "No." I wanted to get it at the same time students got theirs. Things I noticed: • No learning intention or success criteria posted for students to see and reference • Students groaned when packets were distributed (packets are too common?). • Students flipping pages a lot; noisy, but seemed to like examples • Some students took notes, but others didn't. • Lots of questions from students, some of whom seemed frustrated • Lots of repetition in teacher instruction • Students showed anxiety about the due date. Let's meet again as a group and brainstorm some ideas.

Figure 9.3: Professional-observation form template.

minutes. During the last five minutes of the session, share ideas or suggestions for improvement. As you grow comfortable with this process, make whatever changes to the form that will align best with your team's needs and approach.

Although similar to the professional-reflection form, the professional-observation form encourages teachers to observe one another in the classroom. Again, work with your team or a small group of teachers who want to work together and choose one topic of focus. Make a copy of the form for the observer or observers. Determine if teachers want to rotate and observe each other or if one or two teachers might want to observe a colleague. Again, make this form work for you and what you want to learn. Determine how long the observers will watch—the entire class period or another specified length of time. After the observers have watched the lesson and recorded data regarding the topic, the observed teacher should reflect on the lesson. Then, the observers and the teacher can meet for thirty to forty-five minutes to discuss their notes: the observers will discuss the data, and the teacher will share his or her own professional reflection and brainstorm ideas and suggestions to better support students through productive struggle. This brainstorming opportunity can certainly be done one-on-one, but I recommend brainstorming in small groups so all colleagues can benefit from the reflection, even those not directly involved in the observation. Remember, this is an informal observation meant to strengthen the teacher's practice. I recommend conducting observations utilizing this form only occasionally—maybe once a month.

Always remember that, for teachers, self-reflection is meant to heighten pedagogy and practice to maximize student achievement. As part of the not-yet approach, the flexible classroom confronts both success areas and areas for improvement to support students in accepting the need to engage in productive struggle as a means to grow and discover learning in new and imaginative ways. In this way, teachers also embrace setbacks and obstacles in their practice as ways to learn more about their own teaching process.

Student Reflection

Student reflection is as critical to sustaining a flexible classroom as teacher reflection. Teachers want students to be acute observers about their learning process, yes, but also your teaching process. In this way, students become "autonomous learners who take responsibility for their own learning" (O'Grady, 2019). Taking responsibility means that students will be able to meet the demands of productive struggle when realizing that part of their responsibility as students is to accept setbacks and challenges as an opportunity to build their growth mindset and build resilience (grit).

Unfortunately, if teachers don't make time for their own reflection, then there is seldom time to encourage students to reflect and model how to do so effectively. According to coauthors Arthur L. Costa and Bena Kallick (2008):

> Unfortunately, educators don't often ask students to reflect on their learning. Thus, when students *are* asked to reflect on an assignment, they are caught in a dilemma: "What am I supposed to do?

How do I 'reflect'? I've already completed this assignment! Why do
I have to think about it anymore?" (p. 22)

Student reflection is crucial in sustaining a flexible classroom, but it requires students to understand and use metacognitive skills. Teaching students to think about their own thinking is something that any educator can do without the need for extra time by aligning the modeling of metacognitive thinking alongside curriculum content. In *The Metacognitive Student*, educators and authors Richard K. Cohen and colleagues (2021) suggest teachers model the following six simple steps and associated self-questions (what they call *structured SELf-questioning*) for students to use when facing academic, social, or emotional challenges.

1. **Select a focus:** Ask questions such as "What is the problem?" and "What is the task?"

2. **Gather information:** Ask questions such as "What do I know?" and "What do I need to know?"

3. **Brainstorm:** Ask questions such as "How can I solve this problem?" and "What can I do?"

4. **Evaluate:** Ask questions such as "What is the best solution?" and "Does this solution make sense?"

5. **Plan and act:** Ask questions such as "What do I do first, second, and so on?"

6. **Reflect:** Ask questions such as "Did it work?", "How do I know?", and "Do I need to go back and try again?"

By moving steadily from problem identification to brainstorming to acting on a solution to reflecting on that solution, students have a reliable and metacognitive pathway to independently assess and overcome learning challenges. Of course, there are many other ways to ensure student reflection in your flexible classroom. In chapter 2 (page 21), I wrote about how high school visual arts teacher Chad Sperzel-Wuchterl uses digital portfolios with his students that help them "see their shortcomings immediately, which is imperative for student growth" (C. Sperzel-Wuchterl, personal communication, May 27, 2020). He suggests that students seeing their mistakes helps them self-assess and self-reflect, not necessarily relying on the teacher or peers to review their work, but rather focusing inward for guidance.

In addition, Sperzel-Wuchterl says when creating and designing their digital portfolios, students are able to "critique with other students and learn from each other" (personal communication, May 27, 2020). Just as teacher collaboration increases reflective practices for instruction, student collaboration is key in creating a classroom culture of support and encouragement. According to ninth-grade humanities teacher Juli Ruff (2018), "[student] collaboration must be so ingrained in the classroom culture that it is hardly recognized as such. Frequent practice helps students see critique, not as an activity, but rather as a necessary step in a process"—a process that includes obstacles and setbacks.

The self-assessment form (see figure 9.4) and the before-and-after form for student self-reflection (see figure 9.5) are two ways students can reflect in a flexible classroom.

Metacognitive Reflection	Focusing Questions
I can use my metacognitive skills to self-reflect on _____.	How did my mindset affect my work?
	What was my strength in this particular assignment?
	What was my weakness in this particular assignment?
	How can I improve that weakness next time?
	How can I apply my strength in another class or subject?
	How are my skills (specific to this learning) progressing?

Figure 9.4: Student self-assessment form.

Visit go.SolutionTree.com/instruction for a free reproducible version of this figure.

The comprehension self-assessment form asks students to focus on one specific lesson and respond to a series of questions. The purpose of this metacognitive self-assessment is to gather information from the student about his or her own thinking. Teachers can use all or a few of the questions here or add their own. I recommend teachers collect and review students' self-assessment and then confer with students as needed regarding the information they provide. After doing so, ask students you conferenced with to use what they learned from that discussion to metacognitively reflect on how to best approach upcoming classwork or other learning.

1. Did you take the assignment seriously? Why or why not?

My response *before* seeing teacher feedback about my assignment:	My response *after* seeing teacher feedback about my assignment:

2. Were there barriers to your success? If so, what were they, and how can I support you in overcoming these barriers?

My response *before* seeing teacher feedback about my assignment:	My response *after* seeing teacher feedback about my assignment:

3. Did you seek support for the assignment from your peers, me, or other staff?

My response *before* seeing teacher feedback about my assignment:	My response *after* seeing teacher feedback about my assignment:

4. Please share any final thoughts you may have.

My final thoughts *before* teacher feedback about my assignment:	My final thoughts *after* seeing teacher feedback about my assignment:

Figure 9.5: Before-and-after form for student self-reflection.

*Visit **go.SolutionTree.com/instruction** for a free reproducible version of this figure.*

To use the before-and-after form for student self-reflection, give students the form to submit alongside an assignment, assessment, or other product related to their learning. The notion is for students to reflect on the work they did before seeing their teachers' assessment of their learning products. Teachers collect the forms, redistributing them back to students only after teachers have assessed and returned students' work to them. With the teacher feedback in hand, students use the form to *reassess* their own thinking about their work. Because this form is meant as a tool for student reflection, there is no need to collect it back from students after they complete it. That doesn't mean it can't be a part of students' physical or digital portfolio as an interesting way to show progress over time and as a reflection of achievement through productive struggle. While filling out this form requires some time, if you want students to fully engage in the reflection, I do recommend providing classroom time for this exercise, especially as students are first learning how to complete it and learn its value.

The purpose of the before-and-after form is to challenge and perhaps shift student thinking. Initially, students may perceive the work they did in a specific way; but, after reading the teacher's feedback on their paper, they have cause to reflect on their original thinking and change their perspective in a deeper way. For example, if a student wrote his or her paper the night before it was due, his or her response to the form's first question might be that he or she took writing the paper "quite seriously." Then, when the teacher returns the paper, and the student reads the teacher's comments that the work looked incomplete and rushed, the student may change his or her thinking, realizing that trying to write a solid analysis the night before a paper is due is a difficult task to achieve.

Regardless of the reflective approach you use with students, by engaging them in metacognitive self-reflection, teachers support students in learning to be flexible in how they respond to struggle. In this way, students reflect on what they need to be successful without necessarily relying only on the teacher for critique or evaluation, the goal of the not-yet approach.

Student Feedback on Teaching

To ensure students are fully engaged and motivated in learning, teachers must solicit students' feedback and utilize it as a way to process learning. Therefore, the final component in reflective practices that sustain a flexible classroom is for teachers to gather students' voice about the effectiveness of their teaching. Consultants and authors Leigh Colburn and Linda Beggs (2021), who specialize in schoolwide efforts to develop whole child supports rooted in student voice, highlight the importance of this practice: "If educators are sincere in their efforts to support students academically, socially, and emotionally, it's almost impossible to exaggerate the power of listening with respect" (p. 23).

The possibilities you can explore for gathering your students' voice are limitless and rife with opportunities for experimentation. For example, when my students reflected on my teaching practices, I encouraged them to do it in a letter. While we reflected throughout the year using exit slips and other informal methods, every quarter, my students would write a "Dear Mrs. Grafwallner" letter. I gave students very little direction other than for them to tell me what they felt I was doing well to support their learning and what I could do differently to be a more effective teacher. I also requested that they sign their letter. I wanted them to sign it because if I needed to follow up, I wanted to be able to discuss with the student his or her concerns and validate their feelings or explain why I did what I did. I encouraged them to use their notebook to jog their memory for the stories, poems, dramas, and novels we read throughout the year and the various strategies we used that supported their learning. I wanted the letter to be organic and authentic. There was only one caveat: they could not focus on me as a person. Teacher feedback from students is not about wardrobes or hairstyles or favorite movies.

The tricky aspect of this is that it can be difficult for students to feel safe providing teachers with feedback. If they think negative feedback will be used against them (or can be traced back to them if the feedback is anonymous), they may worry it will affect how their work is assessed in the future. So, it's worth emphasizing that for this exercise to work, you need to build trust with them. No matter what a student writes, you cannot react to him or her with anger or with deficit-minded thinking or, worse, punitive actions. *Almost right* language will not serve here. (See chapter 5, page 81.) You must be clear in explaining that the purpose of gathering students' feedback is to "hear their true feelings. . . . Assure them that if they tell you something critical about your class or your teaching, you will not give them a bad grade or punish them in return" (Gonzalez, 2014a).

There are several ways to build an open, trusting classroom community, but here are three that made my classroom a safe space.

1. **Use humor:** Humor (appropriate humor) is always welcome in the
   classroom, sometimes especially when things get tense, and don't be
   afraid to be a little self-deprecating. For example, I had no problem
   making fun of my Diet Coke addiction or my love for the 1960s-era pop
   group, The Monkees. I always wanted students to know that learning
   is fun, and they could laugh at themselves, each other, and me so long

as the spirit of that laughter wasn't mocking, judgmental, or otherwise mean-spirited. Humor doesn't need to be clever or dry in the classroom. Quite the opposite; keep it silly and warm.

2. **Keep an open door:** I always encouraged students to come in after school for extra help in any subject where I might be of some assistance. I often had students who just hung out in my classroom, waiting for their bus or a club or activity to begin. I always had snacks in case students were hungry after school, and I was present if a student needed someone to talk to, even if it was just venting about an assignment, something from class, or something from home. When students realized that my door was always open and that I was there to support their needs, my reputation began to evolve. I was more than just Mrs. G, the English teacher. For many students, I became Mrs. G, a trusted source of encouragement and support.

3. **Be human:** As I mentioned earlier in this book, I was extremely proud of the fact that I only had two late papers in the ten years I taught freshman English at the private school. I'm not sure why that identification was so important to me, but I felt it showed I was a tough, no-nonsense teacher who ran a tight ship. However, it only took a couple of years of teaching to realize that I could have high standards and be human at the same time. Being human simply means incorporating the whole child into the not-yet approach. I quickly realized that being flexible was critical to supporting learning for all and that sometimes all of us need extra support, extra time, extra space, and a whole lot of opportunity to get where we need to go. Always remember that learning must be the constant in your classroom and time the variable (DuFour et al., 2016).

As you consider how you want to go about gathering student feedback for reflection, consider using the student feedback on teaching form (see figure 9.6) as a way to prompt feedback and plan effective classroom action. Give the form to students as is or use the model provided here as inspiration, modifying questions to fit your needs. You can use this form anonymously or explain to your students that you want them to sign it so you can follow up with them to gain their insights on how to work toward being the best teacher you can be. In addition, you will notice the form is positive in tone so it's clear to students that you're hoping to use their voice to take effective action that will ultimately benefit them.

Please share your thoughts on the following comments, adding any specific examples to inform me how to support you and your learning. Thank you.

1. The teacher is prepared and ready for class.

2. The teacher has a good rapport with me.

3. The teacher is respectful of my race.

4. The teacher is respectful of my culture.

5. The teacher is respectful of my learning needs.

6. The teacher creates a good pace for the lesson.

7. The teacher encourages me to participate and gives me opportunities to do so.

8. When I need extra help, it is easy to schedule time with the teacher.

9. The teacher's handouts and resources are respectful of my learning needs (the teacher is willing to modify handouts for me when I ask).

10. I enjoy the teacher's class and would take another class with this teacher.

Figure 9.6: Student feedback on teaching form.

*Visit **go.SolutionTree.com/instruction** for a free reproducible version of this figure.*

Conclusion

Teacher and student reflection are deeply ingrained in the not-yet classroom as the best tools to ensure you and your classroom are flexible in identifying student needs and adjusting teaching practice to more effectively support them as they engage in productive struggle. Teacher reflection gives teachers the chance to improve their methods and pedagogy by asking the why questions to better their teaching practice; student reflection supports students in metacognitively becoming more authentic learners and cautious reviewers of their own learning; and student feedback is a vital way to gather real and pertinent data that teachers can apply immediately as they hone their craft. Before reflection can take place, however, teachers must create safe classrooms where students can offer suggestions and where students value their own desire for sustained process and progress.

A Look Inside

by Kathleen Dimmer, Band Teacher

As part of instilling flexibility and reflection in my band classroom, after each band concert, I ask students to evaluate their performance as a large group in a live discussion. Class begins with everyone watching a video recording of the recent performance, shot from the perspective of an audience member. (I find close-up shots can be an embarrassing distraction for students, which takes away from the listening aspect of the reflection.) Once the video is over, students sit in a circle and share what they felt was the best part of the performance, something that could be improved for their next performance, and if they have one, a comment from a friend or family member who attended the performance. This discussion gets students thinking about ways they could describe what they heard in the performance as part of a written reflection activity at the discussion's conclusion. It's a way for students to form ideas and use the thoughts and opinions of their peers and other audience members to think critically about their performance. For students who find writing outside of an academic setting difficult, it's also an effective way to gather feedback.

The written form then uses previously learned music vocabulary to ask students to respond to more specific questions related to the performance. The submissions are anonymous, and don't require complete sentences or correct spelling or grammar. Questions include items about specific pieces performed and learning targets or goals set for rehearsals and lessons leading up to the performance. The questions also ask students to rate specific aspects of the performance on numeric scales, reflect on their individual preparation for the performance, and evaluate the instruction they received and whether it effectively prepared them to perform their best. I've found that by not requiring students to add their name to this worksheet and providing a place for comments at the end of the worksheet, I get some very honest feedback; students freely share their ideas on what they would like our class to look like.

I carry out this same lesson plan for each of our two annual concerts, but for the second, I also ask students to make comparisons between the first and last concerts. After worksheets are complete, we then go back and watch the first concert, ending the discussion by comparing the two performances.

It's important to note that teachers can accomplish this flexible approach to reflection regardless of the teaching environment—in-person, virtual, or hybrid. It can even be done asynchronously, with students contributing their thoughts and ideas at different times. There are tools available to teachers of any content area to facilitate recording student work and interactions, whether in-person or remote. Teachers and students can review these recordings for reflection purposes. Even the worksheet we use in person is easily adaptable for online distribution. In this way, I'm able to ensure my students engage with the learning process, review the products of that process, and progress in their journey as students and musicians.

Ruminate and Respond

Consider what you've learned in this chapter, and individually or with your team, answer the following questions.

1. Do you allow time for your own professional reflection? If so, why is that time important to you? If not, why not?

2. How do you and your colleagues observe and offer support to each other in improving practice and pedagogy?

3. Why is student reflection so important to student success?

4. What do you do to give students opportunities to reflect on their learning? What do they (and you) do to turn reflection into action?

5. In what ways do you create opportunities for students to offer feedback on your teaching? How do you implement that feedback?

Professional-Reflection Form

List group or team members:

List planned meeting dates:

Topic for today's meeting:

My reflection:

Colleague comments:

Professional-Observation Form

List group or team members:

List observation dates:

Topic for observation:

My reflection:

Observer comments:

The Constructive Classroom

In a perfect teaching world, educators would have unlimited time and no shortage of space or equipment. Imagine what you might accomplish with students and how you might support their learning without having to worry about the bell ringing for recess when you still need ten minutes to complete a lesson or a class change before students can complete a science lab or writing session. Imagine having enough space to do stations work without having to rearrange your classroom or enough room for all your students to test their robotics project. Teachers are often at the mercy of their school's daily schedule and limited on the size of their classroom. It all begs the question of how teachers can maximize their time and space for a constructive classroom that supports students as they process the relevant work they must do, engaging in productive struggle as they go.

In this chapter, you will learn about adopting a constructive approach to your not-yet classroom. With this foundational knowledge, you will see how you can make the most of the learning time you have with your students as well as how to maximize the space you have to engage students in their learning. Lastly, you'll learn about the importance of a culture of stick-withitness and mental muscles as a means to sustain the kind of continuous improvement that is essential to the not-yet approach.

The Not-Yet Approach in the Constructive Classroom

A *constructive classroom* concentrates on process-driven improvements that determine how to focus student learning and maximize time and space available to them as they progress in their learning. *Process-driven improvements* in the classroom enhance the ability of students to perform their work independently by following a process thoroughly and persistently, thus developing their stick-withitness and mental muscles—two concepts you will learn more about later in this chapter. Think of the not-yet approach as your way of delivering process-driven improvements to your students.

The not-yet approach defines *learning process* as "a method, or system, towards building understanding" (Boser, 2020). This "method or system" can look different from student to student. Think of the supportive scaffolds in chapter 8 (page 125) that you can apply for different purposes based on what students need. Ulrich Boser (2020), writing on the science of learning and metacognition for *The Learning Curve*, goes on to explain, "Learning depends on many other skills: such as focusing and centering your attention, planning and sticking to a program; tenacity, resilience, and the ability to reflect on information."

As students struggle productively through their learning, utilizing different methods and applying various modalities to achieve their scaffolded success criteria and vigorous learning intentions, their tenacity and resilience derive from their ability to stick with challenging work (stick-withitness), developing stronger mental muscles in the process. In a clamorous, clutter-filled classroom, one that is filled with heaps of stuff unrelated to learning and unproductive noise (noise that does not reflect learning activities), it can be difficult for students to focus on what they must learn. That's why a constructive classroom focuses on using time and space productively and coherently to support independent learning.

Being a teacher in a constructive classroom means that you, too, must make time and space to hone your pedagogical skills. As a teacher, listing what you do as part of your practice is fairly straightforward, though endless—create vigorous learning intentions and scaffolded success criteria, provide tools (such as graphic organizers, annotation guides, and think sheets) and other products (such as textbooks, articles, and lab equipment) to support students in their learning, assess students' learning and provide feedback in a timely fashion, complete the school and district paperwork correctly—the list goes on. But you must keep in mind that in a constructive classroom, while you may already be doing these things to your satisfaction and that of students, families, and administrators, you must continue to refine your practice so that you are getting the most out of the time and space available to you.

One way to determine potential areas of improvement in your practice is to select an area of *constructive focus* to brainstorm ideas. Let's say you want to improve your turnaround time in returning analytical essays to students. This would be your constructive focus. Based on that selection, there are two vital questions you must answer: (1) What is the process you are currently using? and (2) How can you improve your process? These are simple questions, but maximizing growth for a truly constructive classroom requires genuine and honest reflection on your practice. To facilitate deeper answers, use the constructive-focus chart in figure 10.1. (See page 186 for a reproducible version of this figure.) In this example, I brainstormed a list of three ideas to improve my practice related to how quickly I can turn around student essays. It's a simple process, but it's also highly flexible because it's adaptable to almost any aspect of a teacher's practice.

Constructive Focus	Returning papers to my students in a timely fashion
What is the process I am currently using?	Currently, I read each paper once. Then, I read it a second time, writing my comments and questions in the margin. On average, it takes me nearly ten minutes to grade a paper (with a total of 180 papers).
How can I improve this process?	1. Design a rubric aligned to the curriculum standards using student-friendly language, and create a checklist for students to assess their own work. 2. Set aside class time for students to peer review each other's work for specific elements (such as capitalization, MLA citing, and personal pronouns). 3. Students turn in each essay paragraph individually. I write two pieces of feedback to students after every paragraph. 4. Hand individual paragraphs back to students. Students meet in small groups to help correct their paragraphs. 5. Students correct and work on the next paragraph.

Figure 10.1: Constructive-focus chart.

After completing this form, you can either continue brainstorming ideas or implement any new ideas the next time you engage in that area of constructive focus. In the example in figure 10.1, after implementing this improved feedback model, students increasingly addressed small errors with capitalization, citing, and use of personal pronouns during collaborative time with their peers, which allowed me to focus feedback on supporting high-level learning. I didn't have to use valuable time correcting minor mistakes, and since I only gave two pieces of feedback per paragraph, I was able to assess papers faster. In addition, while students were in their small groups, I worked directly with a group that needed the most support to achieve the learning intentions. When it came time for students to submit their final papers, most needed support with analysis since the minor corrections had already been dispensed and addressed such that I could quickly assess and offer final grades. Giving students this specific group time to help them in the revision process, and offering a quiet place to do it, created a constructive classroom mindset and made more efficient use of my limited time.

If you want to consider an even deeper approach to establishing a constructive focus for improving your practice, consider using the metacognitive process for self-questioning I describe for students in Student Reflection (page 154 in chapter 9). You might also use the other information I provided in chapter 9 (page 145) to collaborate with colleagues to get their suggestions and feedback. To do so, use the professional-reflection form template (see figure 9.2, page 152) and the professional-observation form template (see figure 9.3, page 153). Gathering with like-minded teachers who also want to improve their time management and using these tools establish a foundation for improvement and a more constructive classroom.

Time

You've no doubt heard the adage that time can be your friend or your enemy; it is undeniably true in the education world. A constructive classroom devotes just as much attention to time and space as the other classroom concepts that make up the not-yet approach. Consider how important time, specifically, is to supporting the development of students' growth mindset when engaging them in high-level-thinking tasks such as problem solving and content creation. For example, my school adheres to a block schedule of 90 minutes per class, so there is usually enough time to move through a project. But what happens when a teacher only has forty-five or fifty minutes to teach? Author, international trainer, and keynote speaker Catlin Tucker (2016) writes, "When teachers plan for a 50 minute period, the scope of their lesson is extremely narrow. . . . Too often the default in this scenario is to lecture or verbally present information because it is faster."

Learning purely through lecture, as stated in chapter 9, is a dead end for many students. Direct instruction has its role to play in learning, but instructional units comprised entirely of students listening to lectures cause many students (particularly those who don't learn best from this method) to disengage and act out due to sheer boredom (Kise, 2021). Boredom can just as easily occur in a block schedule, especially when teachers rely exclusively or predominantly on direct instruction for an even longer duration. Instead, Kise (2021) recommends teachers differentiate instruction during classroom time such that, at some point during a unit, all students get to experience learning that aligns with their cognitive processing style. Some examples of this include the following (Kise, 2021).

- **Student-centered discussions:** During these discussions, students work in small or large groups to take an active role in discussing, reasoning, using evidence, and so on to engage at a high level with their learning goals. During these discussions, teachers act as facilitators by adding, prompting, or redirecting students as needed to achieve desired learning outcomes.

- **Curiosity creators:** Students' level of interest in the content you teach will vary based on their own experiences and interests. But teachers can structure learning activities to tap students' natural curiosity and engage them in learning. Consider options like finding compelling audio or visuals as entry points to discussion or independent research, using mystery boxes containing a variety of group or individual tasks from which students draw at random, or implementing anticipation guides that ask students to agree or disagree with a series of statements they must then research to affirm or disprove their thinking.

- **Heuristics:** There are countless tools that aid students in engaging in independent learning. For example, concept maps are heuristics that enable students to organize their thinking or other information as they work toward a learning intention. Further, there are numerous approaches to concept maps that will appeal to different students based on their learning style, such as thinking maps, freeform organizers, graphic recording, and so on. Research several options that might appeal to your students, and allow them to use the process that works best for them.

Whatever options you use, the important factor is to ensure you engage students actively in high-level thinking during the time they're with you. Tucker (2016) contends, "Allowing students to research, discuss, and share their findings takes time. Yet, if we want students to develop these crucial life skills—finding and evaluating information, communicating and collaborating with peers—they *need* time." Without this time to deeply engage in learning, "it's not surprising, then, that half of high school dropouts cite boredom as their primary motivator for leaving" (Jason, 2017). Further, using classroom time to engage students in high-level-thinking activities ensures that when they encounter obstacles or roadblocks, you can use classroom time constructively to support them in overcoming those struggles.

While teachers can access a wealth of sources for engaging students in high-level-thinking activities, a key question often remains: How do teachers manufacture *enough* time to create a constructive classroom where improvement helps guide the process of learning? Here are five ideas that might help you in creating more time.

1. Use the professional-reflection form template (see figure 9.2, page 152) with your colleagues to reflect together on tasks you currently do in the classroom that might be unnecessary. Are there any traditional tasks you and your students are doing that you don't need to do anymore or could be changed to accomplish multiple goals simultaneously? For example, consider the following.

    ○ *Attendance*—While attendance taking is usually necessary, consider how you might take it in ways that are less cumbersome and less time-consuming. My colleague stands outside the hallway during passing time and, as students enter her class, she checks their names off on her clipboard, greeting each student. By the time the bell rings to begin class, attendance is already complete.

    ○ *Announcements*—Classroom announcements are an important way to share information. After greeting students as they walk in, post class announcements on the class whiteboard or as a slide in the front of the classroom. Students can read them and jot them down, as needed, without devoting extra class time to making announcements verbally.

    ○ *Small-group work*—Students enjoy being able to form their own small groups, often being in groups with their friends. However, sometimes getting groups together wastes valuable minutes as students decide who they will group with. To eliminate this wasted time, during the first few months of school, create various student groups to give students the chance to get to know each other and rotate among these groups during the year. To add a bit of fun to the proceedings, consider how you might allow groups to name themselves as teams—the Nighttime Team, the Red Team, and so on.

2. Implement the FRAME model from my book *Ready to Learn* (Grafwallner, 2020). You got a taste of the foundations for this model in chapter 4 (page 51) with an introduction to the importance of vigorous learning intentions and scaffolded success criteria. The FRAME model

uses the following steps to increase teachers' efficiency during instruction (Grafwallner, 2020).

 a. *Focus*—This is the goal for the day's lesson. What do you want your students to know and be able to do? Create a vigorous learning intention and scaffolded success criteria that will focus your students on the learning and then introduce students to that day's focus.

 b. *Reach*—Offer personal attention to each student as you communicate with them. Acknowledging each student's presence with an engaging smile, individual eye contact, and his or her preferred name supports a student's sense of self within the classroom community.

 c. *Ask*—Permit students to ask questions and analyze the expectations for the work they are about to do. Demonstrate how to ask robust questions and how to analyze the *what* of the learning intention and success criteria through a series of clarifying and probing questions.

 d. *Model*—Model a brief overview of the upcoming task. By modeling the process, you take the mystery and frustration out of students' work. Modeling is meant to help students visualize both the finished product and the steps necessary to get there.

 e. *Encourage*—Encourage students' work by praising engagement with the learning process. In this context, praise should act as vital feedback about the work, not about the student.

Introduce the FRAME model during the first ten minutes of class. Initially, this will take time to get students prepared, but once your class is experienced with it (it has been FRAMEd), you will not be spending nearly as much time reteaching, and you will support your students with increased opportunities to be facilitators of their own learning with the limited class time you have.

3. Implement the two-week calendar (see figure 8.2, page 138). Having a two-week calendar prepares students for learning and omits unnecessary downtime. Students specifically know the skills they will be learning and how they can transfer those skills to other content areas.

4. Consider creating an interdisciplinary course. If you are an art teacher, consider collaborating with the history teacher to design units that

focus on the relationship between art and history. For example, consider how World War II affected artists and their art and possibly bring in a guest speaker (digitally or virtually) from an art museum to add expert insights connecting art and history. If you teach to multiple or all disciplines (as in elementary), think about how you might align learning standards from two or more content areas at once, such as teaching literacy concepts as part of a social studies unit.

5. Create learning stations for students to rotate among, engaging in different activities. Learning stations offer students the chance to engage in "diverse tasks; [students are] never doing the same thing for an extended time. Shifting the learning focus from station to station keeps students fresh and engaged" (Sachar, 2016). For example, if you want students to build their note-taking skills and want to give some juice to what might otherwise be a rather dry lesson, instead of lecturing about the different types of note-taking templates, create four stations: (1) concept mapping, (2) annotation, (3) magnet summaries (figure 10.2; Buehl, 2020), and (4) the Cornell method (Cornell University, n.d.). Students can then practice with different ways of learning at their own rate and current ability. See also *Cult of Pedagogy's* "Power Lesson: Note-Taking Stations" (Grafwallner, 2018c).

When focusing on process, teachers can reflect on wasted time, the implementation of a structured routine, the application of skill-building strategies, collaborating with colleagues, or individualized student growth. This reflection helps to eliminate time-wasting procedures and instead uses that time to support students in the classroom. As a result, teachers have more opportunities to offer students experiences that apply productive struggle and move toward progress.

Space

Like time, space is limited. My high school was once a middle school. That means its swim team doesn't have a pool on the premises; lockers are approximately six inches wide; the library is the size of a traditional fifty-year-old middle school library; and the gym is, like the library, the size of a traditional fifty-year-old gymnasium. As a result, space is at a premium, which is a challenge that high schools throughout North America face (Hachem, 2019). Many teachers in schools like mine double up in classrooms because there aren't enough classrooms for every teacher. In such schools, without multi-million-dollar referenda, space will not increase, so teachers must keep their classrooms constructive within the spaces they can access.

Name: _____ **Class:** _____ **Date:** _____

Lesson: _____

Directions: Analyze a portion of the assigned resource, looking for a key term or concept (a *magnet*). Put the magnet word or concept in the middle box of the Main-Idea Chart. In the surrounding boxes, generate four details about the magnet.

Main-Idea Chart

Main-Idea Chart Summary

Using your main-idea chart for reference, write a summary based on your exploration of the magnet term or concept. Write a topic sentence, and then write four sentences that elaborate on the four details from your chart. You may have to add transition words to connect one detail to the next detail, such as *in addition*, *next*, *furthermore*, *last*, and *finally*.

What is the one thing you thought was most important and why based on your selection of and explanation of the magnet term or concept?

Figure 10.2: Magnet summary template.

*Visit **go.SolutionTree.com/instruction** for a free reproducible version of this figure.*

While creating new space is often impossible, it is possible to get creative in making the space you do have work *better*. With classrooms often numbering between twenty and forty students, maintaining a constructive classroom requires flexibility and openness to new ideas. For example, I've seen teachers load up carts with needed classroom materials and simply move them from room to room based on what rooms are available to them at a given point in the school day or week. Gonzalez (2018b) suggests asking students what they think needs to change in your classroom to make it a better environment for them to learn. Your students are creative, and where you might see few or no options, students might have valuable insights to share that will help make better use of your limited space so they can better learn and process information. Sometimes even a simple refresh of the room's decoration, such as putting up different bulletin board messages or posters related to course content, does enough to keep the room fresh and improve student engagement.

If you move between classrooms or share your classroom with one or more other teachers, work together to make the space visually appealing to students. For example, if you are an ELA teacher and share space with a science teacher, could you align common themes between ELA and science curricula in an interesting and creative way? Perhaps create spaces for quiet (writing an essay or conducting research) versus group work (analyzing a text or conducting lab work). Consultants Jennifer Williams and Fran Siracusa (2015) suggest teachers create "collaborative classrooms [that] are alive with action—teaching, learning, innovating, creating, making, and exploring. Innovative learning spaces can encourage both individual and collective voices." Even though teachers might teach different disciplines, connecting these content areas highlights the interconnectedness of all learning and illustrates how interrelated the process of learning truly is.

But, like time, how do you manufacture space to create a constructive classroom where improvement helps guide the process of learning? Here are five process-driven improvements that might help you manufacture space or make your learning space more appealing for your constructive classroom.

1. **Use cheap, flexible seating:** Desks are bulky, and some can be downright uncomfortable. In my skills class, I had a couple of tables (seating for two), a couple of individual desks, two podiums, several single tables, and four cushions. I found most of my seating in donation closets and thrift stores. Eliminating desks makes the room look bigger and gives students the opportunity to choose where they will be most comfortable.

2. **Use more efficient furniture:** Don't restrict thinking about your space to just the seating. There may be ways to adjust your other classroom furniture to free up or more efficiently use space. As a high school ELA teacher, I had a large wooden desk in the front of the classroom. On a side wall was a large table with all the student handouts. Why use up space with both when I could've replaced the table with a tiered shelf to put papers on while adding needed storage space for books or other learning materials?

3. **Use spaces for collaborative work:** Instead of having rows of desks, create learning pods where students sit in groups and work together to solve problems and participate in small-group discussions. Think of how you might establish small-group areas and other stations to make more efficient use of space. When students need to rotate among the stations, the small-group areas are already set up and ready to learn.

4. **Extend your learning space into the library:** If some students are working on a quiet assessment, but others need to practice their speech, move the students who need quiet to the library. Many libraries offer carrel desks that give students privacy, enabling them to concentrate on their individual task in a thorough and persistent way, thus exemplifying a process-driven improvement. Trust them to do their work and use the extra space to process silently.

5. **Ask students what works for them:** As noted earlier in the section, it's never a bad idea to get students' ideas about how to maximize space. Imagine a project where students design their own learning space and then ask for the help of a local contractor, who directs students on how to build that space. This kind of authentic and relevant work is the epitome of 21st century learning and the very foundation of a constructive classroom since it creates student investment in the classroom space.

Whereas teachers have numerous ways to autonomously adjust how they allocate classroom time, many of the ideas that maximize your use of space may require approval (particularly those that require funds), such as from school or district administration. Don't let that deter you from trying to gain more space for your students' learning or make better use of the space you have. I suggest creating a proposal to share with your principal regarding your students' need for more space or space-enhancing tools. Explain clearly and explicitly the rationale behind your request. Then, write a list of benefits this process-driven improvement could provide your students. Finally, determine how much cost is involved with your request. As an example, if you want to have three carrel desks in your classroom for students who appreciate the private space that affords them, research carrel desks and ask for different quotes from nearby office supply stores. By being prepared ahead of time when you talk with your principal about what you want and how that request is of benefit to your students, you may increase your odds of success. Or, even if a principal or other leaders can't approve your request, he or she may have connected ideas that facilitate the same goal.

Ultimately, any change you can implement that enables students to be physically comfortable and get the most out of their academic environment will make your classroom more constructive. Working to improve time and space for students puts the focus on learning and reduces distractions. Part of supporting students through productive struggle means minimizing impediments that aren't related to actually learning.

Process-Driven Improvement

As explained earlier in the chapter, a constructive classroom is one rooted in continuous process-driven improvement where students work by focusing and centering their attention toward building understanding. Process-driven improvement aids students in embracing the opportunity to build understanding through struggle as they realize that learning takes time and mastery isn't the end of growth. Finding new methods to better utilize time and new ways to construct more space can certainly support that improvement. Another part of improvement is growing resiliency and mental agility among students in the form of stick-withitness and the building up of mental muscles, which I explain in more detail in the following sections.

Stick-Withitness

One aspect of establishing and sustaining a culture of continuous improvement is instilling in students continual awareness of what's happening in the classroom and the ability to manage the competing demands of the classroom no matter how tough those demands get (Thompson, 2019). In chapter 3 (page 37), I wrote about grit as one aspect of resiliency (Duckworth, 2016), but there are more ways for teachers to develop resilient students. One such way to keep learning constructive for students as they navigate setbacks and challenging obstacles is to encourage their sense of *stick-withitness*.

In a typical classroom, there are students who will stay with a project, a problem, or a puzzle no matter what. It's almost as if that project, problem, or puzzle becomes a kind of quest that they will stick with until they find their answer. Some students even enjoy being put in situations that seem all but impossible to complete. They dig in and come up for air when they have solved their project, problem, or puzzle. However, as you've explored throughout part 1 (page 9), there are also students who, when faced with a setback or an obstacle, give up as they become increasingly frustrated and discouraged. According to administrator, educator, and author Ben Johnson (2013):

> A common occurrence in classrooms is that the teacher, when he or she sees the students struggle mightily to "think out of the box" will precipitously step in and give the students the answers, or throw the deeper learning activity out all together, thinking that the students aren't ready for it.

In chapter 8 (page 125), I explained the difference between *help* and *support*. This desire to help students by giving them the answers or throwing out the deeper learning activity limits their stick-withitness ability. Teachers want to *support* students in ways that grow their stick-withitness. "What these students and the teachers need is to be patient, practice and build those mental muscles over time" (Johnson, 2013). When building students' stick-withitness, consider the following ideas.

- **Encourage students to seek alternative approaches:** When a student finds their initial approach to a challenge hasn't worked, support them in using self-questions to brainstorm and evaluate alternatives (see Student Reflection, page 154). Authors Emily Mofield and Megan Parker Peters (2018a) suggest, "Students can map out their alternatives and associated potential consequences that could come with each option. They can choose one option for tackling the problem but know that they have other options if the first does not work out" (Mofield & Peters, 2018a).

- **Celebrate successful growth:** One thing a not-yet classroom never runs out of is success stories. Consider setting aside wall space for a "How I Grew Today" posting board where students can write down on a sticky note successes they've had with overcoming mistakes, posting them to the board. These examples don't need to be specific or identifiable, nor do students need to detail the mistake. The purpose is simply for students to see at a glance reminders of their progress, individually or as a class. For example, after students have reflected on a challenging task, ask them to write down one thing they learned about themselves regarding the task or their reflection. Some students may jot down, *I am learning to accept feedback as a way to help me*, or *I realized that I* *need to slow down when focusing on tough problems.* Initially, you may need to model ideas like this while encouraging students to share their own suggestions. Over time, however, students will have accumulated a mountain of evidence to post, and the board will serve as an accessible reminder that mistakes are a part of the learning process.

- **Use the five whys:** In The Not-Yet Approach in the Flexible Classroom (page 146 in chapter 9), you learned about using Sakichi Toyoda's five whys (Tanner, 2020) as a concept map to think through a problem. Teach students how to engage with this same process to enhance their stick-withitness. As an example, maybe a student is feeling trepidation about a unit project. By digging deeper using the five whys, the student might be able to sort out the root cause of that trepidation and begin to implement what he or she might need to be successful, such as planning a schedule and sticking to it or finding a quiet space in which to work.

When encouraging students to stick with it, don't forget that a variety of factors affect students' ability to persevere. Often, these factors come from events outside the classroom. Mofield and Peters (2018b) explain that "sometimes obstacles (e.g., a distraction, lack of focus, changing attitudes, feeling tired, dealing with feelings of fear or anxiety, etc.) hold us back" (p. 62). When this happens, give students a chance to identify what their feelings are and the root cause of what's holding them back, providing supports where necessary.

Mental Muscles

Thinking of the brain as its own muscle that requires exercise is not a new idea; it's an idea built on the concept of *neuroplasticity*, the brain's ability to form new neural connections (change) in response to experiences (Fuller & Fuller, 2021). Building students' mental muscles, as Johnson (2013) states, means ensuring students have opportunities to develop their patience, giving them time to practice the hard stuff. Students can't build mental muscles when classrooms are sit and get or when the work is too easy to engage them in productive struggle. I remember one of my first learning intentions from when I was a new teacher.

Students will be able to write an essay.

The following was the lone success criterion.

Students will know they are successful when they can write an essay.

Clearly, as seen throughout this book, the preceding is not a vigorous learning intention, and the single success criterion is certainly not scaffolded. Instead, my learning intention and success criterion did nothing but check off a box on my lesson plan. My narrow approach, in this case, illustrates how I wasn't supporting my students in growing their mental muscles (or supporting their stick-withitness, for that matter). The learning intention was too broad and clearly didn't give students the chance to dig deep into their analytical writing. In addition, there was no opportunity to self-assess since the success criteria were based on product and not process. If I were to rewrite that learning intention today, it would look like the following.

- **Learning intention:** I can write an analytical argument to support a claim.

- **Success criteria:** I know I am successful because . . .

  1. I can use valid reasoning

  2. I can apply relevant evidence and sufficient evidence

  3. I can combine these concepts to create a well-written paragraph

  4. I can meet with my peers and teacher for feedback

Looking at this new example, you will notice students have a specific vigorous learning intention—to support a claim in their analytical argument. You will also notice the scaffolded success criteria include one where students are able to self-assess their growth. Building up mental muscles isn't complicated. It's about using simple and natural progressions like this one to move students from process to product to progress.

The following are five ways to support students in improving their process to build mental muscles.

1. **Eliminate busy homework:** Chad Ostrowski (2016), science teacher and cofounder of Teach Better (www.teachbetter.com), refers to busy homework as "meaningless repetition [that] does not extend learning or help the student complete learning they started in class." Ask yourself the purpose of the homework; if it does not add value to what students are learning, get rid of it. However, that doesn't mean eliminating all homework. There are creative ways to give students homework so it is of academic value and is worth their time and talent. For example, a digital portfolio (as explained in chapter 2, page 21), helps English teacher Andy Schoenborn's students focus on literacy growth. This growth supports students in developing their mental muscles as they continually revise and improve their skills.

2. **Offer opportunities to try again, but set limits:** Standards-based grading experts Matt Townsley and Nathan L. Wear (2020) stress the benefits of allowing students multiple attempts to achieve learning goals, but also the importance of students meeting key prerequisite criteria before reassessing that learning, such as taking fresh notes or completing practice problems or exercises. For example, Jennifer Inaba, a seventh-grade science teacher, explains that while she offers retakes in her classroom, "if students have missing assignments on the day of the assessment, they'll be working on those assignments instead" (personal communication, May 23, 2020). Students develop patience as they attempt to master the material; but, as Inaba explains, even if everything goes wrong with that attempt, she will meet with them, give them feedback, and reteach if necessary.

3. **Make mistakes in front of your students:** Many students (and adults) feel shame at admitting to making mistakes, but persevering through mistakes is how they build up their mental muscles. Richard Curwin (2014), author and director of the graduate program in behavior disorders at David Yellin College, writes, "Because shame is currently attached to mistakes, students are afraid to take chances, explore, and think for themselves." To mitigate this outcome, show students that mistakes are simply new information to apply to future attempts. Acknowledge your own mistakes and model for students how you would (or did) correct them (or ask students for suggestions about how to correct them).

4. **Provide puzzles:** Puzzles can be a calming influence on students and a way to build collaboration. Writer and educator Jill Staake (2019) writes, "When students work together on puzzles, they learn teamwork, cooperation, and sharing. There's a feeling of satisfaction in fitting the pieces together, one that can be calming for many people." Crossword puzzles, especially content-specific ones, are purposeful vocabulary builders, giving students the chance to learn new words and their definitions. Jigsaw puzzles support students in building their mental muscles by concentrating on patience and practice.

5. **Declare the dilemma of the day:** One of my favorite scenes is from the movie *Apollo 13* (Grazer & Howard, 1995). Jim Lovell (Tom Hanks) and his crew are supposed to land on the moon in 1970; however, due to a malfunction, they are stuck in space. Mission control is trying

to bring them home but faces one setback and obstacle after another, including the need to adapt carbon dioxide scrubbers meant for one type of connector to fit another type. In essence, the astronauts need to fit a "square peg into a round hole" using only materials they have in the spacecraft (Grazer & Howard, 1995). Consider offering your students a similar situation: a table full of nuts, bolts, trinkets, wood pieces—anything they can manipulate to make whatever they determine. No plans, no designs—just their own creativity.

Conclusion

Teachers only have so much control; they cannot manufacture time or conjure adequate space. But teachers can improve time and space to make them work for students and themselves by creating a constructive classroom focused on continuous process-driven improvement. In a constructive classroom, teachers support their students in their ability to engage stick-withitness and engage mental muscles through methods and approaches that yield high-level thinking and persistence through struggle.

A Look Inside

by Melissa Chouinard, Science Teacher

Educators I know who do not have block scheduling envy the extra time it provides. Time is a facet of teaching that we never seem to have enough of. Even with the best-laid plans come days where we run out of it and leave our students awestruck as the bell rings. As a science teacher at Beckendorff Junior High School in Katy, Texas, I struggled with this a lot. Then, I flipped my classroom, adopting blended learning. I have students read articles, watch videos, and create personal podcasts and clips at home before we elaborate and demonstrate in-class concepts with labs and activities. By preloading students with information the week before covering learning intentions in class, when we gather on Monday, it is a week of active learning rather than passive knowledge gathering.

In essence, I do not assign homework. I ask for *home thinking*. I give them one topic for the week—Monday through Thursday—to think about at home and talk with their families about at the dinner table. On Fridays, I assign the preloaded materials due the following Tuesday or Wednesday. This is routine. This is consistent. This is not a week's worth of information but an introduction. Then, we apply this throughout the week in labs, models, and activities.

This keeps in-class time focused and purposeful. We have Socratic seminars, debates, and puppet shows. We collaborate on our graffiti wall and have jigsaw activities. We build giant cells with modeling clay and Makerspace (https://makerspaces.com) supplies. We put on skits and create stop-motion videos. In other words, we get creative and really have time to crush the box and innovate together.

Time and space to me, as an educator, are both precious and coveted. Through my nearly twenty years of teaching, I have changed my outlook and use of time many times. I find blending it works best for me, and that home thinking is important to give time for students to process and analyze. Although space has not always been something my classroom has provided, I am fortunate to have a larger science lab that allows me to get creative with flexible seating. But I still seek to maximize that space by arranging an open floor plan with seating options that provide a center communal experience and place for personal space. In addition to slate tables that provide plenty of counter space, I found three round tables in our district warehouse that are perfect for collaborative grouping. To further fill out my space, I wrote an accepted grant that provided for ten additional standing desks.

With so many options, I can maximize flexibility based on curriculum needs. For example, sometimes I put tables end to end to create one long table I refer to as the *Thanksgiving table*. Other times, I put the tables into smaller groupings, coffee-house style. Then I place the standing desks on the outskirts of the classroom, and students move these around as they see fit. Even when I taught in a smaller classroom, I was able to use pillows and cushions on the floor with students using clipboards rather than desks to open the space up to be more productive and comfortable for students.

Regarding seating, many teachers prefer alphabetical seating or rows for more control, but I find student choice in seating incredibly important. Instead, I set strict rules, routines, and consequences—then allow students to sit where they want. Some days, students sit with their friends; others, they choose to work from a standing desk. The flexibility lets them take ownership of their learning, behavior, and location. My one rule is: if I have to move you for any reason, distraction, or misbehavior, you will not be able to sit with your friends for the rest of the year. It works. I have to redirect every so often, but never more than once, and I have never had to move anyone.

Time and space afford educators a platform to connect with students. Designing a comfortable space and a blended design has allowed me to focus on building relationships and really helping my students be independent thinkers. My motto is, "I am not here to teach them science; I am here to teach them how to teach themselves science." Through flexible seating, a blended classroom, and community building, time and space are on my side.

Ruminate and Respond

Consider what you've learned in this chapter, and individually or with your team, answer the following questions.

1. How much classroom time do you have with your students each day? How can you better structure that time to eliminate wasted actions and procedures and use it more constructively?

2. What are the merits and limitations inherent in your classroom space? What can you do to enhance or even expand on the space available for classroom learning?

3. How do you support process-driven improvements in your classroom?

4. How does your approach to instruction and modeling encourage students to use stick-withitness when faced with learning challenges? How do you know this approach is successful, or how might you improve on it?

5. What practices do you use to encourage students to use their mental muscles, treating learning as a continuous process on the path to progress?

Constructive-Focus Chart

Constructive Focus	
What is the process I am currently using?	
How can I improve this process?	

The Connective Classroom

Collaboration among teaching professionals is essential for achieving improved learning outcomes. Professional learning community (PLC) at Work architects and experts Richard DuFour, Rebecca DuFour, Robert Eaker, Thomas W. Many, and Mike Mattos (2016) write extensively on the importance of a collaborative culture to teaching and learning. For teachers who are not part of a collaborative team, it can be creatively stifling and emotionally isolating to look for collaborative opportunities and find that door closed. Davis (2020) explains, "Teacher collaboration occurs when members of a learning community work together to increase student learning and achievement. If our ultimate destination as educators is student achievement, think of teacher collaboration as the journey."

No doubt, teacher collaboration can certainly be an exhilarating ride where the ultimate victor is the student. To further the not-yet approach, teachers need to connect with each other and experience the same cycle of continuous process-driven improvement they ask students to engage in as part of a constructive classroom (chapter 10, page 167). Davis (2020) adds, "Collaboration is not a task to complete then move on, it's an ever-changing, ongoing process that is only enhanced by social networks and access to new technology." To give students the very best classroom experience, teachers must collaborate—for students' sake and success.

This chapter explores the importance of the connective classroom to the not-yet approach. You will learn about the importance of collegial observation, using pedagogical guiding questions and comments, and how to find collaborative opportunities.

The Not-Yet Approach in the Connective Classroom

When teachers come together with students in mind to share ideas, challenge philosophies, update curricula, and transform perceptions, they operate as part of a *connective classroom*. A connective classroom is acutely embedded in the not-yet approach because learning-focused professional collaboration leads to a classroom culture that encourages the learning process while confronting and overcoming setbacks and obstacles as part of that process. In a connective classroom, collaboration around student learning and the learning process builds toward shared understanding, collective action, and continuous growth for both teachers and students (Boser, 2020; DuFour et al., 2016; Grafwallner, 2018a).

Effective collaboration comes in numerous contexts. Often, it's classroom teachers working with other grade-level or content-area teachers. Sometimes collaboration is vertical, occurring among teachers at lower or higher grade levels or different content areas. In still others, it's among teachers and coaches or administrators. Regardless of the context, the goal is to share knowledge and experience in ways that support student learning. For example, in my role as an instructional coach and reading specialist, it is my goal to support teachers, not tell them what to do or take over their classrooms. I am not in an evaluative role; however, my expertise happens to be literacy, so I work with teachers across disciplines to "embed the four facets of literacy—reading, writing, speaking, and listening—in relation to the subject matter being covered" (Grafwallner, 2017a). In this work, I also explain to teachers that my objective is to make it possible for them to concentrate on their professional practice (teaching, learning, and reflecting) by supporting them with what they need to be successful—research, resources, skills, and strategies.

In my practice, I simply reach out to teachers and ask to meet with them to ask what lesson or unit they may have coming up. When I meet with that teacher, I might offer examples of resources or strategies to help the teacher differentiate for varying levels of readers in his or her class; or, I might offer some vocabulary resources to support students in the disciplinary vocabulary for that particular lesson. I might suggest some articles aligned to that specific topic as student supplements. In this way, instead of teachers having to figure out these concepts for themselves, I facilitate their professional development so they can concentrate on enhancing their not-yet approach, rich with student learning and understanding. In truth, I often don't even ask if I can collaborate with a particular teacher. Because teachers are universally growth oriented, I always assume teachers want to collaborate to continue growing and strengthening their practice.

The not-yet approach relies on some specific collaborative strategies that support productive struggle. The following list offers examples of approaches you and your colleagues might take.

- Many schools, particularly those that operate as PLCs (DuFour et al., 2016), schedule collaborative team time into the master schedule. Most often, grade- or department-level teams meet to plan lessons, score student work and review outcomes, and determine next actions, such as the need to plan specific learning interventions or extensions based on those outcomes. As part of this work, teams determine what they want their students to know and be able to do, share their ideas and suggestions regarding supplemental materials (texts, videos, heuristics, and others), assessments (both formative and summative), and so on. In this way, collaboration becomes purposeful, meaningful, and above all, effective at maximizing student learning.

- Some teachers collaborate with others to create interdisciplinary lessons or units. In this case, two different or content-area teachers meet to determine how they can align their curriculum around shared concepts. While challenging, such collaboration is an exciting opportunity to bring in different perspectives about curricula and learning standards.

- Teachers, coaches, and even administrators can collaborate specifically around productive struggle by establishing shared practices that support students who are struggling or even to enhance learning for students who have mastered learning intentions and would benefit from higher-level challenges. There are many opportunities to be creative in building collaborative relationships along these lines. As an example, sometimes students' report card or grade-point average may negatively affect their opportunity to partake in extracurricular activities, especially athletics. In Wisconsin, the Wisconsin Interscholastic Athletic Association (2020) rules governing high school sports state, "A student-athlete must meet school and DPI requirements defining a full-time student and have received no more than one failing grade (including incompletes) in the most recent school issued grade reporting period" (p. 36). Thus, a teacher, athletic coach, and an administrator might design specific supports to help a student experiencing setbacks in one or more classes to develop needed skills and achieve learning intentions.

These approaches to collaboration exemplify the not-yet approach by using collective action to create authentic classroom and personal experiences that focus on continuous process-driven improvement for both teachers and students.

Collegial Observation

Collegial observation is a nonevaluative and informal opportunity to gain feedback about teachers' practice. In this way, you can think of this section's content as an extension of the Teacher Self-Reflection (page 148) content in chapter 9. Collegial observation also gives teachers a chance to try new methods, strategies, or resources while receiving critical feedback.

In her doctoral dissertation, Angela K. Vincent (2018) describes the benefits of collaboration, which lead to "discussions about instructional design and delivery that encourage teachers to engage in a cycle of constant learning and improvement." When teachers have the opportunity to observe each other, they recognize the importance of growth for the sake of their craft and their students. They embrace a growth mindset, realizing that they are still learning about pedagogy, and want feedback on how to become better educators. Cristi Alberino, a researcher at the University of Pennsylvania's Graduate School of Education and a former New York City teacher, comments, "I think that I learn more from observation than from any other kind of professional development" (as cited in Israel, n.d.). When teachers observe each other, they bring practice to the forefront of their teaching (Israel, n.d.).

When observing colleagues or when being observed, all involved should consider the five Bs.

1. **Be prepared:** Because observer and observed are devoting valuable time to this exercise, you want to make sure all involved have met ahead of time to determine the topic, purpose, and methods of the observation. Autism expert and clinical psychologist Christine Reeve (n.d.) writes, "What are the areas that you think you might be struggling within your classroom? What are the areas you really want to see in this classroom? Are there things you are trying to figure out how to organize, arrange, or teach?" Reeve (n.d.) recommends making a list of these focus areas so there is no losing track of them during the observation.

2. **Be respectful:** After the observation, keep the conversation focused on what you saw, heard, and experienced in the classroom. Les Foltos (2018), coaching trainer and director of Peer-Ed, explains that "successful collaborators discuss student learning, not the teachers. Following this norm keeps the conversation safe by anchoring it on the students, and it provides an avenue to talk about changes needed to meet student needs."

3. **Be curious:** The observed teacher wants to hear the observer's feedback, so it's critical questioning be part of the process. Grafwallner (2017b) writes, "Look for entry points to make suggestions and ideas, using clarifying language to be as clear as possible. Clarifying language communicates that the listener has heard what the speaker said, but might not fully understand."

4. **Be a learner:** Whatever the context for the observation, stay focused on growth. Victoria State Education Department (n.d.) writes, "Peer observation is about teachers observing each other's practice and learning from one another. It aims to support the sharing of best practice and build awareness about the impact of your own teaching."

5. **Be reflective:** Both the observed teacher and observers have the opportunity to reflect on what they saw, heard, and discussed during and following an observation. Catapano (2016) writes, "Reflect on what you observed. What did you see that you would like to emulate? What were they doing that seems particularly effective?"

When I observe a teacher, it is to gather information on how I can support that teacher in his or her lesson. I take notes on the learning intention, success criteria, the teacher-distributed handouts, or the in-class work the teacher explains. I walk around the room and ask students to explain to me what they understand the work to be about or what they are doing. If students seem unclear, I will make a note to share with the teacher.

If I am observing a novice teacher, I rarely ask what he or she needs. Often, a new teacher doesn't know. They are learning their craft, the district mandates, the school's culture, and finally, the names of countless students. Instead, I often bring resources with me—vocabulary strategies, relevant articles related to the discipline, or student relationship–building techniques. From my experiences, I've learned that new teachers benefit most from exposure to new strategies that are straightforward and easy to follow.

When observing veteran teachers, remember that their many experiences inside and outside the classroom impact their perspective on teaching. They have seen mandates come and go and know a recycled idea when they hear one. Often, this means the observer has as much to gain from the collegial observation as the observed teacher. If you're the observer in that circumstance, still conjure your own ideas for process-driven improvement, but be just as prepared to listen and learn from teachers who have years of pedagogical experience (Rutgers Center for Effective School

Practices, 2018). In this way, the experience becomes truly collaborative, as teachers cultivate both new and established ideas to advance each other's practice.

In any case, a post-observation dialogue is necessary to ensure that both the observed and the observer benefit from the experience. This dialogue should occur promptly but not until the observer has had adequate time to reflect on what he or she saw, gather information to support any conclusions, and put together any material that might support the observed teacher's professional development. I recommend this dialogue occur within three days.

The materials I gather vary based on the purpose of my observation. Some of them might include specific reading standards for the learning intention, robust verbs for the success criteria, engaging and motivating videos and graphic organizers, and finally, articles and research about that particular lesson. The purpose of these materials is to support my conversation with teachers as we discuss pedagogical guiding questions and comments that enable teachers to better support students' learning and overcome any roadblocks to learning. You'll learn more about these in the next section. Never forget that, as an observer, preparation is critical. You want to be prepared for the teacher, so he or she knows you are both acting as part of a connective team working for the sole purpose of supporting students' learning. If you are the teacher being observed, support your colleague's efforts by sharing your lesson plan ahead of time, or sending an email with the resource links, or having copies of the lesson's handouts. Give your observer the opportunity to be a part of the classroom experience and culture you have created.

Pedagogical Guiding Questions and Comments

We know that professional collaboration is an opportunity for those involved to confront and overcome setbacks and obstacles in practice just as collaborating with and between students supports process-driven learning (DuFour et al., 2016). As a result, an important aspect of that collaboration is asking pertinent questions, whether as the result of an observation or as part of a collaborative team meeting to discuss the curriculum, pedagogical approaches, assessments, or so on. Therefore, any collaboration should occur with a growth mindset among all participants, and a big part of that is knowing the right questions to ask.

Guiding questions are focused questions that encourage conversation. A high-quality guiding question does not push toward a "correct" answer but does require (and stimulate) high-level thinking and engagement. Pedagogical guiding questions, then, use the same approach but are focused specifically on instructional practice and technique. For example, if you've just observed a teacher and are preparing to reflect on the observation, have a series of questions ready to learn more about the lesson and the teacher's thinking and reasoning behind the lesson. When framing these questions, look for ways they can be practical and useful to the teacher, so he or she can apply his or her answers in the classroom.

When I meet with teachers following an observation, I present the resources and materials I gathered, but I never create a situation where the teacher feels he or she *must* use this information. Instead, we talk about practice, discussing the pedagogical concepts of the lesson. Education researcher and consultant Aakriti Kalra (2020) explains the value of this pedagogical conversation to create knowledge that results in "learning with a shared aim to provide quality learning experiences to . . . students."

Here are some pedagogical guiding questions that can help you and your colleagues define and build a lesson.

1. **What is the lesson's purpose?** When I begin a practice-driven conversation with a colleague about a lesson, I always ask the teacher about the lesson's purpose. It is not unusual for teachers to then reiterate the activities created for the lesson. While activities are important, they don't explain purpose. Even though the teacher might have displayed a vigorous learning intention and scaffolded success criteria, did the teacher, sometime during the lesson, explain the *why* of the learning? After all, it's the why that gives students purpose when diving into the challenging work ahead.

2. **What do you want your students to know?** It's important to find out directly from the teacher what he or she wanted students to gain from the lesson. When the teacher determines what he or she wants students to know, it becomes much easier to write vigorous learning intentions. For example, it's not unusual for a teacher to cite an activity or explain that they wanted their students to know about the Boston Tea Party. But, *what* does he or she want students to know about that event? When students can go on the internet and find answers to almost any question, what specific knowledge makes the lesson so valuable? What learning standards are students achieving? Just reading information isn't the same as digesting it and actually thinking critically and deeply about it.

3. **What do you want your students to be able to do?** This question investigates how teachers plan to get students thinking critically and deeply about the lesson. What will they do with the knowledge they

gain? Answers to this question inevitably lead to a lesson's scaffolded success criteria. The scaffolded success criteria should show those steps to get toward that goal.

4. **What artifacts or other tools support your teaching?** In answering this question, think about the lesson and how much talking and doing a teacher does (or will do) versus how much talking and doing the students do. In general, it's good practice for all teachers to think about the materials they distribute in class. How do those materials support students' skill acquisition? How do they support students in not only showing what they've learned but in overcoming learning obstacles? In The Joy of Learning (page 117 in chapter 7), I related the story of discovered Vietnam-era letters that belonged to my mom and how those became powerful supports to engage students in a curricular unit. What engaging, motivating, and purposeful supplements can you share with your students?

5. **How do you ensure students engage in the learning?** When students are engaged in the lesson, you can see it in their eyes, faces, and body language. Students' eyes are locked in, listening intently or engaged in an animated discussion about the lesson. However, sometimes lessons built on even the most worthwhile purpose, the most vigorous learning intention and scaffolded success criteria, and the most awesome artifacts and tools don't necessarily guarantee students will engage. Many of a teacher's best-laid plans have landed with a thud or haven't led to student acquisition of needed learning. When that happens, the not-yet approach means reflecting on the why of that thud and bouncing back. In meeting with your colleagues, talk about that experience, seeking their feedback on what might've gone wrong or what has worked for them when instructing on the same material. Or, if a colleague relates that experience to you, offer similar suggestions based on your successful experiences. While there is no guarantee these suggestions will enhance student engagement, taking the same approach that failed the first time is sure to be unsuccessful. Further, don't be afraid to ask your students why they disengaged with a lesson. Seek answers. Listen, and take notes. Reflect on the feedback you receive, and try again, modeling explicitly to students how you are engaging productively with this struggle.

When engaging with and discussing pedagogical guiding questions, be mindful of the need for mutual respect. It is important that you listen to the comments from your colleagues and remember that collective growth is not achievable through competitive one-upmanship. When accepting feedback from a teacher, do so with grace and use that feedback to further connect around what practices do or don't lead to student achievement.

Opportunities for Collaboration

As you've seen throughout this chapter, teaching, by nature, is inherently a collaborative enterprise, one that the vast majority of educators I've worked with embrace. The transformative impact of PLCs around the world is a testament to the value of collaboration for improving both pedagogical practice and student achievement (Flanagan, Grift, Lipscombe, Sloper, & Wills, 2021). I have been in education since 1993 and an instructional coach since January 2014, and I rely on collaboration, research, and my experience and expertise to do my job well. I attend and present at local and national conferences and workshops. I read research about instructional practices and reach out to bloggers and authors to learn more. In part, I do all this because I want to share with my colleagues the most up-to-date and reliable thinking and research about best practices for them and their students.

In all that time, I can only think of two instances where a colleague didn't want to work with me, and in both cases, I persevered by sending pertinent articles, relevant strategies, applicable graphic organizers, recent research, and current technology ideas to support students. Eventually, one of the two teachers reached out and thanked me for all the information coming her way and invited me into her psychology classroom to observe how she utilized one of the articles I sent her. The other teacher I found connection with by offering to support him in organizing a mass of case-study papers, an offer he gratefully accepted. As we sorted through the papers, I again explained that I would be happy to collaborate with him on any upcoming lessons. Unfortunately, he ended up leaving the profession after just a year of teaching, but the occasional undesirable outcome doesn't change that seeking collaborative opportunities is *never* a wasted effort.

If you are unable to build a connective relationship with a specific peer, do not give up or take it personally. There might be many reasons why a teacher might not find him- or herself in a collaborative spirit with you—at least for the moment. That is why you persevere. First, there is likely no one teacher, coach, or administrator with whom you simply *must* collaborate. Ideal collaboration is mutually beneficial, and your learning community has numerous colleagues your experience and knowledge will benefit and from whom you will receive the same benefits. Looking to specialists, coaches, and equivalent grade- or course-level teachers is natural. But don't be afraid to seek out teachers of other grade levels or content areas, teachers at other schools in or out of your district, and so on. Second, just because a teacher isn't open to a collaborative effort when you first reach out doesn't mean he or she won't be open to collaborating in the future. Lastly, you need not collaborate with just one colleague at a time. Forming collaborative teams with multiple teachers and building a sense of collective efficacy are incredibly impactful for improving pedagogy and learning outcomes (Donohoo, 2017; DuFour et al., 2016).

When looking for entry points, no matter how subtle, to collaborate with a colleague, consider using the following actions as opportunities for collaboration.

- **Engage in data analysis:** Ultimately, all assignments and assessments are data points. Engaging in data-mining as a grade-level or content-area team offers a collaborative way to analyze student products, assessment trends, and so on. Ultimately, grades represent aggregate outcomes, and collaborative data analysis enables teachers to see more specifically what learning intentions and success criteria students are achieving proficiency with and where there are specific challenges still to overcome. By reflecting on data, teachers can improve the rubrics, grading practices, and more.

- **Share intervention strategies:** Most schools have some policy of intervention, some more effective than others. But when teachers who have their students in class every day (or nearly) work together using collaboratively analyzed data to determine the source of *their* students' struggles, they can more effectively support intervention efforts for students who struggle unproductively. Further, encourage colleagues to share their success stories about how they supported students to overcome negative outcomes or behaviors. Consider sharing one intervention strategy per team or faculty meeting where teachers can benefit from each other's knowledge and experience.

- **Share resources:** Hand deliver teaching and learning resources (reading materials, graphic organizers, and so on) to colleagues. If sending digitally, go out of your way to talk face-to-face with your colleague about them. For example, offer several versions of compare-and-contrast diagrams to a science teacher or provide scaffolded graphic organizers of turn-and-talk student sentence starters to a mathematics teacher. While teachers may not use your specific resources, the resources could inspire them to modify or create their own individualized materials.

- **Demonstrate a lesson for the staff:** If you observe a teacher whose lesson you found particularly impactful, or if you overhear students talking about how great a colleague's class was, ask if he or she would be willing to showcase that lesson for other staff. Or, simply ask colleagues if they have a specific strategy they've been successful with to share at the next team meeting or as part of a forthcoming professional development opportunity.

- **Develop a shared list of guiding questions:** Offer colleagues the list of guiding questions from the previous section, and have a discussion not only about the answers to those questions but what new guiding questions you might explore together that will benefit your school community.

Even if your efforts to collaborate with a particular teacher or staff member meet with rejection, it's important to maintain a positive relationship. Any small success makes a difference and builds a foundation for future collaboration. Ultimately, it resulted in your classroom being more connected and both you and your colleagues finding new and innovative ways to support your students through productive struggle.

Conclusion

Connection with your colleagues is a key component for sustaining successful classroom experiences. That teamwork builds trusting, enduring partnerships where teachers are willing to engage more deeply in their practice and take risks to strengthen student perseverance and achievement. Through collegial observations, discussing pedagogical questions, and seeking out meaningful opportunities to collaborate, teachers show that purpose and process lie at the heart and soul of a not-yet classroom.

A Look Inside

by Victoria Thompson, STEM Coach

The year is 2021, and collaboration with teachers and administrators has been hard for me as a new STEM instructional coach. I began the role in July 2020 and, due to the COVID-19 pandemic, have seldom met any of my new colleagues or even my administration in person. Finding connection in this environment is challenging. Emails go unanswered, professional development sessions end up with no one attending, and so on. It's disheartening, but for many of us teachers, it felt like the world changed overnight, and the playbooks for how to respond were still being written. So I got to work, using the moment as an impetus for change and innovation within my role, one focused on true collaboration as not just a series of check-ins and messages but as genuine opportunities to work together and thrive. These efforts have met with some truly golden moments where changing my strategies achieved results, and it's in those moments where I feel most at home.

In the absence of dedicated collaborative teams, I've found the most effective approach to collaboration in this challenging environment is simply to locate colleagues who are the most invested in mutual mission, vision, and goals. A shared mission lets us know what we want to accomplish, and a shared vision lets us know the steps we need to accomplish to get there as well as *how* we get to accomplish those things. Simple questions, such as "How can I help you?", "What do you need?", and "What can we do together to thrive?" can help spark conversation among colleagues about what they can do together to determine and accomplish shared goals.

It's also important not to overlook the impact technology can have on facilitating collaboration. There are numerous tools I've found to be instrumental not just for my professional growth as a coach but also to reach people remotely. Online storage, such as Google Drive and Microsoft OneDrive, paired with productivity apps like Google Docs and Microsoft Excel, enable collaboration around documents in real time from a few miles away to around the world. Videoconferencing tools such as Zoom, Slack, Google Meet, and Microsoft Teams let us communicate effectively, both synchronously and asynchronously. Learning management systems and whiteboarding tools like Pear Deck and Jamboard can be instrumental for collecting the wisdom and using the results to come up with action items. Collaboration often looks different now than it did even just a few years ago, but it's still there!

With so many opportunities for collaboration, it's fair to ask, "What happens when collaboration *doesn't* work as expected?" I often have ideas or want to work with colleagues who feel they don't have the bandwidth to collaborate ("I'm too busy this week" or "I can't right now") or are hard to get in contact with. Whenever that happens, I don't take that as a personal slight but as an opportunity to reach out to other colleagues who may be interested and available. I've also learned to give time and space to people to process requests for collaboration and ideas for collaboration before moving forward. With a little patience, "I'm too busy this week," turns into, "I had some time open up. Let's talk!" And if a colleague is truly not at a place to collaborate, it's OK to seek out other options with folks who share your mission and your vision.

In endeavoring to sustain a collaborative culture, it's also important to find ways to celebrate collaboration and great instructional efforts. Every Monday, I like to send out "Staff Shout Outs" that highlight faculty and staff members who have done exceptional and innovative work in the classroom and behind the scenes. I usually focus on one instructional highlight, one academic highlight, one innovative highlight, and one collaborative high-light, but I'm always open to highlighting more should there be more to share. I also have open, standing meetings with folks to just discuss collaborative efforts that they have done in their classrooms. From there, we work together on how to sustain that collaboration and continuously refine and improve our practice.

Collaboration may look different in a post-pandemic world, but it's still there, and it's still critical to the cause of continuous improvement and professional growth. During this time, I encourage you all to think about collaboration as an opportunity to create, innovate, and seek new ways to work with others. You might find that your ability to connect and collaborate with your colleagues, improving learning for all students in the process, is better and more sustainable than it's ever been!

Ruminate and Respond

Consider what you've learned in this chapter, and individually or with your team, answer the following questions.

1. What do you do to create a connective classroom that focuses on professional collaboration to benefit students?

2. What arrangements can you make to conduct collegial observations, then set aside time to discuss the benefits of those observations?

3. Does your school organize teachers into collaborative teams? How are they organized, and what are the benefits? If your school does not use collaborative teams, how might you form one with your grade- or department-level colleagues?

4. How does asking pedagogical questions benefit collegial relationships and foster connective classrooms?

5. What opportunities for collaboration can you think of that aren't detailed in this chapter?

The Inclusive Classroom

Student-teacher relationships are fundamental to student achievement. *Education Week* assistant editor Sarah D. Sparks (2019) comments, "Education watchers have long known that the relationship with a teacher can be critically important to how well students learn." When these relationships are positive, students will more critically invest in their education (Sparks, 2019). Positive student-teacher relationships are more than just about what students and teachers like or don't like. Educator and researcher Trynia Kaufman (n.d.) explains the fundamental importance of positive student-teacher relationships: "When students feel supported, they're more likely to engage in learning and have better academic success." It's a win-win for everyone. Rita Pierson (2013) sums this dynamic up best in her iconic TED Talk, "Every Kid Needs a Champion," when she says, "You know, kids don't learn from people they don't like."

It makes sense. If students don't trust their teachers to have their best interests at heart, if they don't think their teachers care about them, what is the incentive to push through learning obstacles and roadblocks? Why should they trust any scaffolds or supports teachers do provide to support their learning? Further, when teachers show clear connections with some students but not others (however inadvertent), it can quickly become an inclusivity issue in which some students feel shut out of learning opportunities.

All teachers have experienced trying to build a relationship with that one particular student who doesn't seem to like them. As practiced educators, that indifference may not hurt teachers' psyche too much, but for that student to feel truly connected to the classroom, the student-teacher relationship must, at the very least, be cordial and focused on learning. In particular, keep in mind that while educators can teach students who don't like them, it can be hard for students to separate the academic from the emotional. Writing for the American Psychological Association, Sara Rimm-Kaufman and Lia Sandilos (2010) conclude, "Those students who have close, positive and supportive relationships with their teachers will attain higher levels of achievement than those students with more conflict in their relationships."

Having that presence of mind can be difficult to summon at times, but it is imperative for you to separate the academic from the emotional for the sake of students' well-being. This is especially the case when you have students who might feel marginalized due to their identity, be that for racial, cultural, religious, or gender-based reasons. This chapter highlights the not-yet approach for an inclusive classroom, ways to develop positive student-teacher relationships, and how to ensure you approach curricula from an inclusive and equitable mindset.

The Not-Yet Approach in the Inclusive Classroom

An *inclusive classroom* is one that is empathetic and compassionate toward all students. Teachers show they recognize, respect, and value who their students are as people, no matter how a student's identity might seem to separate him or her from peers. Teachers must reach out to all students, especially those who separate themselves or have trouble feeling a part of the classroom—those are the students who need their teachers the most. While a teacher can't and shouldn't be a student's friend, veteran educator and diversity, equity, and inclusion specialist Gabriel Benn (2018) explains the importance of connecting with even the most challenging students (perhaps *especially* the most challenging students):

> The students who need the *most* love, support, and encouragement may show their need in rude and disrespectful ways. When a student lashes out in class, you must have the presence of mind in the moment to know that sometimes, poor behavior isn't about you personally.

When observing and assessing how students respond to struggle, teachers must remember students look at and react to those setbacks and obstacles from their particular perspective or their particular lens. In other words, what might seem like a setback to one student might be considered an opportunity to another. Therefore, it is important to give students the chance to see how their peers respond to challenges and learn from them. Part of modeling a growth mindset, grit, stick-withitness, and other essential traits of the not-yet approach in an inclusive way also involves showing students how to recognize and interpret how their peers react to setbacks and obstacles. Because students' lived experiences have a huge impact on how they react to struggle, how you, as a teacher, reserve judgment, show patience and empathy, and adopt an abolitionist mindset toward teaching has a ripple effect on how your students view and react to their peers' academic background, social and emotional contexts, and personal history. These positive reactions of patience and empathy create a classroom culture that reflects the reality that every student is on his or her own journey. As a result, students can see fluctuating degrees of growth among their peers and rejoice as peers move forward successfully from those challenges.

When thinking about inclusivity in their classroom, many educators focus on ensuring representation and equitable practices based on racial, cultural, and religious lines. This is important, but also don't lose sight of how critical it is to ensure inclusive practices for students receiving special education. As the parent of a daughter who is autistic and cognitively impaired, I deeply understand the meaning of *inclusion* in a student population. An inclusive classroom considers every student in the room. No matter where any individual student is in their learning journey, supporting each student to understand his or her individual learning process and progress sets the foundation for their unique learning experience and their ability to face a challenge and say, "Not yet." In so doing, teachers and students learn together to celebrate the learning process and the successes that come from it.

Writing on inclusive classroom practices, authors Lee Ann Jung, Nancy Frey, Douglas Fisher, and Julie Kroener (2019) assert:

> [Inclusion means] dismantling the status quo, disrupting the long-held beliefs about learners and about teaching. Fundamental to this work is replacing a climate of *sorting* and *ranking* students with one of *mastery*—believing and expecting that all students can learn at high levels. (p. 17)

Success for one student will look different than success for another student, and that success is measured in varying ways throughout a student's academic journey. But, students will get there—one step at a time.

Student-Teacher Relationships

Perhaps the most critical understanding teachers must have about student-teacher relationships is the impact those relationships have not only on achievement but on students simply staying in school. Sparks (2019) explains:

> A *Review of Educational Research* analysis of 46 studies found that strong teacher-student relationships were associated in both the short- and long-term with improvements on practically every

measure schools care about: higher student academic engagement . . . and lower school dropout rates.

For many students without a strong student-teacher relationship, there is no reason to stay in school. A teacher can offer guidance, companionship, and hope for some students who may not have an attentive adult in their lives. For example, during the COVID-19 pandemic, many schools and districts had no option but to provide instruction virtually. Teachers, students, and parents were concerned about the lack of relationship building with distance learning. However, the schools that were most effective answered that concern by establishing multiple ways students and teachers could still maintain a connection. In my school, it was "all hands on deck," as all teachers, support staff, and paraprofessionals met with a small group of students—approximately eight to ten students—once a week for an hour. This check-in time was not about academics but rather the sustaining of student-teacher relationships. In this way, we helped students who might otherwise have felt abandoned in this difficult situation feel included.

In writing about *Who You Know: Unlocking Innovations That Expand Students' Networks* by author and researcher Julia Freeland Fisher (2018), education writer Tim Klein (2019) surmises, "When teachers build relationships with students . . . the outcomes are powerful: Students engage with hard academic tasks longer, enjoy working hard, and think that it is okay to make mistakes while pursuing their academic goals." These relationships are the backbone of the not-yet approach, which supports students in overcoming setbacks and obstacles as part of learning and life.

Jensen (2019) frames this kind of approach to student-teacher relationships as part of a relational mindset that will keep students interested in their schooling and less likely to invest their energy in more detrimental or even toxic connections that sometimes come from outside the classroom. The key to this approach doesn't require that teachers know everything about every student. It's about seemingly little things that, all together, communicate to students they matter to their teachers. Jensen (2019) suggests three keys to establishing and sustaining healthy student relationships.

1. **Personalize the learning:** There are no tricks to keeping learning personal. Start with simply knowing and using students' names to establish connections. You might be amazed at how many students don't think their teachers recognize their presence in the classroom. Further, show trust in your students by sharing information about yourself and your own life's challenges, goals, and successes, particularly as they relate to school and academics. Not all students will connect with everything you share, but some will.

2. **Connect students with each other:** Not all students are comfortable being social, but helping students build positive, supportive connections with their peers creates a sense of belonging. Try using a fifty-fifty rule in which classroom activities are split between individual and cooperative learning, then oversee how students interact. Notice and affirm supportive behaviors. When you see unproductive group dynamics at work, interrupt and model the more productive and supportive behaviors you'd like the group members to demonstrate.

3. **Show empathy:** How students feel on any given day affects their ability to engage in learning. When teachers dismiss outside impacts, students will naturally feel their teacher doesn't care about their experience. The key to empathy is that it doesn't require teachers to feel what their students are feeling but to simply understand those feelings and their effects. When students act out or fail to engage in learning, start with concern for their well-being. "Are you OK?" is a simple yet powerful question to ask a student in distress. Further your connections with students by making the rounds before class to check in about how individual students are doing, noticing the things they're interested in or something new about them. Observe students' body language during class for signs of distress, and take a moment before they leave for the day to let them know you're there if they want to talk.

Sometimes, building trust with students gets more complicated than a quick acknowledgement or check in. An unfortunate reality that all teachers must confront is they will have some students who have experienced or are experiencing some kind of significant trauma. Trauma experts Larry K. Brendtro, Martin Brokenleg, and Steve Van Bockern (2019) explain that youth who experience trauma often display one of four pattern behaviors to convey their mistrust of adults or peers: (1) *fight*, characterized by acting out; (2) *flight*, characterized by guarded behavior; (3) *fool*, characterized by the use of masking behavior; and (4) *follow*, characterized as youth who seek out like-minded peers for role models but not adults (Brendtro et al., 2019). Such behaviors test teachers in countless ways, but Brendtro and colleagues (2019) assert each behavior ultimately constitutes a bid for attention. When confronted with such bids, teachers' options are to turn toward (focusing on a positive response and avoiding deficit-minded language), away (ignoring the bid for attention), or against (becoming belligerent or argumentative). Though often difficult, the only response that can build trust and begin to repair damage is to turn toward.

Regardless of how trust is achieved or how long it takes, when students have a positive relationship with their teachers, the rigorous academic tasks and the mistakes that inevitably go along with them are not seen as detriments within the individual but are acknowledged as learning steps forward. Therefore, the inclusive classroom, one rooted in tolerance and understanding, begins when teachers go out of their way to build relationships with their students, creating a culture of patience and purpose, where ultimately, process, product, and progress are the very heart and soul of student success.

Inclusive Curricula

The relationships students have with their teachers and peers aren't the only means teachers have to make them feel part of an inclusive classroom. Teachers often overlook how their approach to grade or course curricula impacts the degree to which students feel valued as part of the classroom community. Onuscheck, Spiller, & Glass (2020) posit three vital questions teachers should ask as they look for ways to make their classrooms more inclusive and equitable:

- "How can our team and school identify and eliminate invisible biases that might influence our instructional approach to students and affect their trust in us?"

- "How can our team and school avoid excluding any student from rigorous learning opportunities in curricula and promote high expectations for all students?"

- "How can our team ensure the resources we select or are asked to use authentically reflect the demographics of our students, diverse perspectives, and the experiences of others?" (p. 218)

When it comes to identifying invisible biases, schools don't have to look far. Often, the big, bold letters on the front of the building or the imagery that makes up the school mascot might say it all. Many school boards have opted to rename their schools or change mascots due to what they convey from a historical context (Delonas, 2020; Mitchell, 2020; Pietsch, 2021). If teachers want schools to be an inclusionary place for *all* students, they must examine every aspect of practice relative to how it supports or inhibits equity in learning, substantive or cosmetic. This examination should occur school- and districtwide, but teachers specifically have a responsibility to examine the messages their classroom conveys about inclusivity. What imagery or messaging might be incendiary or deflating to your students of color, and how might you purge your classroom of those influences?

This thinking should extend to how you structure your classroom for students with special needs. As a parent, I knew what my Ani could and couldn't do in and out of the classroom and that her peers would outperform her in various tasks and situations. However, I wanted her to have opportunities to acquire learning that would benefit her, like the example you read about in Using Data to Personalize Learning Intentions and Success Criteria (page 69 in chapter 4). For example, when Ani was ten years old, our local recreation department sponsored scuba lessons in the high school pool. Knowing how much Ani loved to swim, I signed her up, explaining that she was a visual learner due to her autism and cognitive impediments. The recreation department told me she could not take scuba lessons with her peers because of her disability, despite the reality that she had passed the recreation department's swimming levels. When I asked to speak to the scuba instructor, I also asked if Ani wasn't allowed to take scuba lessons with the other children, what lessons would they be offering for students with disabilities to be compliant with federal law? Needless to say, Ani took scuba lessons with her peers. But it should never have come to that, and parents shouldn't have to similarly visit with you when it comes to supporting an equitable learning experience for their child.

Consider the similarity of this experience to the student experience in schools that *track* them, which refers to "the practice of grouping high school students by ability into a series of courses with differentiated curriculums; students take high-, middle-, or low-level courses related to the track they have selected or been assigned to (academic, general, or vocational)" (Futrell & Gomez, 2008). By its nature, tracking doesn't give students the same chance as their peers, often determining their educational future based on standardized test scores, which any teacher can tell you is a problematic mindset. Halley Potter (2019), a senior fellow at the Century Foundation focusing on educational inequity, writes:

> Academic tracking—and the racial and socioeconomic segregation it often creates—raises a number of concerns about equity. First, academic tracking and other forms of homogeneous ability grouping such as gifted programs frequently do a poor job at the main goal they are designed to achieve: sorting students by ability.

Although the word *tracking* has rightfully fallen out of use, high school teacher Michelle Higgins (2019), writing for *Learning for Justice*, explains that the practice hasn't gone away, just evolved:

> But many schools and districts still engage in tracking—they just use a different name. Students are sorted into gifted and talented programs, selected to join honors classes or guided onto AP tracks—extended opportunities that their classmates may never see.

When curricula are inclusive, all students receive the same opportunities to learn as their peers, even if those opportunities and that learning journey look different (as they must). That effort should also be reflected in the resources teachers use in their instruction. ELA teachers especially have long relied on a list of usual suspects: Shakespeare, Dickens, Twain, and so on, with an occasional Langston Hughes thrown in to offer something resembling a multicultural perspective in the curriculum. While updating the canon to include more voices that represent LGBTQ issues, gender diversity, people of color, people with disabilities, and ethnic, cultural, and religious minorities, Jill Anderson (2018) of the Harvard EdCast and cofounder of #Disrupttexts, writes:

> But even as teachers appear aware of a need to diversify the curriculum, there can be roadblocks to making it happen. For example, there's a diversity gap in the book publishing industry regarding who gets published (mostly white authors), who gets awarded (mostly white authors), and which books make it onto school vendor booklists (mostly white creators).

Those roadblocks mean students miss out on reading authors who look like them or have similar life experiences. Writing for Scholastic, Jodie Rodriguez (2018) encourages teachers to select texts that offer students cultural connections, stating, "Kids also need to see kids just like themselves doing ordinary kid stuff like visiting the library, going to the pool, and playing in the backyard." An example of this ordinary kid stuff is Matthew A. Cherry's (2019) bestseller, *Hair Love,* about a father who must do his daughter's hair for the first time. While this is an ordinary act, the book became an extraordinary sensation because it delightfully shared the bond between a father and daughter of color as he did his best to style his daughter's hair. Readers of color saw themselves in Zuri, the main character, and rejoiced in the fact that her daddy is proud of her beautiful hair.

When teachers go beyond what they know from past lived experiences and instead focus on reflecting their *students'* lives and diverse experiences, they forge relationships with students that are authentic and respectful. Through those relationships, teachers sustain an inclusive classroom that supports students through productive struggle.

Conclusion

Do not underestimate the critical importance of inclusive student-teacher relationships and curricula. Many educators fondly remember positive relationships with their teachers. I remember Rosemary Link, my ninth-grade English teacher. I became an English teacher because of Miss Link. She saw in me something I didn't necessarily see in myself at the time—a confidence and desire to make literature relevant in my life. Creating classrooms of inclusion and tolerance where students can foster relationships with their teachers and their peers supports students in learning about their world and, ultimately, themselves.

A Look Inside

by Peg Grafwallner, Instructional Coach and Reading Specialist

It was five minutes before my first freshman skills class of the day. I stood outside my door and greeted students as they walked in. When the bell rang, I moved away from the door to the front of the classroom. I began to share the learning intention with the class while taking attendance.

About ten minutes later, Mike charged in.

Mike was a tough kid—rough around the edges and totally disengaged from school. Mike and his buddies caused enough classroom headaches that teachers were weary of them. He and I had, for the most part, a working relationship. He did what I asked him to do with minimum pushback, and I sometimes gave him space to do what he needed.

This morning, something was wrong. He was angry; his face was contorted and red. He stormed to his desk and sat down with a thump. I continued explaining the morning's goal along with the pertinent skills. I asked students to take out paper along with their text.

Mike did nothing. I gave him a couple of sheets of paper and a pencil. He moved them aside and put his head down. I stood next to him and gave the next set of directions. As students were moving their desks to make teams, I leaned over and encouraged him to move to a group.

"Leave me alone!" he shouted into the crook of his arm. A few heads turned in our direction.

"Mike," I said softly, "join Devon's group. You can follow along with him." He lifted up his head. "I told you, leave me alone! Shut up and leave me alone!" he screamed.

Before the situation escalated further or the language turned colorful, I said, "Mike, let's go in the hallway for a minute." I turned to my class and asked them to please review their vocabulary note cards.

Mike stood up with such force that his desk tipped over. I followed him into the hallway where he paced back and forth. I gently closed the classroom door about halfway—wide enough to see and hear my class, but narrow enough to give Mike the attention he deserved.

"OK, what do you need from me?" I asked. I didn't ask him what was wrong—that answer would come in time. I didn't need to know what had happened.

The situation would reveal itself eventually. Right then, I needed to know how I could get him to a place of learning.

Mike stopped, looked at me, and began ranting about his mother. There had been a disagreement that morning, and he left the house angry, hurt, and frustrated.

I listened and kept quiet, focusing solely on him. I kindly reminded him to keep his voice down because I didn't want to bother the students working in my room or alert administration. I didn't want Mike to feel that his honesty would get him in trouble. This didn't need to end with another referral.

I didn't correct his language, nor did I correct his feelings. He was angry at his mother, and I was the first adult female he saw that morning. When I asked him to join a group, I was one more person asking one more thing of an already stressed and disenfranchised kid.

When he was done, I asked him to quietly wait in the hallway. I went into my room and grabbed a paper cup and a hallway pass. I explained to my students that I needed to finish the hallway conversation.

Mike had settled down. He wasn't pacing anymore but leaning against the wall with his head on his chest. I gave him the paper cup and began to write out a pass.

"What are you doing?" he asked.

"Go get some water. Take the pass and walk around the building. I expect you back in five minutes."

"Wait, you're not going to write me up?"

"For what? For being angry? No. I need you to do the best you can to put this away for now. I need you in my room and focused. We'll talk to the social worker later."

"Thanks, Mrs. G.," he said sheepishly.

Mike returned to my room within five minutes. He joined a group and did the best he could to be the best student he could on this particular morning.

Could I have handled the situation differently? *Yes*—but I'm not sure how. I could have sent him to the office for being late to class, but he would have missed more learning. I could have called our safety officer and had him removed for his behavior, but to what end? Had I done either of those things, he never would have trusted me again.

The way I handled this situation caused Mike to rethink our relationship. Although it was acceptable, it became stronger. He never raised his voice to me again. He became tardy less often. And most important, I saw a change in his attitude. He was willing to be a part of our classroom community— whatever that meant for him. And every morning, there was an empty cup on his desk that he filled with water. It was my way of saying, relax, breathe, and focus as you begin your day.

About six years later, I had a visitor. Sure enough, it was Mike. He was working as a heating and cooling apprentice with his uncle. He came back to high school for the first time since graduation. He came back to apologize to me.

"I'm sorry, Mrs. G. I know I wasn't easy. I know I gave you a hard time. Thanks for putting up with me. Thanks for listening," he said awkwardly.

I knew what he meant. Years later, Mike remembered what I had done. I had the chance to get it right, and I did. I put my hand on his shoulder and thanked him for coming in and told him how much I appreciated his visit. He told me he was "in the neighborhood and decided to stop in," but had to get to work. He thanked me again and left.

As he walked down the hall, I smiled. Thank *you*, Mike. He gave me the opportunity to know that I made a difference. Although all teachers hope that to be true with their students, many of us don't get the chance to actually hear it. A cup of water, a walk, and a little humanity go a long way for students like Mike—and for all of us.

Ruminate and Respond

Consider what you've learned in this chapter, and individually or with your team, answer the following questions.

1. Why are student-teacher relationships so vital to student success?

2. What do you do to build student relationships that are centered on trust and respect?

3. What are some methods and techniques you can use to make students feel a part of your classroom, encouraging them to persist in their learning?

4. How might you make changes to your curriculum materials to better reflect the lived experiences of your students?

5. How will the not-yet approach and productive struggle encourage your students to achieve success?

Epilogue

Thank you for joining me on the not-yet journey to make education as practical, transformational, productive, supportive, flexible, constructive, connective, and inclusive as possible. These eight lenses provide context for how you might view your approach to building a classroom culture of *not yet* in response to the learning obstacles and struggles students encounter. I hope these themes and the research-based best practices, suggestions, and examples support and inspire your approach to the teaching and learning that occur in your classroom, empowering you with the flexible perspective all teachers need to support student achievement.

While educators don't have all the answers, they do have a desire to design and create a classroom culture that encourages the process of learning while accepting that setbacks and obstacles are part of that process. As the expert on your classroom and students, it's up to you to decide which aspects of the not-yet classroom will most benefit the cause of learning through productive struggle.

Through this book's numerous strategies and tools, the firsthand accounts you read about in the many A Look Inside sections, and the opportunities for reflection that the Ruminate and Respond reproducibles provide, I hope you find purposeful and meaningful support in this book's contents. Remember, you can use all the not-yet classroom strategies I offer as is or modify them to better fit your and your students' needs. There is no judgment here, just a chance for teachers to learn from one another and support student learning in unique and authentic ways.

Thank you for the opportunity to share with you my years of experience and expertise. I hope you find this book helpful, and I look forward to working with you again!

References and Resources

ACT. (n.d.). *Reading college and career readiness standards.* Iowa City, IA: Author. Accessed at www.act.org/content/act/en/college-and-career-readiness/standards/reading-standards .html on December 7, 2020.

Ainsworth, L. (2017, October 9). *The clarity problem—and the teacher solution.* Accessed at www.larryainsworth.com/blog/the-clarity-problem-and-the-teacher-solution on March 20, 2021.

Alber, R. (2014, January 24). *6 scaffolding strategies to use with your students.* Accessed at www .edutopia.org/blog/scaffolding-lessons-six-strategies-rebecca-alber on March 19, 2021.

Allen, J. (2008). *More tools for teaching content literacy.* Portland, ME: Stenhouse.

Amaro, M. (2016, October 20). *Why teacher expectations are important for student achievement.* Accessed at https://thehighlyeffectiveteacher.com/why-teacher-expectations-are-important -for-student-achievement on March 14, 2021.

American Academy of Child and Adolescent Psychiatry. (n.d.). *Your adolescent—Anxiety and avoidant disorders: Excerpts from* Your Adolescent: Emotional, behavioral, and cognitive development from early adolescence through the teen years *on anxiety and avoidant disorders.* Accessed at www.aacap.org/AACAP/Families_and_Youth/Resource_Centers /Anxiety_Disorder_Resource_Center/Your_Adolescent_Anxiety _and_Avoidant_Disorders.aspx on December 7, 2020.

American Civil Liberties Union of Wisconsin. (2020, June 17). *ACLU of Wisconsin offering virtual summer justice institute for high school students.* Accessed at www.aclu-wi.org/en /news/aclu-wisconsin-offering-virtual-summer-justice-institute-high-school-students on March 23, 2021.

Anderson, J. (2018). Hooked on classics: A classic problem: The push to modernize reading lists is challenging traditional definitions of literature. Surprise: Not everyone is happy about it. *Harvard Ed.* Magazine. Accessed at www.gse.harvard.edu/news/ed/19/08/ hooked-classics on April 4, 2021.

Anderson, J. (2021). *The agile learner: Where growth mindset, habits of mind, and practice unite.* Bloomington, IN: Solution Tree Press.

Anderson, L. W., & Krathwohl, D. R. (2001). Revised Bloom's taxonomy action verbs. In *A taxonomy for learning, teaching, and assessing: A revision of Bloom's taxonomy of educational objectives.* Boston: Allyn & Bacon. Accessed at www.apu.edu/live_data /files/333/blooms_taxonomy_action_verbs.pdf on March 20, 2021.

Anderson, M. (2016). *Learning to choose, choosing to learn: The key to student motivation and achievement.* Alexandria, VA: Association for Supervision and Curriculum Development.

Anderson, M. (2017, June 27). *Scaffolding and success criteria.* Accessed at https://schoolecosystem.org/2017/06/27/scaffolding-success-criteria on March 20, 2021.

Armida, G. (2018, January 24). *A zero does nothing but hurt education.* Accessed at https://theteacherandtheadmin.com/2018/01/24/a-zero-does-nothing-but-hurt-education on March 16, 2021.

Association for Supervision and Curriculum Development. (n.d.). *The whole child.* Accessed at www.ascd.org/whole-child.aspx on March 21, 2021.

Bain, P. (2018, October 31). *The secret to student success? Teach them how to learn.* Accessed at www.edsurge.com/news/2018-10-31-the-secret-to-student-success-teach-them-how-to-learn on March 19, 2021.

Barnett, J. E. H. (2017). Helping students with ADHD in the age of digital distraction. *Physical Disabilities: Education and Related Services, 36*(2), 1–7.

Barshay, J. (2019, January 14). *Five years after Common Core, a mysterious spike in failure rate among NY high school students.* Accessed at https://hechingerreport.org/five-years-after-common-core-a-mysterious-spike-in-failure-rate-among-ny-high-school-students on April 6, 2021.

Bellow, A. (2020, June 22). *The 101 hottest tech tools according to education experts.* Accessed at https://tutorful.co.uk/blog/the-82-hottest-edtech-tools-of-2017-according-to-education-experts on March 23, 2021.

Benn, G. (2018). Relationships and rapport: "You don't know me like that!" *Educational Leadership, 76*(1), 20–25.

Bjork, E. L., & Bjork, R. A. (2014). Making things hard on yourself, but in a good way: Creating desirable difficulties to enhance learning. In M. A. Gernsbacher and J. Pomerantz (Eds.), *Psychology and the real world: Essays illustrating fundamental contributions to society* (2nd ed., pp. 59–68). New York: Worth.

Blackburn, B. R. (2018). Productive struggle is a learner's sweet spot. *Productive Struggle for All, 14*(11). Accessed at www.ascd.org/ascd-express/vol14/num11/productive-struggle-is-a-learners-sweet-spot.aspx on February 3, 2021.

Boser, U. (2020, May 17). *The learning process and why it matters.* Accessed at www.the-learning-agency-lab.com/the-learning-curve/six-key-steps-to-learn-better on March 25, 2021.

BrainyQuote. (n.d.). *Mark Twain quotes.* Accessed at https://brainyquote.com/quotes/mark_twain_389874 on December 7, 2020.

Brendtro, L. K., Brokenleg, M., & Van Bockern, S. (2019). *Reclaiming youth at risk: Futures of promise* (3rd ed.). Bloomington, IN: Solution Tree Press.

British Psychological Society. (2014, September 21). *Fear of failure from a young age affects attitude to learning.* Accessed at https://sciencedaily.com/releases/2014/09/140921223559.htm on December 7, 2020.

Brookfield, S. D. (2017). *Becoming a critically reflective teacher* (2nd ed.). San Francisco: Jossey-Bass.

Brookhart, S. M. (2007/2008). Feedback that fits. *Educational Leadership, 65*(4), 54–59. Accessed at www.ascd.org/publications/educational-leadership/dec07/vol65/num04 /Feedback-That-Fits.aspx on December 7, 2020.

Brookhart, S. M. (2019). A perfect world is one with no grades. *ASCD Express, 14*(31). Accessed at www.ascd.org/ascd-express/vol14/num31/a-perfect-world-is-one-with -no-grades.aspx on December 7, 2020.

Buehl, D. (2020). *Classroom strategies for interactive learning* (4th ed.). Portsmouth, NH: Stenhouse.

Buffum, A., Mattos, M., & Malone, J. (2018). *Taking action: A handbook for RTI at Work.* Bloomington, IN: Solution Tree Press.

Burns, E., & Frangiosa, D. (2021). *Going gradeless, grades 6–12: Shifting the focus to student learning.* Thousand Oaks, CA: Corwin Press.

Busch, B. (2015, November 15). *Four questions that encourage growth mindset among students.* Accessed at www.theguardian.com/teacher-network/2015/nov/15/four-questions -encourage-growth-mindset-students on March 19, 2021.

Canonica, P. (2019, June 5). *The danger of growth mindset.* Accessed at www.sec-ed.co.uk /blog/the-danger-of-growth-mindset on March 18, 2021.

Catapano, J. (2016). Observing other teachers. *Pershing WAAG.* Accessed at www.smore .com/f1dgz-pershing-waag on April 21, 2021.

Chang, B. (2019). Reflection in learning. *Online Learning, 23*(1), 95–110.

Cherry, M. A. (2019). *Hair love.* New York: Kokila.

Chiaravalli, A. (2017, April 18). *Teachers going gradeless: Toward a future of growth not grades* [Blog post]. Accessed at https://medium.com/teachers-going-gradeless/teachers-going -gradeless-50d621c14cad on March 20, 2021.

Cohen, R. K., Opatosky, D. K., Savage, J., Stevens, S. O., & Darrah, E. P. (2021). *The metacognitive student: How to teach academic, social, and emotional intelligence in every content area.* Bloomington, IN: Solution Tree Press.

Colburn, L., & Beggs, L. (2021). *The wraparound guide: How to gather student voice, build community partnerships, and cultivate hope.* Bloomington, IN: Solution Tree Press.

Coley, R. J., & Goertz, M. E. (1990, June). *Educational standards in the 50 states: 1990* (ETS Research Report Series). Princeton, NJ: Educational Testing Service.

Common Core State Standards Initiative. (n.d.). *Development process.* Accessed at www .corestandards.org/about-the-standards/development-process on March 16, 2021.

Common Sense Education. (n.d.). *Ten great free websites for high school.* Accessed at www .commonsense.org/education/top-picks/10-great-free-websites-for-high-school on March 23, 2021.

Conley, D. T. (2015, October 13). *Breadth vs. depth: The deeper learning dilemma* [Blog post]. Accessed at http://blogs.edweek.org/edweek/learning_deeply/2015/10/breadth_vs_depth _the_deeper_learning_dilemma.html on December 7, 2020.

Cornell University. (n.d.). *The Cornell note taking system.* Accessed at http://lsc.cornell.edu /study-skills/cornell-note-taking-system on March 3, 2020.

Costa, A. L., & Kallick, B. (Eds.). (2008). *Learning and leading with habits of mind: Sixteen essential characteristics for success.* Alexandria, VA: Association for Supervision and Curriculum Development.

Crosnoe, R. (2002). High school curriculum track and adolescent association with delinquent friends. *Journal of Adolescent Research, 17*(2), 143–167.

Curwin, R. (2014, October 28). *It's a mistake not to use mistakes as part of the learning process* [Blog post]. Accessed at https://edutopia.org/blog/use-mistakes-in-learning-process -richard-curwin on December 7, 2020.

Csikszentmihalyi, M. (1990). *Flow.* New York: Harper Perennial.

Darling-Hammond, L. (2016, March 1). Research on teaching and teacher education and its influences on policy and practice. *Educational Researcher.* Accessed at https://journals .sagepub.com/doi/10.3102/0013189X16639597 on March 27, 2021.

Davis, L. (2020, February 1). *Teacher collaboration: How to approach it in 2020* [Blog post]. Accessed at https://schoology.com/blog/teacher-collaboration on December 7, 2020.

Davis, V. (2015, July 28). *True grit: The best measure of success and how to teach it* [Blog post]. Accessed at https://edutopia.org/blog/true-grit-measure-teach-success-vicki-davis on December 7, 2020.

Delonas, L. (2020, October 17). *Decades of research supports mascot change.* Accessed at www.idahostatejournal.com/opinion/columns/decades-of-research-supports-mascot -change/article_0b6a7239-c8e2-5d6c-a1a6-23c24956ee0d.html on April 21, 2021.

Deslauriers, L., McCarty, L. S., Miller, K., Callaghan, K., & Kestin, G. (2019, September). Measuring actual learning versus feeling of learning in response to being actively engaged in the classroom. *Proceedings of the National Academy of Sciences, 116*(39), 19251–19257. Accessed at www.pnas.org/content/116/39/19251 on March 24, 2021.

Donohoo, J. (2017). *Collective efficacy: How educators' beliefs impact student learning.* Thousand Oaks, CA: Corwin Press.

Dr. Seuss. (1957). *The cat in the hat.* New York: Random House.

Dr. Seuss. (1960). *Green eggs and ham.* New York: Random House.

Duckworth, A. (n.d.a). *Grit scale.* Accessed at https://angeladuckworth.com/grit-scale on December 7, 2020.

Duckworth, A. (n.d.b). *Media.* Accessed at https://angeladuckworth.com/media on March 19, 2021.

Duckworth, A. (n.d.c). *Publications.* Accessed at https://angeladuckworth.com/publications on March 19, 2021.

Duckworth, A. (2009, October 18). *True grit: Can perseverance be taught?* [Video file]. Accessed at https://youtu.be/qaeFnxSfSC4 on March 19, 2021.

Duckworth, A. (2016). *Grit: The power of passion and perseverance.* New York: Scribner.

DuFour, R., DuFour, R., Eaker, R., Many, T. W., & Mattos, M. (2016). *Learning by doing: A handbook for Professional Learning Communities at Work* (3rd ed.). Bloomington, IN: Solution Tree Press.

Dweck, C. S. (2006). *Mindset: The new psychology of success.* New York: Ballantine Books.

Dweck, C. S. (2015, November 3). *Teaching a growth mindset—Carol Dweck* [Video file]. Accessed at https://youtu.be/isHM1rEd3GE on March 18, 2021.

Dweck, C. S. (2016). *Mindset: The new psychology of success* (Updated ed.). New York: Ballantine Books.

The Education Hub. (n.d.). *How to develop high expectations teaching.* Accessed at https://theeducationhub.org.nz/wp-content/uploads/2018/06/How-to-develop-high-expectations-teaching.pdf on March 14, 2021.

Education Oasis. (2006). *Graphic organizer: Character trait chart with word bank* [Free reproducible]. Accessed at https://educationoasis.com/printables/graphic-organizers/character-traits-chart on December 7, 2020.

Eva, A. L. (2017, February 22). *How to help students feel powerful at school: Educators can exert power over students—or they can create an environment where students feel energized and capable themselves.* Accessed at https://greatergood.berkeley.edu/article/item/how_to_help_students_feel_powerful_at_school on March 18, 2021.

Evans, B. E. (2017, June 27). *11 brutal truths about creativity that no one wants to talk about.* Accessed at https://thenextweb.com/creativity/2017/06/21/11-brutal-truths-about-creativity-that-no-one-wants-to-talk-about on March 23, 2021.

Fail. (n.d.a). In *Dictionary.com.* Accessed at https://dictionary.com/browse/fail?s=t on December 7, 2020.

Fail. (n.d.b). In *Merriam-Webster.com.* Accessed at www.merriam-webster.com/dictionary/fail on February 2, 2021.

Feldman, D. L., Smith, A. T., & Waxman, B. L. (2017). *"Why we drop out": Understanding and disrupting pathways to leaving school.* New York: Teachers College Press.

Feldman, J. (2017, November/December). Do your grading practices undermine equity initiatives? *Leadership,* 8–11. Accessed at https://crescendoedgroup.org/wp-content/uploads/2014/03/Equitable-grading-Leadership-Mag_NovDec.pdf on December 21, 2020.

Fessler, L. (2018, March 26). *"You're no genius": Her father's shutdowns made Angela Duckworth a world expert on grit.* Accessed at https://qz.com/work/1233940/angela-duckworth-explains-grit-is-the-key-to-success-and-self-confidence on March 19, 2021.

Fisher, D., & Frey, N. (2018). Show & tell: A video column / A map for meaningful learning. *Educational Leadership, 75*(5), 82–83.

Fisher, D., Frey, N., & Rothenberg, C. (2008). *Content-area conversations: How to plan discussion-based lessons for diverse language learners.* Alexandria, VA: Association for Supervision and Curriculum Development.

Fisher, J. F. (2018). *Who you know: Unlocking innovations that expand students' networks.* San Francisco: Jossey-Bass.

Fisher, M. (2019, May 30). *Updating your teaching to something messier.* Accessed at https://teachthought.com/pedagogy/8-tips-for-updating-your-teaching on December 7, 2020.

Flanagan, T., Grift, G., Lipscombe, K., Sloper, C., & Wills, J. (2021). *Transformative collaboration: Five commitments for leading a professional learning community.* Bloomington, IN: Solution Tree Press.

Foltos, L. (2018, January 29). *Teachers learn better together.* Accessed at www.edutopia.org /article/teachers-learn-better-together on March 26, 2021.

Fournier, D. (2018, April 24). *The only way to eat an elephant: How we set our goals has everything to do with whether or not we achieve them.* Accessed at www.psychologytoday .com/us/blog/mindfully-present-fully-alive/201804/the-only-way-eat-elephant on April 13, 2021.

Freibrun, M. (2019, March 5). *Spark motivation in your students with success criteria.* Accessed at www.teachingchannel.com/blog/spark-motivation-in-your-students-with-success -criteria on March 20, 2021.

Fuller, A., & Fuller, L. (2021). *Neurodevelopmental differentiation: Optimizing brain systems to maximize learning.* Bloomington, IN: Solution Tree Press.

Fulleylove, R. (n.d.). *Es Devlin on her creative process and embracing mistakes.* Accessed at https://artsandculture.google.com/theme/es-devlin-on-her-creative-process-and -embracing-mistakes/aAKy4tUEpwQkLg?hl=en on December 7, 2020.

Futrell, M. H., & Gomez, J. (2008). Special topic / how tracking creates a poverty of learning. *Education Week, 65*(8), 74–78. Accessed at www.ascd.org/publications /educational-leadership/may08/vol65/num08/How-Tracking-Creates-a-Poverty-of -Learning.aspx on April 4, 2021.

Garcia, H. (2018, August 9). *Sharing student work—online network of educators.* Accessed at https://onlinelearningconsortium.org/sharing-student-work on March 20, 2021.

Gehr, L. (2020, February 11). *How to make student choice work.* Accessed at www.edutopia .org/article/how-make-student-choice-work on March 28, 2021.

Gershenson, S. (2020a). End the "easy A." *Education Next, 20*(2). Accessed at https:// educationnext.org/end-easy-a-tougher-grading-standards-set-students-up-success on December 7, 2020.

Gershenson, S. (2020b, February). *Great expectations: The impact of rigorous grading practices on student achievement.* Washington, DC: Thomas B. Fordham Institute. Accessed at https:// fordhaminstitute.org/sites/default/files/publication/pdfs/20200204-great-expectationsthe -impact-rigorous-grading-practices-student-achievement0.pdf on March 14, 2021.

Gibson, W. (1959). *The miracle worker.* New York: Scribner.

Glossary of Education Reform. (2017, November 9). *Standards-based.* Accessed at https:// edglossary.org/standards-based on December 7, 2020.

Gonser, S. (2020, March 16). *Four reasons teachers are going gradeless.* Accessed at https:// edutopia.org/article/4-reasons-teachers-are-going-gradeless on December 7, 2020.

Gonzalez, J. (2014a, October 23). *Five reasons you should seek your own student feedback.* Accessed at www.cultofpedagogy.com/student-feedback on December 7, 2020.

Gonzalez, J. (2014b, June 7). *The gut-level teacher reflection.* Accessed at https:// cultofpedagogy.com/gut-level-reflection-questions on December 7, 2020.

Gonzalez, J. (2015, December 12). *How and why we should let our students fail.* Accessed at https://cultofpedagogy.com/gift-of-failure on December 7, 2020.

Gonzalez, J. (2018a, November 4). *To learn, students need to do something.* Accessed at www .cultofpedagogy.com/do-something on March 18, 2021.

Gonzalez, J. (2018b, March 18). *Twelve ways to upgrade your classroom design.* Accessed at https://cultofpedagogy.com/upgrade-classroom-design on December 7, 2020.

Grafwallner, P. (2017a, September 5). *Coaching the novice teacher.* Accessed at https://edutopia .org/article/coaching-novice-teacher on December 7, 2020.

Grafwallner, P. (2017b, October 16). *Coaching the veteran teacher.* Accessed at www.edutopia .org/article/coaching-veteran-teacher on March 26, 2021.

Grafwallner, P. (2017c, August 5). *"It's a check-up!"* [Blog post]. Accessed at https://ncte.org /blog/2017/08/its-a-check-up on December 7, 2020.

Grafwallner, P. (2017d, November 2). *Keeping learning real, relevant, and relatable: Reading and writing exercises teachers can use to tap students' interests and experiences in a variety of classes.* Accessed at https://edutopia.org/article/keeping-learning-real-relevant-and-relatable on December 7, 2020.

Grafwallner, P. (2017e, December 19). *What I've learned from special ed teachers.* Accessed at www.edutopia.org/article/what-ive-learned-special-ed-teachers on March 27, 2021.

Grafwallner, P. (2018a). *Lessons learned from the special education classroom: Creating opportunities for all students to listen, learn, and lead.* Lanham, MD: Rowman & Littlefield.

Grafwallner, P. (2018b, August 14). *On being an instructional coach* [Blog post]. Accessed at https://inservice.ascd.org/on-being-an-instructional-coach on December 7, 2020.

Grafwallner, P. (2018c, December 16). *Power lesson: Note-taking stations.* Accessed at https:// cultofpedagogy.com/note-taking-stations on December 7, 2020.

Grafwallner, P. (2020). *Ready to learn: The FRAME model for optimizing student success.* Bloomington, IN: Solution Tree Press.

The Graide Network. (n.d.). *The 7 hallmarks of effective feedback.* Accessed at www.thegraide network.com/7-hallmarks-philosophy on April 12, 2021.

Gray, P. (2016, October 3). *What's behind America's insistence on instilling grit in kids?* Accessed at https://theconversation.com/whats-behind-americas-insistence-on-instilling-grit-in -kids-65314 on December 7, 2020.

Grazer, B. (Producer), & Howard, R. (Director). (1995). *Apollo 13* [Motion picture]. United States: Universal Pictures.

Greene, P. (2018, July 12). *Whatever happened to Common Core?* Accessed at www.forbes.com /sites/petergreene/2018/07/12/what-ever-happened-to-common-core on March 16, 2017.

Gross-Loh, C. (2016, December 16). How praise became a consolation prize. *The Atlantic.* Accessed at https://theatlantic.com/education/archive/2016/12/how-praise-became-a -consolation-prize/510845 on December 7, 2020.

Guskey, T. R. (2011). Five obstacles to grading reform. *Educational Leadership, 69*(3), 16–21.

Hachem, H. (2019, October 4). *Overcrowding in schools: Why is it a huge issue?* Accessed at https://patch.com/michigan/dearborn/overcrowding-schools-why-it-huge-issue on March 26, 2021.

Hattie, J. (2012). *Visible learning for teachers: Maximizing impact on learning.* New York: Routledge.

The Hechinger Report. (2017, December 4). Kids asked to learn in ways that exceed attention spans. *U.S. News & World Report.* Accessed at www.usnews.com/news/national-news /articles/2017-12-04/teachers-often-ask-kids-to-learn-in-ways-that-exceed-adult-sized -attention-spans-study-finds on March 19, 2021.

Hedberg, P. R. (2009). Learning through reflective classroom practice: Applications to educate the reflective manager. *Journal of Management Education, 33*(1), 10–36.

Heflebower, T., Hoegh, J. K., Warrick, P. B., & Flygare, J. (2019). *A teacher's guide to standards-based learning.* Bloomington, IN: Marzano Resources.

Heineke, A. J., & McTighe, J. (2018). Language matters: Giving students the words to learn and understand. *ASCD Express, 13*(23). Accessed at www.ascd.org/ascd-express /vol13/Language-Matters-Giving-Students-the-Words-to-Learn-and-Understand.aspx on December 7, 2020.

Help. (n.d.). In *Dictionary.com.* Accessed at https://dictionary.com/browse/help?s=t on December 7, 2020.

Herrmann, E. (2018, February 14). *Using affixes, roots, and base words to improve English language learners' skills.* Accessed at https://exclusive.multibriefs.com/content/using -affixes-roots-and-base-words-to-improve-english-learners-language-ski/education on March 27, 2018.

Hertz, M. B. (2020, January 6). *Tools for creating digital student portfolios.* Accessed at www .edutopia.org/article/tools-creating-digital-student-portfolios on March 20, 2021.

Higgins, M. (2019, Summer). Getting on the right track: How one school stopped tracking students. *Learning for Justice, 62.* Accessed at www.learningforjustice.org/magazine /summer-2019/getting-on-the-right-track-how-one-school-stopped-tracking-students on April 4, 2021.

Hilppo, J., & Stevens, R. (2020). "Failure is just another try": Re-framing failure in school through the FUSE studio approach. *International Journal of Educational Research, 99*(101494). Accessed at www.sciencedirect.com/science/article/pii/S08830355 18316525 on March 15, 2021.

Homer. (1999). *The odyssey* (R. Fagles, Trans.). New York: Penguin Classics. (Original work published circa 750 BC)

Intercultural Development Research Association. (2018, May). *Failing in-grade retention.* Accessed at www.idra.org/wp-content/uploads/2018/05/eBook-Failing-In-Grade -Retention-IDRA-2018.pdf on March 15, 2021.

International Baccalaureate. (n.d.). *MYP command terms for language and literature.* Accessed at www.d11.org/site/handlers/filedownload.ashx?moduleinstanceid=13274&dataid=23051 &FileName=Command%20Terms%20in%20Language%20and% 20Literature.pdf on December 7, 2020.

International Reading Association. (1996). *Standards for the English language arts.* Newark, DE: Author. Accessed at https://cdn.ncte.org/nctefiles/resources/books/sample/standards doc.pdf on December 7, 2020.

International Society for Technology in Education. (n.d.). *ISTE standards for students.* Accessed at www.iste.org/standards/for-students on April 8, 2021.

Israel, M. (n.d.). Teachers observing teachers: A professional development opportunity for every school. *Education World.* Accessed at www.educationworld.com/a_admin/admin/admin297.shtml on March 26, 2021.

Jarvis, M-A., & Baloyi, O. B. (2020). Scaffolding in reflective journaling: A means to develop higher order thinking skills in undergraduate learners. *International Journal of Africa Nursing Sciences, 12*(100195). Accessed at www.sciencedirect.com/science/article/pii/S2214139119302057 on March 27, 2021.

Jason, Z. (2017, Winter). Bored out of their minds. *Harvard Ed. Magazine.* Accessed at www.gse.harvard.edu/news/ed/17/01/bored-out-their-minds on December 7, 2020.

Jensen, E. (2019). *Poor students, rich teaching: Seven high-impact mindsets for students from poverty* [Rev. ed.]. Bloomington, IN: Solution Tree Press.

Johnson, B. (2013, May 20). *Teaching students to dig deeper* [Blog post]. Accessed at www.edutopia.org/blog/teaching-students-dig-deeper-ben-johnson on December 7, 2020.

Johnson, M. (2018). The struggle is real: How difficult work strengthens student achievement. *ASCD Express, 14*(11). Accessed at www.ascd.org/ascd-express/vol14/num11/the-struggle-is-real-how-difficult-work-strengthens-student-achievement.aspx on December 7, 2020.

Johnson, P. N. (2018, April). *In-grade retention national trends and civil rights concerns.* Accessed at www.idra.org/resource-center/in-grade-retention-national-trends-and-civil-rights-concerns on March 15, 2021.

Joy. (n.d.). In *Merriam-Webster.com.* Accessed at www.merriam-webster.com/dictionary/joy on February 16, 2021.

Jung, L. A., Frey, N., Fisher, D. & Kroener, J. (2019). *Your students; my students; our students: Rethinking equitable and inclusive classrooms.* Alexandria, VA: Association for Supervision and Curriculum Development.

Kalra, A. (2020, September 24). *Teacher collaboration in challenging learning environments.* Accessed at https://oecdedutoday.com/teacher-collaboration-challenging-learning-environments on March 27, 2021.

Kallick, B., & Zmuda, A. (2017). *Students at the center: Personalized learning with habits of mind* [Kindle version]. Alexandria, VA: Association for Supervision and Curriculum Development.

Kamenetz, A. (2016, March 3). Is "grit" doomed to be the new self-esteem? *NPR.* Accessed at https://npr.org/sections/ed/2016/03/03/468870056/is-grit-doomed-to-be-the-new-self-esteem on December 7, 2020.

Kanold, T. D. (2017). *HEART! Fully forming your professional life as a teacher and leader.* Bloomington, IN: Solution Tree Press.

Kaplan, T., & Dance, R. (2018, July 26). Developing a classroom community where students feel safe to talk. *Talking in Math, 13*(22). Accessed at www.ascd.org/ascd-express/vol13/1322-kaplan.aspx on March 18, 2021.

Kaufman, J. (2013). *The first 20 hours: How to learn anything . . . fast.* New York: Penguin.

Kaufman, T. (n.d.). *Building positive relationships with students: What brain science says.* Accessed at www.understood.org/en/school-learning/for-educators/empathy/brain-science-says-4-reasons-to-build-positive-relationships-with-students on March 22, 2021.

Kaufmann, R. (2020). Negative instructor communication behaviours: Exploring associations between instructor misbehaviours and the classroom learning environment. *Learning Environments Research, 23*(1), 185–194.

Khan Academy. (n.d.). *Making inferences from random samples.* Accessed at www .khanacademy.org/math/cc-seventh-grade-math/cc-7th-probability-statistics/cc-7th -population-sampling/e/making-inferences-from-random-samples on March 28, 2021.

Klein, T. (2019, June 13). Why every student needs caring adults in their life. *Greater Good Magazine.* Accessed at https://greatergood.berkeley.edu/article/item/why_every_student _needs_caring_adults_in_their_life on December 7, 2020.

Kipman, S. (2021, March 2). *15 highly successful people who failed on their way to success.* Accessed at www.lifehack.org/articles/productivity/15-highly-successful-people-who -failed-their-way-success.html on March 15, 2021.

King, M. L., Jr. (1963). *I have a dream* [Speech]. Accessed at https://kinginstitute.stanford .edu/king-papers/documents/i-have-dream-address-delivered-march-washington-jobs -and-freedom on March 5, 2021.

Kise, J. A. G. (2021). *Doable differentiation: Twelve strategies to meet the needs of all learners.* Bloomington, IN: Solution Tree Press.

Kohn, A. (2017, May 11). *What's the problem with grades?* [Blog post]. Accessed at https:// blogs.ibo.org/blog/2017/05/11/whats-the-problem-with-grades on December 7, 2020.

Kommers, C. (2019, April 22). *What's the point of standardized testing?* [Blog post]. Accessed at www.psychologytoday.com/us/blog/friendly-interest/201904/whats-the-point -standardized-testing on December 7, 2020.

Kounin, J. S. (1977). *Discipline and group management in classrooms.* Huntington, NY: Krieger.

Lemon, N., & McDonough, S. (2020). *Building and sustaining a teaching career: Strategies for professional experience, wellbeing and mindful practice.* New York: Cambridge University Press.

Love, B. L. (2019a, March 18). Dear White teachers: You can't love your Black students if you don't know them. *Education Week.* Accessed at https://edweek.org/ew/articles/2019/03/20 /dear-white-teachers-you-cant-love-your.html on December 7, 2020.

Love, B. L. (2019b, February 12). "Grit is in our DNA": Why teaching grit is inherently anti-Black. *Education Week.* Accessed at https://edweek.org/ew/articles/2019/02/13/grit-is-in -our-dna-why-teaching.html on December 7, 2020.

Loveless, B. (n.d.). *Scaffolding in education.* Accessed at www.educationcorner.com/scaffolding -education-guide.html on March 27, 2021.

Martin, A. J. (2012). Fear of failure in learning. In N. M. Seel (Ed.), *Encyclopedia of the sciences of learning.* Boston: Springer.

Marzano, R. J. (2007). *The art and science of teaching: A comprehensive framework for effective instruction.* Alexandria, VA: Association for Supervision and Curriculum Development.

Marzano, R. J. (2017). *The new art and science of teaching.* Bloomington, IN: Solution Tree Press.

McCarthy, J. (2015, May 13). *Teachers are in control: Myth-busting DI, Part 4*. Accessed at www.edutopia.org/blog/differentiated-instruction-myth-teachers-control-john-mccarthy on March 28, 2021.

McGee, K. (2017, November 28). *What really happened at the school where every graduate got into college*. Accessed at https://npr.org/sections/ed/2017/11/28/564054556/what-really -happened-at-the-school-where-every-senior-got-into-college on December 7, 2020.

Meador, D. (2018, April 9). *Essential questions concerning grade retention*. Accessed at www.thoughtco.com/essential-questions-concerning-grade-retention-3194685 on March 15, 2021.

Meredith, T. (2015, May 15). *Starting student feedback loops*. Accessed at www.edutopia .org/blog/starting-student-feedback-loops-taylor-meredith on March 22, 2021.

Midwest Comprehensive Center. (2018, May). *Student goal setting: An evidence-based practice*. Accessed at https://files.eric.ed.gov/fulltext/ED589978.pdf on March 17, 2021.

Minero, E. (2018, July 3). *Do no-zero policies help or hurt students?* Accessed at www.edutopia .org/article/do-no-zero-policies-help-or-hurt-students on March 21, 2021.

Miller, S. R. (1998). Shortcut: High school grades as a signal of human capital. *Educational Evaluation and Policy Analysis, 20*(4), 299–311.

Mitchell, C. (2020, December 18). *With name changes, schools transform racial reckoning into real-life civics lesson*. Accessed at www.edweek.org/teaching-learning/with-name-changes -schools-transform-racial-reckoning-into-real-life-civics-lessons/2020/12 on April 21, 2021.

Mofield, E., & Peters, M. P. (2018a, October 26). *5 tips for teaching tenacity and resilience*. Accessed at www.prufrock.com/5-Tips-for-Teaching-Tenacity-and-Resilience.aspx on March 26, 2021.

Mofield, E., & Peters, M. P. (2018b). *Teaching tenacity, resilience, and a drive for excellence: Lessons for social-emotional learning for grades 4–8*. Waco, TX: Prufrock Press.

Moss, C. M., Brookhart, S. M., & Long, B. A. (2011). Knowing your learning target. *Educational Leadership, 68*(6), 66–69. Accessed at www.ascd.org/publications /educational-leadership/mar11/vol68/num06/Knowing-Your-Learning-Target.aspx on April 12, 2021.

Mulvahill, E. (2018, August 31). *10 ways to scaffold learning*. Accessed at www.weareteachers .com/ways-to-scaffold-learning on March 27, 2021.

National Council of Teachers of English. (1996). *Standards for the English language arts*. Newark, DE: International Reading Association. Accessed at https://cdn.ncte.org /nctefiles/resources/books/sample/standardsdoc.pdf on December 7, 2020.

National Governors Association Center for Best Practices & Council of Chief State School Officers. (2010). *Common Core State Standards for English language arts and literacy in history/social studies, science, and technical subjects*. Washington, DC: Authors. Accessed at www.corestandards.org/assets/CCSSI_ELA%20Standards.pdf on December 7, 2020.

Needham, B. L., Crosnoe, R., & Muller, C. (2004). Academic failure in secondary school: The inter-related role of health problems and educational context. *Social Problems, 51*(4), 569–586. Accessed at https://ncbi.nlm.nih.gov/pmc/articles /PMC2846654 on December 7, 2020.

Newman, S. (2015, August 11). *How allowing children to fail helps them succeed: Seven secrets to children's success* [Blog post]. Accessed at https://psychologytoday.com/us /blog/singletons/201508/how-allowing-children-fail-helps-them-succeed on December 7, 2020.

Niguidula, D. (2010). Digital portfolios and curriculum maps: Linking teacher and student work. In H. H. Jacobs (Ed.), *Curriculum 21: Essential education for a changing world* (pp. 153–167). Alexandria, VA: Association for Supervision and Curriculum Development.

Nordengren, C. (2019, July 15). *Goal-setting practices that support a learning culture.* Accessed at https://kappanonline.org/goal-setting-practices-support-learning-culture-nordengren on April 8, 2021.

Nordengren, C. (2020, July 27). *How to use goal setting to carve a new path for learning growth this fall.* Accessed at www.nwea.org/blog/2020/how-to-use-goal-setting-to-carve-a-new -path-for-student-growth-this-fall on March 17, 2021.

Nucaro, A. (2017, October 2). *Positive words go a long way.* Accessed at www.edutopia.org /article/positive-words-go-long-way on March 20, 2021.

O'Brien, T. (2009). *The things they carried.* New York: Mariner Books.

O'Connor, K. (n.d.). Making the grades: Ensure accuracy, meaning, consistency, and support for learning. *ASCD Express.* Accessed at www.ascd.org/ascd-express/vol5/503-newvoices .aspx on December 7, 2020.

O'Connor, K. (2018). *How to grade for learning: Linking grades to standards* (4th ed.). Thousand Oaks, CA: Corwin Press.

O'Grady, K. (2019, December 13). *Stop and think: Teaching students to reflect.* Accessed at www.responsiveclassroom.org/stop-and-think-teaching-students-to-reflect on March 25, 2021.

Ofoghi, N., Sadeghi, A., & Babaei, M. (2016). Impact of class atmosphere on the quality of learning (QoL). *Psychology, 7*(13), 1645–1657.

Onuscheck, M., Spiller, J. (Eds.), & Argentar, D. M., Gillies, K. A. N., Rubenstein, M. M., & Wise, B. R. (2020). *Reading and writing strategies for the secondary English classroom in a PLC at Work.* Bloomington, IN: Solution Tree Press.

Onuscheck, M., Spiller, J. (Eds.), & Glass, K. T. (2020). *Reading and writing instruction for fourth- and fifth-grade classrooms in a PLC at Work.* Bloomington, IN: Solution Tree Press.

Oregon State University. (n.d.). *Make better to-do lists.* Accessed at https://success.oregonstate .edu/learning/better-lists on March 20, 2021.

Ostrowski, C. (2016, December 7). *Is it homework or busy work?* Accessed at www.teachbetter .com/blog/homework-or-busy-work on March 26, 2021.

Pandolpho, B. (2018, May 4). *Putting students in charge of their learning.* Accessed at https:// edutopia.org/article/putting-students-charge-their-learning on December 7, 2020.

Parker, F., Novak, J., & Bartell, T. (2017). To engage students, give them meaningful choices in the classroom. *Phi Delta Kappan, 99*(2), 37–41. Accessed at https://kappanonline.org /engage-students-give-meaningful-choices-classroom on March 28, 2021.

Peixoto, F., Monteiro, V., Mata, L., Sanches, C., Pipa, J., & Almeida, L. S. (2016). "To be or not to be retained . . . That's the question!" Retention, self-esteem, self-concept, achievement goals, and grades. *Frontiers in Psychology, 7*(1550). Accessed at https://doi .org/10.3389/fpsyg.2016.01550 on December 21, 2020.

Peterson, A. (2020, March 23). *Literacy is more than just reading and writing* [Blog post]. Accessed at https://ncte.org/blog/2020/03/literacy-just-reading-writing on March 20, 2021.

Pierson, R. (2013, May). *Rita Pierson: Every kid needs a champion* [Video file]. Accessed at www.ted.com/talks/rita_pierson_every_kid_needs_a_champion?referrer=playlist-the _official_ted_talk_guide_pl on December 7, 2020.

Pietsch, B. (2021, January 7). San Francisco scraps 44 school names, citing reckoning with racism. *The New York Times.* Accessed at www.nytimes.com/2021/01/27/us/san-francisco -schools-lincoln-feinstein.html on April 4, 2021.

Piros, G. (2019, March 27). *Sparking change in teaching practices.* Accessed at https://edutopia .org/article/sparking-change-teaching-practices on December 7, 2020.

Poetry slam. (n.d.). In *Wikipedia.* Accessed at https://en.wikipedia.org/wiki/Poetry_slam on March 23, 2021.

Poorvu Center for Teaching and Learning. (2021, Spring). *Transfer of knowledge to new contexts.* Accessed at https://poorvucenter.yale.edu/TransferKnowledge on March 20, 2021.

Potter, H. (2019, January 29). *Integrating classrooms and reducing academic tracking.* Accessed at https://tcf.org/content/report/integrating-classrooms-reducing-academic-tracking -strategies-school-leaders-educators on April 4, 2021.

Pruitt, D. B. (2000). *Your adolescent: Emotional, behavioral, and cognitive development from early adolescence through the teen years.* New York: HarperCollins.

Rashid-Doubell, F., O'Farrell, P. A., & Fredericks, S. (2018). The use of exemplars and student discussion to improve performance in constructed-response assessments. *International Journal of Medical Education, 9,* 226–228. Accessed at www.ncbi.nlm.nih .gov/pmc/articles/PMC6129159 on March 20, 2021.

Razzetti, G. (2018, September 18). *How to overcome the fear of change* [Blog post]. Accessed at https://psychologytoday.com/us/blog/the-adaptive-mind/201809/how-overcome-the-fear -change on December 7, 2020.

Reeve, C. (n.d.). *Observing others' classrooms: What to look for from another teacher.* Accessed at https://autismclassroomresources.com/observing-others-classrooms on March 26, 2021.

Reeves, D. (2004). The case against the zero. *Phi Delta Kappan, 86*(4), 324–325. Accessed at https://researchgate.net/publication/285846142_The_Case_against_the_Zero on December 7, 2020.

Reeves, D. (2011). From differentiated instruction to differentiated assessment. *ASCD Express, 6*(20). Accessed at www.ascd.org/ascd-express/vol6/620-reeves.aspx on December 7, 2020.

Reeves, D., Jung, L. A., & O'Connor, K. (2017, May). What's worth fighting against in grading? *Educational Leadership.* Accessed at www.creativeleadership.net/s/EducationalLeadership -LiftingSchoolLeaders-WhatsWorthFightingAgainstinGrading.pdf on March 14, 2021.

Renwick, M. (2017). Chapter 1: Defining digital portfolios. In *Digital portfolios in the classroom: Showcasing and assessing student work*. Alexandria, VA: Association for Supervision and Curriculum Development. Accessed at www.ascd.org/publications/books/117005/chapters /Defining-Digital-Portfolios.aspx on December 7, 2020.

Responsive Classroom. (2012, April 10). *Want positive behavior? Use positive language.* Accessed at www.responsiveclassroom.org/want-positive-behavior-use-positive-language on December 7, 2020.

Rimm-Kaufman, S., & Sandilos, L. (2010). *Improving students' relationships with teachers to provide essential supports for learning.* Accessed at www.apa.org/education/k12 /relationships on March 31, 2021.

Robb, L. (2018, April 19). *Independent reading and choice* [Blog post]. Accessed at https:// edublog.scholastic.com/post/independent-reading-and-choice on December 7, 2020.

Rodriguez, J. (2018, March 1). *Why it's important for kids to see themselves in books.* Accessed at www.scholastic.com/parents/books-and-reading/raise-a-reader-blog/why-its-important -kids-to-see-themselves-books.html on April 4, 2021.

Rogers, K. (2019, July 7). *How digital portfolios empower student ownership of learning.* Accessed at www.gettingsmart.com/2019/07/how-digital-portfolios-empower-student -ownership-of-learning on March 17, 2021.

Rollins, S. P. (2015, November 15). *The precious first few minutes of class.* Accessed at www. teachthought.com/pedagogy/the-precious-first-few-minutes-of-class on March 20, 2021.

Rosenbaum, J. E., DeLuca, S., Miller, S. R., & Roy, K. (1999). Pathways into work: Short- and long-term effects of personal and institutional ties. *Sociology of Education, 72*(3), 179–196.

Rosser, J. (2016, June 13). *Teacher learns the value of sometimes scary communication with parents.* Accessed at www.ednc.org/teacher-learns-value-sometimes-scary-communication -parents on April 13, 2021.

Rubel, D. (2018, December). *2017–18 New York state Regents Exams results policy alert.* Accessed at www.davidrubelconsultant.com/wp-content/uploads/2019/01/2017-18 -Algebra-and-ELA-Regents-exam-policy-alert-1-1.pdf on March 15, 2021.

Ruff, J. (2018, October 2). *Collaboration, critique, and classroom culture* [Blog post]. Accessed at http://blogs.edweek.org/edweek/learning_deeply/2018/10/collaboration_critique_and _classroom_culture.html on December 7, 2020.

Rutgers Center for Effective School Practices. (2018, August 21). *12 teaching management techniques learned from teaching veterans.* Accessed at https://cesp.rutgers.edu/blog/12 -classroom-management-techniques-learned-teaching-veterans on March 26, 2021.

Sachar, C. O. (2016, October 21). *6 tips for supercharging your learning stations.* Accessed at www.edutopia.org/article/creating-meaningful-learning-stations-cassandra-sachar on March 25, 2021.

Sackstein, S. (2015). *Hacking assessment: 10 ways to go gradeless in a traditional grades school.* Cleveland, OH: Times 10 Publications.

Salazar, R. (2019, April 4). *Why I still give my students zeroes.* Accessed at www.nbpts.org /why-i-still-give-my-students-zeros on March 16, 2021.

Sawchuk, S. (2017a, November 13). *Even when states revise standards, the core of the Common Core remains*. Accessed at www.edweek.org/teaching-learning/even-when-states-revise -standards-the-core-of-the-common-core-remains/2017/11 on April 8, 2021.

Sawchuk, S. (2017b, September 26). *Learning how to learn could be a student's most valuable skill*. Accessed at www.edweek.org/teaching-learning/learning-how-to-learn-could-be-a -students-most-valuable-skill/2017/09 on March 3, 2021.

Schaaf, R. L. (n.d.). *Overcoming a "that's the way we've always done it" mindset in schools*. Accessed at https://thelearningcounsel.com/article/overcoming-%E2%80%9C%E2 %80%99s-way-we-have-always-done-it%E2%80%9D-mindset-schools on March 22, 2021.

Schawbel, D. (2013, May 30). *Josh Kaufman: It takes 20 hours not 10,000 to learn a skill*. Accessed at www.forbes.com/sites/danschawbel/2013/05/30/josh-kaufman-it-takes -20-hours-not-10000-hours-to-learn-a-skill on April 13, 2021.

Schippers, M. C., Morisano, D., Locke, E. A., Scheepers, W. A., Latham, G. P., & de Jong, E. M. (2020). Writing about personal goals and plans regardless of goal type boosts academic performance. *Contemporary Education Psychology*, *60*(101823). Accessed at www.sciencedirect.com/science/article/pii/S0361476X1930428X on March 27, 2021.

Serra, R. (2015, March 11). *What is reflective teaching and why is it important?* [Blog post]. Accessed at https://richmondshare.com.br/what-is-reflective-teaching-and-why-is-it -important on December 7, 2020.

Shahar, G. (2015). *Erosion: The psychopathology of self-criticism*. New York: Oxford University Press.

Shakespeare, W. (2004). *Romeo and Juliet*. New York: Simon & Schuster. (Original work published 1597)

Shanahan, T. (2017, March 15). *Disciplinary literacy: The basics* [Blog post]. Accessed at https:// shanahanonliteracy.com/blog/disciplinary-literacy-the-basics#sthash.h02N6esJ.dpbs on December 7, 2020.

Sheninger, E. (2019, June 3). *The problem with zeros* [Blog post]. Accessed at http://esheninger .blogspot.com/2019/06/the-problem-with-zeros.html on March 16, 2021.

Slavin, R. E., Karweit, N. L., & Wasik, B. A. (1992/1993). Preventing early school failure: What works? *Educational Leadership*, *50*(4), 10–18. Accessed at www.ascd.org /publications/educational-leadership/dec92/vol50/num04/Preventing-Early-School -Failure@-What-Works%C2%A2.aspx on December 7, 2020.

Southern Poverty Law Center. (n.d.). *Learning for justice*. Accessed at www.splcenter.org /learning-for-justice on March 19, 2021.

Spady, W. G. (2002). Re-forming the reforms: How total leaders face education's biggest challenge. *Principal Leadership*, 57–62. Accessed at https://education.sa.gov.au/sites /default/files/how_total_leaders_face_educations_biggest_challenge.pdf?v=1456968489 on December 21, 2020.

Sparks, S. D. (2019, March 12). Why teacher-student relationships matter. *Education Week*. Accessed at https://edweek.org/ew/articles/2019/03/13/why-teacher-student-relationships -matter.html on December 7, 2020.

Staake, J. (2019, January 22). *Why every classroom needs jigsaw puzzles, plus our top picks* [Blog post]. Accessed at https://weareteachers.com/jigsaw-puzzles on December 7, 2020.

Stanley, B. L. (2018, June 12). *Teachers need time to reflect on their teaching* [Blog post]. Accessed at https://medium.com/whats-the-plus/teachers-need-time-to-reflect-on-their-teaching-190f72967f62 on December 7, 2020.

Stipek, D., & Lombardo, M. (2014, May 20). *Holding kids back doesn't help them* [Blog post]. Accessed at www.edweek.org/ew/articles/2014/05/21/32stipek.h33.html on December 7, 2020.

Stoltzfus, K. (2019). Abolitionist teaching in action: Q and A with Bettina Love. *Education Week, 61*(12). Accessed at www.ascd.org/publications/newsletters/education-update/dec19/vol61/num12/Abolitionist-Teaching-in-Action@-Q$A-with-Bettina-L.-Love.aspx on March 19, 2021.

Strauss, V. (2017, September 15). Of course algebra is important. It's also a huge problem. *The Washington Post.* Accessed at https://washingtonpost.com/news/answer-sheet/wp/2017/09/15/of-course-algebra-is-important-its-also-a-huge-problem/?utm_term=.8bc8a3cb5286 on December 7, 2020.

Stuart, D., Jr. (2015, October 17). *The 300-word guide to pop-up debate* [Blog post]. Accessed at https://davestuartjr.com/pop-up-debate on December 7, 2020.

Support. (n.d.). In *Merriam-Webster.com.* Accessed at https://www.merriam-webster.com/dictionary/support on June 21, 2021.

Syrie, M. (2016, February 16). *The uncomfortable truth about grading practices.* Accessed at www.edutopia.org/discussion/uncomfortable-truth-about-grading-practices on March 14, 2020.

Tanner, R. (2020). *Five whys: Act like a child and improve problem solving.* Accessed at https://managementisajourney.com/five-whys-act-like-a-child-and-improve-problem-solving on April 19, 2021.

Taylor, J. (2009, September 3). *Parenting: Don't praise your children!* [Blog post]. Accessed at https://psychologytoday.com/us/blog/the-power-prime/200909/parenting-dont-praise-your-children on December 7, 2020.

Taylor, J. (2011, November 17). *Prime family alert! Fear of failure is a childhood epidemic* [Blog post]. Accessed at www.huffpost.com/entry/parenting-alert-fear-of-f_b_709099 on December 7, 2020.

TeacherLists. (2021, February 11). *15 ways to get kids moving in the classroom* [Blog post]. Accessed at www.teacherlists.com/blog/15-ways-to-get-kids-moving-in-the-classroom on March 27, 2021.

TeachersFirst. (n.d.). *Involving students in creating rubrics.* Accessed at www.teachersfirst.com/lessons/rubrics/involving-students.cfm on March 20, 2021.

Thompson, J. G. (2019, February 19). *Develop your sense of "with-it-ness"* [Blog post]. Accessed at https://sharemylesson.com/blog/develop-your-sense-it-ness%E2%80%99 on December 7, 2020.

Thomsen, B. S., & Ackermann, E. (2015, April 3). *Whole child development is undervalued.* Accessed at www.edutopia.org/blog/changemakers-whole-child-development-undervalued-bo-stjerne-thomsen-edith-ackermann on March 21, 2021.

Thought Leaders. (2018, March 12). *Equity in education: What it is and why it matters.* Accessed at www.thinkingmaps.com/equity-education-matters on March 22, 2021.

Townsley, M., & Wear, N. L. (2020). *Making grades matter: Standards-based grading in a secondary PLC at Work.* Bloomington, IN: Solution Tree Press.

Tucker, C. (2016, August 30). *Are fifty minute periods killing teacher creativity?* [Blog post]. Accessed at https://catlintucker.com/2016/08/50-minute-periods-are-killing-teacher -creativity on December 7, 2020.

U.S. Department of Justice Civil Rights Division and U.S. Department of Education Office for Civil Rights. (n.d.). *Information for limited English proficient (LEP) parents and guardians and for schools and school districts that communicate with them.* Accessed at www2.ed.gov/about/offices/list/ocr/docs/dcl-factsheet-lep-parents-201501.pdf on March 22, 2021.

Victoria State Education Department. (n.d.). *Peer observation.* Accessed at www.education.vic .gov.au/school/teachers/teachingresources/practice/improve/Pages/peerobservation.aspx on June 21, 2021.

Vincent, A. K. (2018). Collaborating with teachers to create peer observations as a means of effective professional development. Doctoral dissertation, University of South Carolina, Columbia. Accessed at https://scholarcommons.sc.edu/etd/4758 on March 26, 2018.

Wabisabi Learning. (n.d.). *7 ways to achieve high levels of classroom productivity.* Accessed at https://wabisabilearning.com/blogs/future-fluencies/7-ways-to-achieve-high-levels-of -classroom-productivity on March 23, 2021.

Ward, R. (2017, March 17). *The fallacy of failure* [Blog post]. Accessed at https://inservice .ascd.org/the-fallacy-of-failure on December 7, 2020.

Westerberg, T. R. (2016). *Charting a course to standards-based grading: What to stop, what to start, and why it matters.* Alexandria, VA: Association for Supervision and Curriculum Development.

Willis, J. (2016, October 25). *Conquering the multitasking brain drain.* Accessed at www .edutopia.org/blog/conquering-the-multitasking-brain-drain-judy-willis on March 22, 2021.

Wiesel, E. (2006). *Night* (M. Wiesel, Trans.). New York: Hill and Wang.

Wiggins, G. (2015). *How student work models make rubrics more effective.* Accessed at www .teachthought.com/pedagogy/how-to-use-a-rubric-without-stifling-creativity on March 20, 2021.

Wiggins, G., & McTighe, J. (2005). *Understanding by design* (Expanded 2nd ed.). Alexandria, VA: Association for Supervision and Curriculum Development.

Williams, J., & Siracusa, F. (2015, October 16). *Collaborative learning spaces: Classrooms that connect to the world* [Blog post]. Accessed at https://edutopia.org/blog/collaborative -learning-spaces-connect-to-world-jennifer-williams-fran-siracusa on December 7, 2020.

Wisconsin Interscholastic Athletic Association. (2020). *Senior high handbook 2019–20.* Accessed at www.wiaawi.org/Portals/0/PDF/Publications/2019-20handbook.pdf on March 26, 2021.

Wisconsin Policy Forum. (2020, January). *State's college readiness slips.* Accessed at https:// wispolicyforum.org/research/states-college-readiness-slips on March 20, 2021.

Wolk, S. (2008). Joy in school. *Educational Leadership*, 66(1), 8–15. Accessed at www
.ascd.org/publications/educational-leadership/sept08/vol66/num01/Joy-in-School.aspx
on December 7, 2020.

Wolpert-Gawron, H. (2017, June 29). *Scaffolding grit [Blog post]*. Accessed at www.edutopia
.org/blog/scaffolding-grit-heather-wolpert-gawron on March 19, 2021.

Wolpert-Gawron, H. (2018, November 18). *Why choice matters to student learning*. Accessed
at www.kqed.org/mindshift/52424/why-choice-matters-to-student-learning on March
28, 2021.

Wormeli, R. (2020, April). *Descriptive feedback tips for teachers and parents, part 1*. Accessed
https://6192b46b-a555-41bd-98e4-f89abb0dfd7b.filesusr.com/ugd/10b7c9_410a8029
aa6a4d4a94f2d8db8b580d12.pdf on March 21, 2021.

Zakrzewski, V. (2013, December 5). How to help kids overcome fear of failure. *Greater Good
Magazine*. Accessed at https://greatergood.berkeley.edu/article/item/how_to_help_kids
_overcome_fear_of_failure on December 7, 2020.

Index

A

abolitionist teaching, 7, 38, 45–48, 94
academic transformation and personal success feedback form, 96–100, 103–104, 108–109
acceleration, 4
achievement, 4
   iterative process of, 12–13
   student-teacher relationships and, 203–204
   trying as, 11–12
action verbs, 57–58
after-school tutoring, 5–6
agency, 31, 38
Alberino, C., 190
algebra, 13–14
Almeida, L. S., 15
Amaro, M., 4
American Academy of Child and Adolescent Psychiatry, 93
American Civil Liberties Union of Wisconsin, 114
Anderson, J., 40, 208
Anderson, M., 58, 130
announcements, 172
anxiety, 93
Apollo 13 movie, 182–183
apps, 92, 114
Armida, G., 24
art, posting, 130–131
artifacts, 194
assessment, 29–34
   check-ups, 103–104, 129–133
   deficit language in, 84–86
   differentiated, 116–117
   grading and, 21–36
   language about, 103
   portfolios for, 32–34
   self-, 54, 62–63
   success criteria and, 54
   summative, 53
   supportive check-ups in, 129–133
Association for Supervision and Curriculum Development, 47–48, 91
assumptions, 47
attendance taking, 172

authenticity, 95, 208
   of learning progressions and success criteria, 65
autonomy, 38

B

Babaei, M., 111
Bain, P., 54
Baloyi, O. B., 128
before-and-after form for student self-reflection, 156, 157–158
Beggs, L., 158–159
Benn, G., 202
biases, 206–207
Blackburn, B. R., 1–2
block schedules, 170–171, 183–184
Bloom's Taxonomy, 57–58
boredom, 171
Boser, U., 168
brainstorming, 168–169
Brendtro, L. K., 205–206
Brokenleg, M., 205–206
Brookfield, S. D., 149
Brookhart, S. M., 30, 33, 55
Buncee, 114
Burns, E., 30
busy homework, 181
buzz words, 151

C

Callaghan, K., 148
Canonica, P., 39
Catapano, J., 191
celebrating, 179–180
   failure, 39
   grit, 45
Chang, B., 145–146
change, coping with, 93–94
character-trait charts, 133–136
Charting a Course to Standards-Based Grading (Westerberg), 24
check-ups, 103–104, 129–133
Cheney, C., 140–141
Cherry, M. A., 208
choice, 56
   character-trait charts and, 133–136
   in reading, 136–140
   tools to support, 133–140

Chouinard, M., 183–184
cognitive processing styles, 116–117, 170–171
Cohen, R. K., 155
Colburn, L., 158–159
Coley, R. J., 27–28
collaboration, 177, 187–200
   collegial observation and, 190–192
   context and, 188–189
   guiding questions and comments for, 192–195
   opportunities for, 194–197
   strategies for, 189
collegial observation, 190–192
Common Core State Standards (CCSS), 28–29, 57
Common Sense Education, 113
concept maps, 129, 147, 174, 180
confidence, 42
   grit and, 44
connective classroom, 7, 187–200
   collegial observation and, 190–192
   definition of, 188
   guiding questions and comments for, 192–195
   a look inside, 197–199
   not-yet approach in, 188–189
   opportunities for collaboration in, 194–197
   reflection on, 200
constructive classroom, 7, 167–186
   definition of, 167
   a look inside, 183–185
   not-yet approach in, 167–170
   process-driven improvement in, 178–183
   reflection on, 185
   space use in, 174–178
   time use in, 170–174
constructive focus, 168–169
constructive-focus chart, 169, 186
content-focused design, 26–27, 29
core proficiency skills, 66–67
Costa, A. L., 154–155
Council of Chief State School Officers (CCSSO), 28
COVID-19 pandemic, 204

creativity, 111–123
Crescendo Education Group, 104
critical reflection, 149
critical thinking, 128
critical-input experiences, 145–146
Csikszentmihalyi, M., 118
Cult of Pedagogy, 37–38
culture, 2, 72
    change as part of, 93–94
    choice in classroom, 130–131
    core traits of not-yet, 7
    flexibility in, 45
    fostering grit with, 45
    language use and, 81–90
    negative classroom, 111–112
    not-yet, 5
    productive, 111–123
curiosity, 41, 191
curiosity creators, 171
curriculum
    inclusive, 206–208
    standards-based, 31
Curwin, R., 182

D

Dance, R., 39
Darling-Hammond, L., 127
data, 196
    personalizing learning intentions
        and success criteria with,
        69–72
Davis, L., 29, 187
Davis, V., 43
deficit model, 83–86, 87
desirable difficulty, 1–2
Deslauriers, L., 148
developmental appropriateness, 55
Devil, E., 114–115
differentiated learning approaches,
    94, 115–116
    self-differentiation in, 132
    time use and, 170–171
Digital Civics Toolkit, 113
digital student portfolios, 32–33,
    155–156
dilemma of the day, 182–183
Dimmer, K., 162–163
disciplinary instruction
    deficit language in, 83–86
    front-loading concept-specific
        vocabulary in, 127–128
discussions, student-centered, 171
diversity issues
    abolitionist teaching and, 45–48
    curriculum, 206–208
    inclusivity and, 206–207
    language barriers, 104
    sharing personal passions, 114
Doable Differentiation (Kise),
    116–117
dropping out, 3, 171
    failure's role in, 13–14
    student-teacher relationships and,
        203–204

Duckworth, A., 43–44
DuFour, R., 187
Dweck, C. S., 39, 40
Dyson, J., 18

E

Eaker, R., 187
Education Hub, 4
empathy, 201–212
empowerment, 2
    assessment and, 30
    language for, 83
    from setbacks, 13
encouragement, 173
engagement, 7, 148
    choice and, 131–133
    language encouraging, 85
    learning intentions and, 54–55
    lesson planning and, 194
    vigorous learning intentions
        and, 52
equality, 104–105
equity, 104–105, 206. *See also*
        inclusive classroom
eudaimonic joy, 117–118
Eva, A. L., 38
Evans, B. E., 115
exemplars, 63, 65
expectations, 4
    of failure, 13–17
    success criteria and, 63
experts, 44
extracurricular activities, 189

F

failure, 11–20
    as an end and beginning, 17–19
    avoidance of, 17
    celebrating, 39
    definitions of, 11
    effects of on student psyches, 7,
        13–17
    encouraging, 114–115
    fear of, 11, 17
    to learn, 2
    learning through, 18–19
    long-term effects of, 13–17
    normalization of, 18–19
    passing students to avoid, 5–6,
        37–38
    redos, retakes, and, 5–6
    reflecting on, 20
    trying and, 11–12
    world's view of, 4
failure mindset, 14–17
false-growth mindset, 40
families and communities, 44
    academic transformation and
        personal success feedback
        form for, 96–100
    check-ups with, 103–104
    communicating with, 91–92
    in feedback loops, 96
    language barriers and, 104

fear
    of failure, 11, 17, 18
    growth mindset and, 39
Fearless Culture, 93
feedback
    for academic transformation,
        95–100
    in assessment, 33
    best practices for, 100–102
    collegial observation and,
        190–192
    confidence and, 44
    success criteria and, 63
    useful language in, 82
feedback loops, 95–96, 100
Feldman, D. L., 3
Feldman, J., 104
fight response, 205–206
The First 20 Hours (Kaufman),
    87–88
Fisher, D., 51, 128, 203
Fisher, J. F, 204
Fisher, M., 53
five whys, 147–148, 180
fixed mindset, 39, 41
flexibility, 94
    in seating, 130
flexible classroom, 7, 145–166
    definition of, 146
    a look inside, 162–163
    not-yet approach in, 146–148
    reflection on, 164
    student feedback on teaching in,
        158–161
    student reflection in, 154–158
    teacher self-reflection and,
        148–154
flight response, 205–206
Flipgrid, 114
flow, 118
focus, 41, 43, 173
    constructive, 168–169, 186
follow response, 205–206
follow-up, 100
Foltos, L., 190
fool response, 205–206
FRAME model, 172–173
Frangiosa, D., 30
Freibrun, M., 57
Frey, N., 51, 128, 203
frustration, 87–88, 115
Fulleylove, R., 114–115
furniture, 176–177, 184

G

games, 121–122
Garcia, H., 63
Gehr, L., 130
Gershenson, S., 3, 126
Glass, K. T., 206
goals
    clarity in, 51, 66
    gradeless assessment and student,
        30–32

teachers', 30–31
uncertainty and, 93–94
Goertz. M. E., 27–28
Gonzalez, J., 18, 37–38, 149–151
grading, 3–6, 7, 21–36
abolishing, 29–34
equity and equality in, 104–105
explaining, 104
extracurricular activities and, 189
failure and, 13–17
as measure of learning, 24
motivation and, 25–26
as necessary evil, 37–38
points and zeroes in, 23–26
reflection on, 36
standards-based, 25, 26–29
supportive classroom, 126
teacher training in, 21–23
transformative, 102–105
Grafwallner, P., 54, 55–56, 172–173,
191, 209–211
Graide Network, 96
graphic organizers, 128–129
Gray, P., 44
Greater Good Science Center, 38
Greene, P., 28
grit, 7, 38, 42–45, 94, 113
modeling, 202–203
grit scale, 43
Grit: The Power of Passion and
Perseverance (Duckworth), 43
group reflection, 151–153
growth mindset, 7, 38, 39–42, 54,
94, 113
collegial observation and, 190
false-, 40
grading and, 27–29
habits and strategies for, 40–41
modeling, 202–203
guiding questions, 192–195, 197
Guskey, T. R., 30
gut talk, 149–151

H

Hacking Assessment (Stackstein), 30
Hair Love (Cherry & Harrison), 208
Harrison, V., 208
HEART? Fully Forming Your
Professional Life as a Teacher
and Leader (Kanold), 112
Hedberg, P. R., 145
hedonic joy, 117
Heflebower, T., 29
Heineke, A. E., 82
help vs. support, 125, 179
helplessness, 38
Herrmann, E., 128
Hertz, M. B., 32
heuristics, 171
Higgins, M., 207–208
home lives of students, 202–203,
205–206
abolitionist teaching and, 45–48
after-school tutoring and, 5–6

getting to know students and,
44–45
grading and, 22
grit and, 45–46
stick-withitness and, 180
home thinking, 183–184
Homer, 117
homework, 181, 183–184
hopelessness, 3, 5–6, 38
humor, 159–160

I

I can statements, 57
inclusive classroom, 7, 201–212
curricula in, 206–208
definition of, 202–203
a look inside, 209–211
not-yet approach in, 202–203
reflection on, 212
student-teacher relationships in,
203–206
individualized inquiry, 132
intentional language, 55
interdisciplinary courses, 173–174,
189
International Center for Leadership
in Education, 26
International Society for Technology
in Education (ISTE), 33–34
intervention strategies, 196

J

Jarvis, M-A., 128
Jensen, E., 43, 45, 117, 204–205
Johnson, B., 179
Johnson, M., 25
joy, 111–123
types of, 117–118
Jung, L. A., 4, 203

K

Kallick, B., 154–155
Kalra, A., 193
Kamenetz, A., 43
Kanold, T. D., 112
Kaplan, T., 39
Karweit, N. L., 14–15
Kauffman, R., 111–112
Kaufman, J., 87–88, 92–93
Kaufman, T, 95
Kestin, G., 148
Khan Academy, 113
Kipman, S., 18
Kise, J., 116–117
Klein, T., 204
Knight, T., 73–74
Kohn, A., 34–35
Kommers, C., 69–70
Kroener, J., 203

L

language, 81–90
barriers in, 104

buzz words, 151
common definition of success
and, 101
concise, student-friendly, 56–58
deficit, in disciplinary instruction,
83–86, 87
focused, 82
grading and, 103
intentional, in learning intentions, 55
in learning intentions, 56–58
not-yet, 86–88
practical, 86
reflection on, 90
right, almost right, never right,
82–83, 84
student feedback on teaching
and, 159
in success criteria, 60
for supportive classroom culture,
131
used in support/praise, 40, 42
useful, 82
learning
appropriate difficulty and, 25–26
choice in approaches to, 131–133
desire to share, 38
differentiated approaches for, 94,
115–116
facilitating vs. owning, 130
grading as a measure of, 24–26
joy and creativity in, 111–123
to learn, 31
love of, encouraging, 118
personalization of, 204–205
reflecting on, 32
showing, 69
standards-based, 35
students' desire for, 37–38
workshops, 34
learning intentions, 51–78
applying, 65–69
character-trait charts and,
133–136
clarity in, 56
crafting, 54–65
data in personalizing, 69–72
definition of, 51
language in, 56–58
a look inside, 73–74
planning, 52
reflection on, 75
student access to, 65
template for, 57, 58, 76
vigorous, 52
learning outcomes, 1
learning processes, 168
learning progressions, 52, 65
learning stations, 174
learning styles, 56, 94, 98, 116–117
Lemon, N., 147
lessons, building, 193–194
libraries, 177
Link, R., 209

literacy skills, 66–69
Lombardo, M., 15
Long, B. A., 55
lovable loser stereotype, 17–18
Love, B. L., 46, 47–48
Loveless, B., 126–127
Lovell, J., 182–183
Lynn, A., 121–122

M

magnet summaries, 174, 175
Many, T. W., 187
Marzano, R. J., 145
mascots, 206–207
MasterClass, 115
mastery, 87–88
Mata, L., 15
Mattos, M., 187
McCarty, L. S., 148
McDonough, S., 147
McTighe, J., 26–27, 82
Meador, D., 15
mental muscles, 180–183
Meredith, T., 95–96
metacognition, 41, 54
    flexible classrooms and, 148
    self-questioning and, 170
    student reflection and, 154–158
The Metacognitive Student
        (Cohen, et al), 155
Midwest Comprehensive Center, 31
Miller, K., 148
Milwaukee's Finest Scholarship
        Foundation, 114
mind maps, 129
mindset
    content-focused, 29
    of control, 130
    failure, 14–17
    fixed, 39, 41
    growth, 7, 27–29, 39–42
    not-yet, 38, 148
    prototyping, 115
    reflection on, 49
    relational, 204–205
*Mindset: The New Psychology of
        Success* (Dweck), 39
Minero, E., 22
mistakes, encouraging, 114–115
modeling, 2, 173, 202–203
    being human, 160
    failure, 18–19
    grit, 45
    mistakes, 182
    success criteria, 62–63
Mofield, E., 179, 180
Monteiro, V., 15
Moss, C. M., 55
motivation, 31, 130
    autonomy and, 38
    choice and, 131–133
    grading and, 25–26
    learning intentions and, 54–55

vigorous learning intentions
        and, 52
music, 131

N

Nagel, A., 88–89
National Council of Teachers of
        English (NCTE), 33–34
National Governors Association
        (NGA)Center for Best
        Practices, 28
negative classroom culture, 111–112
neuroplasticity, 180
Newman, S., 18
Night (Wiesel), 15–16
Niguidula, D., 32–33
Nordengren, C., 31–32
note-taking templates, 174
not-yet approach, 6, 7–8
    concepts supporting, 37–49
    to grading, 23–36
    grit and, 42–45
    growth mindset in, 39–42
    growth over time in, 34
    initiating, 53–54
    standards in, 27–29
Nucaro, A., 83

O

O'Brien, T., 118–119
observation, collegial, 190–192
O'Connor, K., 4, 22
The Odyssey (Homer), 117
off-task behavior, 43
Ofoghi, N., 111
Online Learning Consortium, 63
online resources, 113–114
Onuscheck, M., 206
open door policy, 160
Ostrowski, C., 181
outputs, 27–29
ownership, 130

P

Padlet, 114
Pandolpho, B., 134–135
Parker Peters, M., 179, 180
Patterson, W., Jr., 15–17
Peixoto, F., 15
perseverance, 7, 38, 42–45, 178–180
    student-teacher relationships
        and, 74
    teaching, 43–44
personal interests/passions, 114,
        118–119
personalization, 204–205
physical education, 67–68
Pierson, R., 201
Pipa, J., 15
Piros, G., 148
poetry slams, 114
Poor Students, Rich Teaching (Jensen),
        117

portfolios, 32–34, 155–156
Potter, H., 207
practical classroom, 7, 81–90
    definition of, 82
    a look inside, 88–89
practices
    for feedback, 100–102
    grading, 3–6
    shared support, 189
praise, 40, 42, 95, 173
prior knowledge, activating, 127
process, 2
    learning approach driven by, 6
process-driven improvement, 167–
        168, 178–183
    mental muscles, 180–183
    stick-withitness, 177–180
product, 2
productive classroom, 7, 111–123
    definition of, 112
    differentiation and creativity in,
        115–116
    a look inside, 121–122
    not-yet approach in, 112–115
    online resources for, 113–114
    reflection on, 123
productive struggle, 1–2
    collaborative strategies for, 189
    deficit language and, 83–86
    effective effort and, 40
    frustration and, 112–113
    grading *vs.*, 24–26
    in-grade retention and, 14–15
    learning intentions, success
        criteria, and, 54
    openness to, 40–41
    scaffolding and, 58
    showing progress and, 70
professional learning communities
        (PLCs), 187, 189, 195
professional-observation form
        template, 153–154, 166, 170
professional-reflection form
        template, 151–153, 165,
        170, 172
progress, 2
    measuring, 101
    showing, 70 (*See also* success
        criteria)
    students' perception of, 32–33
prototyping, 115
puzzles, 182

Q

quality, focus on, 55
questions, 173
    for critical thinking, 128
    to elicit student voice, 44–45
    guiding, 192–195, 197
    structured SELF-questioning, 155

R

Razzetti, G., 93
reach, 173

reading, 136–140, 208
Ready to Learn (Grafwallner), 54, 55–56, 172–173
redoing and retaking, 5–6
  grading and, 24–25
  mental muscle building and, 182
Reeve, D., 190
Reeves, D., 4, 25–26, 116
reflection, 8
  assessment and, 32–34
  before-and-after form for student self-, 156, 157–158
  collegial observation and, 191
  on connective classrooms, 200
  on constructive classrooms, 185
  critical, 149
  critical-input experiences and, 145–146
  on failure, 20
  five whys for, 147–148, 180
  on flexible classrooms, 164
  on grading, 36
  group, 151–153
  growth from, 147–148
  gut talk and, 149–151
  on inclusive classrooms, 212
  on language, 90
  learning intentions and, 54
  on learning intentions and success criteria, 75
  on mindset, 49
  on productive classrooms, 123
  self-criticism *vs.*, 146–147, 149
  student, 154–158
  student goal setting and, 32
  student self-assessment form for, 156
  on supportive classrooms, 142
  teacher self-, 148–154, 190
  in transformational classrooms, 94
  on transformational classrooms, 107
Regents Exam, 13–14
relevance, 118–119
Remind, 92
Renwick, M., 32–33
resiliency, 178–180
resource sharing, 196
respect, 190, 194–195
Responsive Classroom, 84
results-focused design, 27
retention, in-grade, 14–15
Ridriguez, J., 208
Rimm-Kaufman, S., 202
Robb, L., 136–137
Rogers, K., 33
Romeo and Juliet (Shakespeare), 12, 133–134
Ronald W. Reagan College Preparatory High School, Milwaukee, Wisconsin, 66–70

learning intentions and success criteria at, 73–74
not-yet language at, 88–89
productive classrooms at, 121–122
transformational classrooms in, 106
Rothenberg, C., 128
routines, 2, 52, 93, 174, 183–184
Rubel, D., 13–14
rubrics, 62–63, 65
Ruff, J., 156

S

Sadeghi, A., 111
Salazar, R., 24
Sanches, C., 15
Sandilos, L., 202
scaffolding, 1–2. *See also* success criteria
  activating prior knowledge, 127
  choice and, 130–133
  chunking with, 126–127
  data in personalizing, 69–72
  disrupting patterns of failure with, 15–17
  graphic organizers, 128–129
  methods for, 127–129
  success criteria, 51–78
  in supportive classrooms, 126–143
  talking with students, 128
  writing and, 128
Schaaf, R. L., 102
Schoenborn, A., 33–34, 181
seating arrangements, 130, 176
Seesaw, 92
self-assessment form, 156
self-criticism, 146–147
self-differentiation, 132
self-efficacy, 13–17
setbacks and obstacles, 2
  deficit language about, 83–86
  as empowerment opportunities, 13
  encouraging, 45
  joy in overcoming, 112–113
  mindset toward, 38
  modeling, 202–203
  normalizing, 2
  online resources for, 113–114
Shakespeare, W., 12, 133–134
Sheninger, E., 26
Siracusa, F., 176
Slavin, R. E., 14–15
small-group work, 172
Smith, A. T., 3
Smithsonian Open Access, 113
social media, 17–18
Southern Poverty Law Center, 46
space use, 130, 168, 174–178, 184
Sparks, S. D., 201, 203–204
speaking skills, 119–120

special education, 203
special needs, 207
Sperzel-Wuchterl, C., 34, 155
Spiller, J., 206
spontaneous joy, 117
Staake, J., 182
Stackstein, S., 30
stakeholders
  common language with, 101
  communication with all, 91–92
standardized tests, 69, 70
standards
  assessment based on, 33–34
  grading based on, 25, 26–29, 35
  student goals and, 31
  verbs in, 57
Stanley, B. L., 148–149
stick-withitness, 178–180
  modeling, 202–203
Stipek, D., 15
Strauss, V., 13
student exemplars, 63, 65
student feedback on teaching form, 160–161
student self-assessment form, 156
students
  connecting with, 202–203
  connecting with each other, 205
  engaging, 194
  feedback of on teaching, 158–161
  getting to know, 44–45
  personal passions of, 114, 118–119
  prototypes by, 115
  reflection by, 154–158
  trauma responses of, 205–206
  voice of, 44–45, 65, 94
student-teacher relationships, 74, 159–160, 201–212
  feedback and trust in, 95–100
success
  common language about, 101
  ensuring feedback for, 95–100
success criteria
  achievable, 55
  applying, 65–69
  character-trait charts and, 133–136
  clarity in, 55, 56
  common language for defining, 101
  crafting, 54–65
  data in personalizing, 69–72
  definition of, 51
  dos and don'ts of, 60
  examples of, 60–62
  a look inside, 73–74
  reflection on, 75
  revising, 70–71
  rubrics for, 62–63
  scaffolded, 51–78
  student access to, 65
  template for, 63–65, 77–78

writing, 58–65
summative assessment, 53
support
    academic transformation, personal success, and, 99–100
    choice in, 131–133
    collaboration and, 155–156
    help *vs.,* 125, 179
    language used in, 40, 42
    shared practices for, 189
    of stick-withitness, 179–180
supportive classroom, 7, 125–143
    check-ups in, 129–133
    choice in, 130–133
    definition of, 126
    a look inside, 140–141
    not-yet approach in, 126
    reflection on, 142
    tools for, 133–140
Syrie, M., 3

T

Taylor, J., 17–18, 42
Teach for America, 46
TeachBetter, 181
teachers and teaching
    abolitionist, 7, 38, 45–48
    collaboration in, 187–200
    collegial observation and, 190–192
    empathy in, 205–206
    group reflection for, 151–153
    guiding questions and comments for, 192–195
    gut talk and, 149–151
    observing others', 153–154
    opportunities for collaboration in, 195–197
    pedagogical skill improvement for, 168–170
    perseverance, 43–44, 45
    self-reflection by, 148–154, 190
    student feedback on, 158–161
    timeless *vs.* mindless, 53
templates
    learning intention, 57, 58, 76
    magnet summary, 174, 175
    professional-observation form, 153–154, 166
    professional-reflection form, 151–153, 165
    success criteria, 63–65, 77–78
    writing learning intentions, 57, 58
The Things They Carried (O'Brien), 118–119
thinking charts, 67–68
Thompson, V., 197–199
time, 168, 170–174, 183–184
    for collaboration, 189
    creating more, 172–174
    for student reflection, 154–155
Toyoda, S., 147, 180
tracking, 207–208
transformational classroom, 7, 91–109
    academic transformation and personal success feedback form, 96–100
    definition of, 92

feedback best practices in, 100–102
feedback in, 95–100
grading in, 102–105
a look inside, 106
not-yet approach in, 92–95
reflection on, 107
trauma, 205–206
trial and error, 2
trust, 95–100, 159–160, 201
trying, 40
    new things, 40–41
    perseverance and, 7, 38, 42–45
Tucker, C., 171
tutoring, 5–6
Twain, M., 81
two-week instructional calendar, 137, 143, 173

U

ultimate (sport), 67–68
uncertainty, coping with, 93–94
University of Wisconsin-Milwaukee, 114
U.S. Department of Education Office for Civil Rights, 104
U.S. Department of Justice Civil Rights Division, 104

V

Van Bockern, S., 205–206
verbs, robust, 56–58, 73
Victoria State Education Department, 191
Vietnam conflict, 118–119, 194
vocabulary, front-loading concept-specific, 127–128
voice, student, 44–45, 65, 94
    about space use, 177

W

Wabisabi Learning, 112
wall art, 130–131
Wander, P., 140–141
Ward, R., 5, 12–13, 106
Wasik, B. A., 14–15
Watanabe-Crockett, L., 112
Waxman, B. L., 3
Weeblys, 92
Westerberg, T. R., 24
Who You Know: Unlocking Innovations That Expand Students' Networks (Fisher & Klein), 204
whole child approach, 91–92, 93
Why We Drop Out (Feldman, Smith, & Waxman), 3
Wiesel, E., 15–16
Wiggins, G., 26–27
Williams, J., 176
Wisconsin Interscholastic Athletic Association, 189
Wolk, S., 111
Wolpert-Gawron, H., 43, 132
Wormeli, R., 83
writing, 128

Y

Youth Social Justice Forum, 114